The Practitioner's Guide to

Trials Before the Patent Trial and Appeal Board

THIRD EDITION

Kathleen A. Daley, Michael J. Flibbert, and Joshua L. Goldberg
EDITORS

AMERICAN BAR ASSOCIATION
Intellectual Property Law Section

Cover design by Amy Mandel, ABA Section of Intellectual Property Law; Jill Tedhams, ABA Design/ABA Design

Printed in the United States of America.

26 25 24 23 22 5 4 3 2 1

A catalog record for this book is on file with the Library of Congress.

Contents

About the Authors

Cory C. Bell (coauthor) is a partner at Finnegan, Henderson, Farabow, Garrett & Dunner, LLP. Since working on the first ever PGR of a covered business method CBM patent, Cory has represented patent owners and petitioners in over 200 PGR and IPR trials before the Patent Trial and Appeal Board and in related matters before the U.S. Court of Appeals for the Federal Circuit. He coauthored both prior versions of the American Bar Association's *The Practitioner's Guide to Trials before the Patent Trial and Appeal Board* and teaches a course he created on post-grant practice at the Suffolk University Law School.

Daniel C. Cooley (coauthor) is a partner at Finnegan, Henderson, Farabow, Garrett & Dunner, LLP, where he handles litigation at both the trial and appellate level. Dan has acted as lead or cocounsel in dozens of Federal Circuit matters, including appeals from PTAB proceedings. Dan also practices before the PTAB, handling all aspects of post-grant proceedings for petitioners and patent owners. Dan served as a law clerk at the U.S. Court of Appeals for the Federal Circuit.

Kathleen A. Daley (coeditor) is a partner at Finnegan, Henderson, Farabow, Garrett & Dunner, LLP, where she has extensive experience in trial, appellate, and PTAB litigation. She has led litigation teams before district courts, the U.S. International Trade Commission, the PTAB, and the Federal Circuit. Kathleen has also made post-grant proceedings before the PTAB, including reexaminations and inter partes review proceedings, a focus of her practice. Her work encompasses a wide range of technologies with an emphasis on medical devices.

Pier DeRoo (coauthor) is a partner at Finnegan, Henderson, Farabow, Garrett & Dunner, LLP. Pier has represented parties in dozens of proceedings before the PTAB, including as lead counsel, with a particular emphasis on proceedings in the chemical, pharmaceutical, and biotechnology fields. He also has broad experience in patent litigation and appeals, regularly litigating PTAB proceedings in parallel with U.S. district court actions.

Michael J. Flibbert (coeditor) is a partner at Finnegan, Henderson, Farabow, Garrett & Dunner, LLP. With more than 25 years of patent litigation experience, he serves as lead counsel in district court litigations, post-grant proceedings before the Patent Trial and Appeal Board, and appeals before the U.S. Court of Appeals for the Federal Circuit. Mike represents clients in patent cases involving pharmaceuticals, biotechnology, chemistry, chemical engineering, agriculture, and materials science. He has particular experience representing pharmaceutical patent holders in litigations arising under the Hatch-Waxman Act.

Joshua L. Goldberg (coeditor) is a partner at Finnegan, Henderson, Farabow, Garrett & Dunner, LLP, where he leads the firm's PTAB trials section. He is also a director of the PTAB Bar Association. As lead or backup counsel in more than 300 PTAB proceedings, Josh splits his time approximately 60/40 between representing petitioners and patent owners. He also regularly argues appeals from PTAB trials to the U.S. Court of Appeals for the Federal Circuit.

Timothy P. McAnulty (coauthor) is a partner at Finnegan, Henderson, Farabow, Garrett & Dunner, LLP, and a former patent examiner. Tim has a diverse practice including district court litigation and strategic counseling spanning portfolio development, licensing, and enforcement, especially related to medical devices and drug delivery combination products. Tim has several thousand hours of experience on contentious proceedings before the PTAB and regularly serves as lead counsel representing both petitioners and patent owners. Tim's PTAB experience also includes Federal Circuit appeals as well as strategic use of reexaminations and reissues.

Amanda Murphy (coauthor) is a partner at Finnegan, Henderson, Farabow, Garrett & Dunner, LLP. Amanda focuses her practice on strategic client counseling, including due diligence investigations, patent portfolio management, and post-grant proceedings, with an emphasis on biotechnology and life sciences inventions. Her experience includes prosecuting and appealing applications within the U.S. Patent and Trademark Office, as well as post-grant proceedings, supplemental examinations, and opinion work.

Chapter 1

Introduction[1]

This book seeks to assist practitioners representing patent owners and challengers in trials before the Patent Trial and Appeal Board (PTAB) of the U.S. Patent and Trademark Office (the Office). It is intended to be a concise, practical desk reference for practicing attorneys, in-house counsel, and non-attorney professionals (e.g., patent agents) involved in PTAB proceedings.

When the Leahy-Smith America Invents Act (AIA) was signed into law on September 16, 2011, it created a new practice in patent law—patent trials before the newly created PTAB. PTAB trials are a hybrid of conventional patent prosecution and patent litigation practices. Successfully navigating a PTAB trial may involve such varied tasks as analyzing highly technical prior art, drafting persuasive petitions or patent owner responses, arguing motions, deposing scientific experts, drafting patent-claim amendments, and arguing at an oral hearing before an expert three-judge panel. This book's authors and editors, all seasoned patent office practitioners and experienced patent litigators, are uniquely qualified to provide guidance to practitioners faced with the myriad challenges of a PTAB trial.

More than ten years have passed since the AIA was enacted, and it is fair to say that the legislation has fundamentally changed U.S. patent litigation in a number of significant ways. With the third edition of this guide, we

1. The authors thank Nicholas Cerulli, Michael Galgano, Mingi Jin, Sydney Kestle, Leon Lin, Joey Myles, Kassandra Officer, Cara Regan, Michele Rice, Bradley Richards, Melissa Santos, Lulu Wang, and Brooke Wilner for their assistance with this book.

attempt to encapsulate what we have learned over the last decade about proceedings before the PTAB. The case law about the AIA in general and post-grant proceedings in particular from the PTAB, the Court of Appeals for the Federal Circuit, and the Supreme Court is much more developed than it was when we published the first edition. We have included those advancements in this edition, along with explanations of how they have been implemented. As a result, we have reorganized this edition and expanded our discussion of each aspect of a PTAB trial. In Chapter 2, we discuss strategic issues to consider before filing a post-grant proceeding. We also address the relationship between post-grant proceedings and other proceedings, such as a parallel litigation or another proceeding before the Office, and the impact on those proceedings such as through estoppel. In Chapter 3, we walk through preparation of a petition, including the requirements and strategic considerations. And in Chapter 4, we provide guidance on and a discussion of patent owner preliminary responses.

In Chapters 5–7, we cover the proceeding at the PTAB once trial is instituted. In Chapter 5, we cover the briefing and discovery that take place after trial has been instituted. We discuss motions to amend in Chapter 6. And in Chapter 7, we address oral argument before the Board, rehearing options and procedures, and the Precedential Opinion Panel. We discuss procedures for appeals to the Federal Circuit and strategic considerations in Chapter 8. Finally, in Chapter 9, we discuss other practices that may arise during a post-grant proceeding such as settlement and termination, PTAB programs and resources, and nonscheduled motions practice. Throughout all of these chapters, we have strived to make this edition not a treatise on the law but a practical guide to all aspects of PTAB trials.

Disclaimer

We provide the material in this guide for information purposes only and do not render legal advice or provide a substitute for legal counsel. The information found here may or may not reflect the most current legal developments or rules. Accordingly, practitioners must review current rules to identify changes the PTAB may have adopted and conduct independent research to ensure that they are relying on the most recent case law.

While we have attempted to provide information as accurately as possible based on the rules and procedures of the PTAB in effect at the time of publishing, the guide may contain errors or omissions, including those resulting from changes in the PTAB's rules and procedures made after the guide was authored, for which we disclaim any liability. Readers should not take any actions, or refrain from taking any actions, based on information in this guide without first consulting their own attorneys.

Chapter 2

Prefiling Considerations and Relationship between Proceedings

The Leahy-Smith America Invents Act (AIA) provided several new tools for challenging patents that affect how challengers and patent owners alike approach litigation strategy. Patent owners should consider how these tools may be used to challenge their patents when forming patent-assertion strategies as well as when developing portfolios. And defendants (or potential defendants) should understand the options, requirements, and outcomes of the procedures available to them to determine whether to challenge a patent in district court, the U.S. Patent and Trademark Office (the Office), or both and the types of challenges to bring (or not bring) in the different forums.

A. Preliminary Considerations

A patent may be challenged before the Office through post-grant review (PGR), inter partes review (IPR), or ex parte reexamination.[1] For a limited period under the AIA, patents could also be challenged by covered business method (CBM) review, but this option is no longer available.[2] The strategic

1. While third parties may challenge the validity of a patent, a patent owner may seek to confirm the validity of its patent through ex parte reexamination. *See* 35 U.S.C. § 302; 37 C.F.R. § 1.510(a); *see also* Manual of Patent Examining Procedure § 2212 (9th ed., rev. 10, 2019) (last revised June 2020) [hereinafter MPEP].
2. Leahy-Smith America Invents Act, Pub. L. No. 112-29, § 18(a)(3) (2011).

value or limitations of these proceedings may depend upon the timing of the challenge, whether there are any parallel proceedings in other forums (or whether any previously existed), and the relationship between the parties, which may limit the challenger's rights on appeal.

1. Timing

Timing is an important consideration and may limit the options available for a challenger at the Office. For example, any third party (not the patent owner) may challenge a patent via PGR only if (1) the challenged claims have an effective filing date of March 16, 2013, or later, and (2) the petition is filed within nine months of the patent's issue or reissue date.[3] If either condition is not met, a third party must consider an alternative means at the Office, like IPR or ex parte reexamination.

For patents that are PGR-eligible,[4] IPR becomes available (1) after the nine-month window for filing a PGR passes or (2) if a PGR petition is filed and instituted,[5] after the PGR terminates.[6] For all other patents, IPR is available immediately after issuance[7] for any third party "who is not the owner of a patent."[8] A related litigation also impacts when an IPR can be filed. A petitioner, real party in interest, or privy of the petitioner must file any IPR petition within one year of service of a complaint asserting infringement (the one-year time bar).[9] Similarly, a petitioner or real party in interest cannot file an IPR after filing a civil action challenging the validity of

3. 35 U.S.C. § 321(c).

4. *Id.* § 100(i)(1).

5. *Id.* § 311(c); 37 C.F.R. § 42.102(a).

6. 35 U.S.C. § 311(c). The waiting period for petitioning for an IPR filing does not apply to pre-AIA patents. *See* To Correct and Improve Certain Provisions of the Leahy-Smith America Invents Act and Title 35, H.R. 6621, 112th Cong. § 1(d) (2012). If no decision on whether to institute a PGR has been made, a party may file an IPR after nine months from issuance. *See* Changes to Implement Inter Partes Review Proceedings, Post-Grant Review Proceedings, and Transitional Program for Covered Business Method Patents, 77 Fed. Reg. 48,680, 48,696, Response to Comment 18 (Aug. 14, 2012).

7. 37 C.F.R. § 42.102(a) was revised on March 25, 2013, to implement the Leahy-Smith America Invents Technical Corrections, Pub. L. No. 112-274, § (1)(d)(1); *see* Changes to Implement the Technical Corrections to the Leahy-Smith America Invents Act as to Inter Partes Review, 78 Fed. Reg. 17,871, 17,874 (Mar. 25, 2013).

8. 35 U.S.C. § 311(a).

9. *Id.* § 315(b).

the patent.[10] Notably, however, these time bars do not apply if a petitioner files a counterclaim of invalidity[11] or a declaratory judgment action for noninfringement.[12]

As an alternative to PGR and IPR, a third party may also request ex parte reexamination of a patent at any time during the period of enforceability for the patent, provided that party is not otherwise estopped.[13] One thing to keep in mind is that reexamination is available even if a petition is denied after the one-year time bar, provided that the requestor can still show a "substantial new question of patentability."[14] The Office conducts ex parte reexaminations with "special dispatch,"[15] but, unlike IPRs and PGRs, there is no statutory deadline to complete a reexamination proceeding.

The schedule for a PGR or IPR can be faster than a reexamination proceeding and is typically faster than most district court schedules. The majority of PGRs and IPRs are completed approximately 18 to 20 months after the petition is filed.[16] Office regulations require a patent owner to file any preliminary response within three months of an accepted petition receiving a filing date, and governing statutes require the Board to issue a decision whether to institute within three months of the patent owner's preliminary response (or the date a preliminary response would otherwise be due if one is not filed).[17] Thus, the Board typically issues a decision on whether to institute within six months of the petition being filed.[18] If a trial is instituted, the Board must issue a final written decision within 12 months, unless that

10. *Id.* § 315(a)(1). If the petitioner or real party in interest files a civil action on or after the date on which the petitioner files a petition, the civil action is automatically stayed. *See id.* § 315(a)(2).

11. *Id.* § 315(a)(3).

12. *See* Ariosa Diagnostics v. ISIS Innovation Ltd., IPR2012-00022, Paper 20, at 7 (Feb. 12, 2013).

13. MPEP, *supra* note 1, § 2209.

14. *See* 35 U.S.C. § 302 (noting request for reexamination may be filed at any time); 84 Fed. Reg. 16,654, 16,656 ("A patent owner also may . . . fil[e] a request for *ex parte* reexamination before, during, or after an AIA trial proceeding concludes with a final written decision."); *see, e.g.*, Reexamination Control No. 90/014036 (reexamination ordered after a one-year time bar).

15. 35 U.S.C. § 305; MPEP, *supra* note 1, § 2209.

16. *See* 35 U.S.C. § 316(11).

17. *Id.* §§ 314(b), 324(c).

18. *See id.* § 314(b).

deadline is extended by "not more than 6 months" for good cause.[19] The Board has rarely extended this 12-month deadline.

In contrast, the average time from filing to trial for civil cases was 28.3 months for the 12-month period ending June 30, 2021.[20] This timing was a primary consideration and goal of the AIA. Thus, if a petition is filed soon after a complaint, the PGR or IPR will likely conclude well before the district court trial. There are exceptions, however. For example, some district courts—like the Eastern District of Virginia and Western and Eastern Districts of Texas—and the International Trade Commission (ITC) have especially fast schedules and may keep pace with or be faster than the Board, reaching trial before the Board would issue its final written decision. When a petition is filed matters, particularly as parallel cases go to appeal.

Timing of proceedings at the Board may also impact other strategic considerations in district court. Timing of a petition and the overall schedule will impact the likelihood of getting a stay in district court, the availability of prior art, the interplay of claim construction for validity and infringement, and the timing and record building for appeal. To that end, it is usually important to coordinate discovery efforts with any related litigations. Supplemental information discovered in a parallel litigation that might be relevant to a claim under review at the Board must be submitted within one month of institution.[21] As such, a party may consider front-loading strategies, like serving discovery requests in the parallel litigation, that may lead to information relevant to a party's positions.

2. Considerations for Parallel Proceedings

While the post-grant mechanisms available at the Office (PGR, IPR, ex parte reexamination) are intended to provide an alternative to challenging a patent's validity in district court, they are relatively limited in scope. In district court, a number of affirmative defenses are available, including

19. *Id.* §§ 316(11), 326(11).

20. *U.S. District Courts—Combined Civil and Criminal Federal Court Management Statistics, National Judicial Caseload Profile* (June 30, 2021), https://www.uscourts.gov/sites/default/files/data_tables/fcms_na_distprofile0630.2021.pdf.

21. 37 C.F.R. §§ 42.123, 42.223.

invalidity,[22] noninfringement,[23] unenforceability,[24] statute of limitations,[25] estoppel,[26] laches,[27] and failure to mark.[28] In contrast, IPR, PGR, and ex parte reexaminations are limited to patentability challenges.

Of the post-grant Office mechanisms, PGR offers the widest range of grounds for challenging a patent, including prior art, statutory subject matter, written description, indefiniteness, and enablement.[29] The unpatentability grounds available in IPR and ex parte reexaminations are more circumscribed. IPR is limited to anticipation and obviousness challenges based on prior art patents or printed publications.[30] Ex parte reexamination is likewise limited to unpatentability challenges based on prior art patents or printed publications.[31]

In addition to the different grounds available in PGR, IPR, and ex parte reexamination, each proceeding generates different estoppel relative to parallel proceedings. A petitioner (including any real parties in interest and/or privies of the petitioner) in an IPR or PGR that results in a final decision is estopped in a later or ongoing proceeding before the Office, including an ex parte reexamination, and before a district court or ITC, from raising any ground that was *raised or reasonably could have been raised* in an earlier proceeding.[32] For a PGR, this can mean that a petitioner will be estopped from challenging patentability based on prior art, statutory subject matter, written description, indefiniteness, and/or enablement. In contrast, because IPR is limited to anticipation and obviousness challenges based on prior art patents or printed publications, a petitioner may be able to file an IPR without the risk of being estopped from raising other types of challenges

22. 35 U.S.C. §§ 282(b)(2), 282(b)(3).
23. *Id.* § 282(b)(1).
24. *Id.*
25. Fed. R. Civ. P. 8(c).
26. *Id.*
27. *Id.*
28. 35 U.S.C. § 287(a).
29. *Id.* §§ 321(b) (relating to invalidity of the patent or any claim), 324(b) (relating to any unsettled legal question).
30. *Id.* § 311(b).
31. *Id.* § 302; MPEP, *supra* note 1, §§ 2210, 2258.
32. *See* 35 U.S.C. §§ 315(e), 325(e); *see also infra* Chapter 2, section E.1.

or defenses—like those under 35 U.S.C. §§ 101 and 112—in another proceeding.[33] There is no estoppel for a reexamination proceeding.[34]

PGR, IPR, and ex parte reexamination proceedings also have different threshold standards for institution. The standard for instituting a PGR requires the petitioner to establish that it is *more likely than not* that at least one challenged claim is unpatentable.[35] For an IPR, the petitioner need only show a *reasonable likelihood* that it will prevail with respect to at least one challenged claim.[36] The Office has explained that the "more likely than not" threshold for instituting a PGR is designed to be higher than the "reasonable likelihood" threshold for IPRs.[37] For ex parte reexamination, the *substantial new question of patentability* (SNQ) standard applies.[38] The AIA's legislative history indicates the institution standards for PGR and IPR were intended to be higher than the SNQ threshold for ex parte reexamination.[39]

There are several differences between challenging validity in district court and challenging patentability at the Board. For example, in post-grant proceedings before the Office, a petitioner must prove unpatentability by a preponderance of the evidence.[40] This burden is lower than an accused infringer's burden in district court, where it must prove invalidity by clear and convincing evidence.[41] Likewise, challenges at the Board are before a

33. *See infra* Chapter 2, section E.1.

34. *See* MPEP, *supra* note 1, § 2259.

35. 35 U.S.C. § 324(a).

36. *Id.* § 314(a).

37. Changes to Implement Inter Partes Review Proceedings, Post-Grant Review Proceedings, and Transitional Program for Covered Business Method Patents, 77 Fed. Reg. 48,680, 48,702, Response to Comment 59 (Aug. 14, 2012); *see also* Message from Chief Judge James Donald Smith, Board of Patent Appeals and Interferences: USPTO Discusses Key Aspects of New Administrative Patent Trials, USPTO, http://www.uspto.gov/aia_implementation/smith-blog-extravaganza.jsp (last updated May 21, 2012).

38. 35 U.S.C. § 303(a).

39. *See* 112 Cong. Rec. S1375 (daily ed. Mar. 8, 2011) (statement of Sen. Kyl) ("Among the most important protections for patent owners added by the bill are its elevated thresholds for instituting inter partes and post grant reviews. The present bill dispenses with the test of substantial new question of patentability, a standard that currently allows 95% of all requests to be granted. It instead imposes thresholds that require petitioners to present information that creates serious doubts about the patent's validity.").

40. *In re* Baxter Int'l, Inc., 678 F.3d 1357, 1365 (Fed. Cir. 2012); 37 C.F.R. § 42.1(d).

41. Microsoft Corp. v. i4i Ltd. P'ship, 564 U.S. 91, 95 (2011) (holding that the standard of proof for all invalidity claims is clear and convincing evidence).

panel of administrative patent judges, who are experienced in patent law and have a technical background or experience, often relevant to the subject matter of the challenged patent.[42] In contrast, in district court, validity may be decided by a judge or lay jury with little knowledge of the technology and patent law.[43] Board proceedings are generally conducted on a written record, except for an oral hearing after all briefing, with limited discovery, often only expert declarations and deposition transcripts. Depending on the technology at issue, and the nature of the challenges presented, one forum may be more beneficial than the other. To that end, it is worthwhile to consider if positions will benefit from explanation by witnesses (expert or fact) and whether the credibility of those witnesses will be best appreciated by a jury as opposed to the written record generally used by the Board (e.g., declarations and deposition transcripts). A challenger may also consider a tiered approach, raising some challenges at the Board (benefiting from the expertise of the Board), while raising other challenges before a judge or lay jury in district court.[44] Regardless of the forum, petitioners and patent owners alike need to coordinate parallel proceedings, taking into account, among other things, inconsistent positions, contrary rulings, and findings of fact.

3. Appellate Standing

Although any party "who is not the owner of a patent" may file a petition for IPR or PGR,[45] not all petitioners automatically have standing to appeal an adverse decision by the Board. A petitioner-appellant must still meet Article III requirements, including showing a cognizable injury in fact,

---

42. 35 U.S.C. §§ 326(c) (PGR), 316(c) (IPR); MPEP, *supra* note 1, § 2233.

43. *See, e.g.*, *In re* Tech. Licensing Corp., 423 F.3d 1286, 1290 (Fed. Cir. 2005).

44. *See, e.g.*, Clinicomp Int'l, Inc. v. Athenahealth, Inc., No. A-18-CV-00425, 2020 WL 7011768, at *2 (W.D. Tex. Oct. 28, 2020) ("Estoppel does not extend to other types of prior art, such as prior-art devices. Therefore defendants can rely on the prior-art systems in their invalidity contentions to argue anticipation or obviousness." (internal citations omitted)); Medline Indus., Inc. v. C.R. Bard, Inc., No. 17-C-7216, 2020 WL 5512132, at *4 (N.D. Ill. Sept. 14, 2020). *But see* Wasica Fin. GmbH v. Schrader Int'l, Inc., 432 F. Supp. 3d 448, 455 (D. Del. 2020).

45. 35 U.S.C. §§ 311(a), 321(a).

before that petitioner may successfully appeal an adverse Board determination to the Federal Circuit.[46]

The statute broadly provides that any "person who is not the owner of a patent may file with the Office a petition to institute"[47] and does so without limitation. As the Supreme Court has explained, "[p]arties that initiate the [IPR] proceeding need not have a concrete stake in the outcome."[48] "[A]lthough Article III standing is not necessarily a requirement to appear before an administrative agency, once a party seeks review in a federal court, 'the constitutional requirement that it have standing kicks in.'"[49] And, as the Federal Circuit explained, to "meet the constitutional minimum for standing," the petitioner-appellant (1) "must show that it has suffered an 'injury in fact' that is both concrete and particularized, and actual or imminent (as opposed to conjectural or hypothetical"; (2) must show that the injury is "fairly traceable to the challenged action"; and (3) must show "it is likely, rather than merely speculative, that a favorable judicial decision will redress the injury."[50] Because Congress "has accorded a procedural right to" appeal to a petitioner-appellant, immediacy, redressability, and prudential requirements are relaxed,[51] but the injury-in-fact requirement remains "a hard floor of Article III jurisdiction that cannot be removed by statute."[52]

In the context of appeals from IPR and PGR final written decisions, the Federal Circuit has explained that petitioner-appellants can meet the injury-

46. *See, e.g.*, JTEKT Corp. v. GKN Auto. Ltd., 898 F.3d 1217, 1219–21 (Fed. Cir. 2018); Phigenix, Inc. v. Immunogen, Inc., 845 F.3d 1168, 1170–76 (Fed. Cir. 2017); *see also, e.g.*, Argentum Pharms. LLC v. Novartis Pharms. Corp., 956 F.3d 1374, 1376–78 (Fed. Cir. 2020); AVX Corp. v. Presidio Components, Inc., 923 F.3d 1357, 1361–67 (Fed. Cir. 2019); Momenta Pharms., Inc. v. Bristol-Myers Squibb Co., 915 F.3d 764, 767–70 (Fed. Cir. 2019); E.I. DuPont de Nemours & Co. v. Synvina C.V., 904 F.3d 996, 1003–05 (Fed. Cir. 2018).

47. 35 U.S.C. §§ 311(a), 321(a).

48. Cuozzo Speed Techs., LLC v. Lee, 136 S. Ct. 2131, 2143–44 (2016).

49. Consumer Watchdog v. Wis. Alumni Rsch. Found., 753 F.3d 1258, 1261 (Fed. Cir. 2014) (quoting Sierra Club v. E.P.A., 292 F.3d 895, 899 (D.C. Cir. 2002)).

50. *Id.* at 1260–61 (quoting Lujan v. Defenders of Wildlife, 504 U.S. 555, 560–61 (1992)).

51. *Id.* at 1261 (citing Massachusetts v. E.P.A., 549 U.S. 497, 517–18 (2007)); *see also* 35 U.S.C. § 319 ("A party dissatisfied with the final written decision of the Patent Trial and Appeal Board under section 318(a) may appeal the decision pursuant to sections 141 through 144. Any party to the inter partes review shall have the right to be a party to the appeal.").

52. *Consumer Watchdog*, 753 F.3d at 1261 (quoting Summers v. Earth Island Inst., 555 U.S. 488, 497 (2009)).

in-fact "hard floor" if they can show that (1) they face a risk of infringing the challenged patent; (2) they are an actual or prospective licensee of the patent; or (3) they otherwise plan to take actions that would implicate the challenged patent.[53] Said another way, a petitioner-appellant can show injury in fact if it shows "that it is engaged or will likely engage 'in an[] activity that would give rise to a possible infringement suit,' or has contractual rights that are affected by a determination of patent validity."[54]

In *JTEKT v. GKN*, the Federal Circuit explained that having no product on the market "does not preclude Article III standing."[55] But it cautioned that when a petitioner-appellant is not currently engaging in infringing activity, "it must establish that it has concrete plans for future activity that creates a substantial risk of future infringement or likely cause the patentee to assert a claim of infringement."[56] While petitioner-appellant had submitted two declarations in support of standing, the declarations did not "establish that its planned product could create a substantial risk of" infringement or would "likely lead to charges of infringement."[57] The declarations only showed that (1) the patent owner has not alleged infringement; (2) the petitioner-appellant and patent owner were "competitors generally"; and (3) the product remains "in development," is not "yet finalized," and "will continue to evolve," as the petitioner-appellant was still "validating its design, including tuning and conducting demonstrations."[58] The Federal Circuit held that petitioner-appellant could not show its products created a concrete, substantial risk of infringement or would likely lead to an infringement suit and dismissed the appeal for lack of standing.[59]

In contrast, in *E.I. DuPont v. Synvina*, the Federal Circuit held that the petitioner-appellant had standing.[60] The court found it particularly

53. Phigenix, Inc. v. Immunogen, Inc., 845 F.3d 1168, 1173–74 (Fed. Cir. 2017).
54. JTEKT Corp. v. GKN Auto. Ltd., 898 F.3d 1217, 1221 (Fed. Cir. 2018) (quoting *Consumer Watchdog*, 753 F.3d at 1262) (citing MedImmune, Inc. v. Genentech, Inc., 549 U.S. 118, 137 (2007)).
55. *Id.*
56. *Id.* at 1221.
57. *Id.*
58. *Id.*
59. *Id.*
60. E.I. DuPont de Nemours & Co. v. Synvina C.V., 904 F.3d 996, 1003–05 (Fed. Cir. 2018).

persuasive that (1) the petitioner-appellant had built a demonstration plant that was capable of operating under conditions falling within the ranges claimed in the challenged patent; (2) the patent owner was a competitor and alleged copying during the IPR; and (3) the patent owner rejected the petitioner-appellant's request for a covenant not to sue.[61] In such circumstances, the court found the petitioner-appellant had taken and planned to take sufficient action that would implicate the challenged claims, including sufficient involvement in research and commercial activities involving the claimed subject matter.[62]

In view of these cases, it is important for a petitioner to appreciate the risk that it may file a petition, fail to show all challenged claims are unpatentable, and then be unable to appeal to the Federal Circuit. As estoppel attaches upon issuance of a final written decision, there is the concurrent risk that a petitioner may lose before the Board, be unable to appeal, and also be estopped in future proceedings from raising any ground that was raised or that reasonably could have been raised before the Board, although the Federal Circuit has not yet addressed whether estoppel would apply in such a situation.[63]

B. Stays of Parallel Proceedings

1. District Courts

The AIA imposes an automatic stay of any civil action filed by a petitioner challenging the validity of a patent filed on or after the date on which the

61. *Id.*

62. *Id.* at 1005.

63. *See, e.g.*, AVX Corp. v. Presidio Components, Inc., 923 F.3d 1357, 1363 (Fed. Cir. 2019) ("[T]his court has not decided whether the estoppel provision would have the effect that AVX posits—specifically, whether § 315(e) would have estoppel effect even where the IPR petitioner lacked Article III standing to appeal the Board's decision to this court. For this court to so hold, we would have to consider whether that reading of § 315(e) is tied to § 319's right to appeal for any 'party dissatisfied with the final written decision' of the Board. Relatedly, we would also have to consider whether § 315(e) should be read to incorporate a traditional preclusion principle—that neither claim nor issue preclusion applies when appellate review of the decision with a potentially preclusive effect is unavailable. We have not addressed those and other considerations bearing on the proper application of § 315(e). We decline to do so here." (internal citations omitted)).

petitioner files a petition for IPR or PGR.[64] The stay continues until the patent owner either moves the court to lift the stay or files a civil action or counterclaim that the petitioner (or real party in interest) infringes the patent.[65] A counterclaim challenging the validity of a patent does not, however, trigger this automatic stay.[66]

The AIA provides no guidance on the remaining circumstances for staying a civil action in view of a pending IPR or PGR. These circumstances are left to the inherent power of district courts to decide whether to stay an action or permit concurrent judicial and Board review. In deciding whether to stay an action, district courts typically consider three factors:

(1) whether granting a stay will simplify issues for trial;
(2) the status of the litigation, particularly whether discovery is complete and a trial date is set; and
(3) whether a stay would cause the nonmovant to suffer undue prejudice or allow the movant to gain a clear tactical advantage.[67]

The first factor—whether granting a stay will simplify the issues for trial—is viewed as the most important factor when evaluating a motion to stay.[68] Simplification of the issues for trial depends on whether the Board institutes review,[69] and an instituted proceeding usually weighs more heavily

64. 35 U.S.C. §§ 315(a)(2), 325(a)(2).
65. *Id.*
66. *Id.* §§ 315(a)(3), 325(a)(3).
67. *See, e.g.*, Found. Med., Inc. v. Guardant Health, Inc., No. CV-17-807, 2018 WL 950261, at *1 (D. Del. Feb. 15, 2018); Trover Grp., Inc., et al. v. Dedicated Micros USA, No. 13-CV-1047, 2015 WL 1069179, at *2 (E.D. Tex. Mar. 11, 2015); Lennon Image Techs., LLC v. Macy's Retail Holdings, Inc., Nos. 2:13-CV-00235, 2:13-CV-00239, 2014 WL 4652117, at *2 (E.D. Tex. Sept. 17, 2014); Universal Elecs., Inc. v. Universal Remote Control, Inc., 943 F. Supp. 2d 1028, 1030–31 (C.D. Cal. 2013); Semiconductor Energy Lab. Co. v. Chimei Innolux Corp., No. SACV 12-21, 2012 WL 7170593, at *1 & n.1 (C.D. Cal. Dec. 19, 2012); Star Envirotech, Inc. v. Redline Detection, LLC, No. SACV 12-01861, 2013 WL 1716068, at *1 (C.D. Cal. Apr. 3, 2013) (applying reexamination inquiry to considerations of stay pending IPR); Gryphon Networks Corp. v. Contact Ctr. Compliance Corp., 792 F. Supp. 2d 87, 90 (D. Mass. 2011) (citation omitted); Softview LLC v. Apple Inc., No. 10-389, 2012 WL 3061027, at *2–5 (D. Del. July 26, 2012); Soverain Software LLC v. Amazon.com, Inc., 356 F. Supp. 2d 660, 662 (E.D. Tex. 2005).
68. Scorpcast, LLC v. Boutique Media Pty Ltd., No. 20-CV-00193, 2020 WL 7631162, at *3 (E.D. Tex. Dec. 22, 2020).
69. *Id.*

in favor of a stay.[70] District courts will also consider the degree of overlap between the Office proceeding and the litigation when determining if a stay will simplify issues.[71] In particular, courts often examine the overlap of the claims asserted in the litigation and the claims challenged at the Board, as well as any causes of action, counterclaims, or defenses that may not be resolved by the Board.[72] Courts will also take into account the extent to which codefendants are willing to be bound by estoppel of the parallel proceeding.[73]

The second factor—the status of the litigation, particularly whether discovery is complete and a trial date has been set—requires district courts to weigh the resources already spent in the litigation against the potential economies to be gained by staying the ligation and allowing the parallel proceeding to play out. District courts generally view a stay as reasonable

70. *See, e.g.*, *Scorpcast*, 2020 WL 7631162, at *3; CRFD Rsch., Inc. v. Dish Network Corp. et al., No. 14-064 (D. Del. June 3, 2015).

71. Snyders Heart Valve LLC v. St. Jude Med. S.C. Inc., No. 18-2030, 2021 WL 1063005, at *5 (D. Minn. Mar. 19, 2021).

72. *See, e.g.*, Versata Software v. Callidus Software, 771 F.3d 1368, 1371 (Fed Cir. 2014), *vacated as moot*, 780 F.3d 1134 (Fed. Cir. 2015) (granting a stay "even when a CBM proceeding does not address all asserted patents, claims, or invalidity defenses"); Bonutti Skeletal Innovations, L.L.C. v. Zimmer Holdings, Inc., No. 12-CV-1107, 2014 WL 1369721 (D. Del. Apr. 7, 2014) (granting stay where IPR was instituted for four of six patents in suit); Robert Bosch Healthcare Sys., Inc. v. Cardiocom, LLC, 12-CV-3864, 2012 WL 6020012 (N.D. Cal. Dec. 3, 2012) (granting a stay where most, but not all, of the asserted claims were subject to Office review); Card-Monroe Corp. v. Tuftco Corp., No. 14-CV-292, 2015 WL 11109362, at *4 (E.D. Tenn. Feb. 19, 2015) ("[T]he benefit of such a review would be limited because it would only have the potential to resolve issues with one of the three patents at issue in the instant litigation."); Unifi Sci. Batteries, LLC v. Sony Mobile Commc'ns AB, No. 12-CV-221, 2014 WL 4494479 (E.D. Tex. Jan. 14, 2014) (denying review where a large number of the claims at issue were not in inter partes review); US Nutraceuticals LLC v. Cyanotech Corp., No. 5:12-CV-00366, at *5 (M.D. Fla. Oct. 15, 2013).

73. Semiconductor Energy Lab. Co. v. Chimei Innolux Corp., No. SACV 12-21, 2012 WL 7170593 (C.D. Cal. Dec. 19, 2012) (granting stay because "Defendants who did not file the IPR petitions have agreed to be bound by the estoppel provisions of the IPR proceedings."); Pi-Net Int'l, Inc. v. Focus Bus. Bank, No. C-12-4958, 2013 WL 4475940, at *5 (N.D. Cal. Aug. 16, 2013); Achates Reference Publ'g, Inc. v. Symantec Corp., No. 11-CV-00294, at *1–2 (E.D. Tex. Apr. 17, 2013); Evolutionary Intelligence, LLC v. Sprint Nextel Corp., No. C-13-4513, 2014 WL 819277 (N.D. Cal. Feb. 28, 2014); *Semiconductor Energy Lab. Co.*, 2012 WL 7170593, at *2 ("The estoppel effect of *inter partes* review carries less weight when there are several defendants that are not parties to, and thus are not bound by, the estoppel effects of the proceedings."); e-Watch Inc. v. Avigilon Corp., No. H–13–0347, 2013 WL 6633936, at *2 (S.D. Tex. Dec. 17, 2013).

if little substantive activity has occurred in the litigation when the stay is sought.[74] But district courts are less likely to find that a stay will economize resources if, for example, claim construction and discovery are complete.[75] Thus, to improve the possibility of getting a stay, a defendant should file a petition as early as possible.

The third factor—whether a stay would cause the nonmovant to suffer undue prejudice or allow the movant to gain a clear tactical advantage—allows district courts to consider whether the moving party delayed in filing its petition, used dilatory tactics, or demonstrated bad faith; whether a stay will do nothing but delay the proceedings; and whether monetary damages would not sufficiently compensate a patent owner for the alleged infringement.[76] But the potential for delay, alone, is insufficient to show the undue prejudice needed to deny a stay, particularly in view of the 12-month timeline for completing a post-grant proceeding.[77] District courts will look at the specific facts of the case to determine whether a stay would unfairly advantage the movant to the disadvantage of the patent owner, such as in cases where the litigants are direct competitors and the stay would impact market share or revenue.[78]

---

74. *See, e.g.*, NFC Tech. LLC v. HTC Am., Inc., No. 13-CV-1058, 2015 WL 1069111, at *4 (E.D. Tex. Mar. 11, 2015) (granting motion to stay filed four months after service of infringement contentions); Destination Maternity Corp. v. Target Corp., 12 F. Supp. 3d 762, 766–68 (E.D. Pa. 2014) (granting motion to stay filed less than four months after infringement contentions); Software Rights Archive, LLC v. Facebook, Inc., No. C-12-3970, 2013 WL 5225522, at *6 (N.D. Cal. Sept. 17, 2013) (granting motion to stay filed just over four months after identification of asserted claims); *Semiconductor Energy Lab. Co.*, 2012 WL 7170593, at *3; VirtualAgility, Inc. v. Salesforce.com, Inc., No. 13-CV-00011, 2014 WL 94371, at *6 (E.D. Tex. Jan. 9, 2014); VirtualAgility, Inc. v. Salesforce.com, Inc., 759 F.3d 1307, 1318 (Fed. Cir. 2014).

75. *See, e.g.*, *Snyders Heart Valve LLC*, 2021 WL 1063005, at *5 (D. Minn. Mar. 19, 2021); Universal Elecs., Inc. v. Universal Remote Control, Inc., 943 F. Supp. 2d 1028, 1031–32 (C.D. Cal. 2013) (stay denied where plaintiff had already served written discovery, trial date was set, and the court had held Markman hearing and issued claim construction ruling).

76. *Snyders Heart Valve LLC*, 2021 WL 1063005, at *4.

77. *See, e.g.*, Neste Oil Oyj v. Dynamic Fuels, LLC, No. 12-662, 2013 WL 424754, at *2 (D. Del. Jan. 31, 2013) (finding that "the potential for delay does not, by itself, establish undue prejudice" and that concerns about direct competitiveness were not persuasive in that case); Market-Alerts Pty. Ltd. v. Bloomberg Fin. L.P., 922 F. Supp. 2d 486 (D. Del. 2013); *VirtualAgility*, 2014 WL 94371, at *5 & n.4.

78. *See, e.g.*, Davol v. Atrium Med. Corp., No. 12-958, 2013 WL 3013343, at *6 (D. Del. June 17, 2013) (denying stay and finding that "Davol will suffer undue prejudice should it be forced to continue competing with Atrium's accused products without being permitted

Litigants should consider the strategic advantages and disadvantages of seeking a stay. Advantages for patent owners and defendants alike may include saving or delaying litigation expense and simplifying issues and the litigation. Disadvantages may include taking positions on claim construction early without the benefit of robust discovery and delaying resolution of the parties' claims if the IPR or PGR is not fully case dispositive.

The Supreme Court's decision in *SAS v. Iancu*,[79] holding that the Board's final written decision must address every claim challenged in an IPR petition, may impact district courts' evaluation of motions to stay. For example, because the Board has a binary decision—institute all challenged claims or none at all—there is no chance the Board will review only a subset of claims asserted in the district court (if all asserted claims are challenged). This binary decision also simplifies issues at the district court because, for every instituted petition, each of the challenged claims will either be (1) confirmed, resulting in estoppel of all challenges the petitioner raised or could have reasonably raised in the IPR, or (2) canceled, reducing the number of issues remaining for the district court.[80] On the other hand, *SAS* may weigh against a stay because the Board need only determine whether the petitioner is likely to succeed on at least one claim to institute, which can ultimately lead to a mixed outcome where the Board confirms some claims and cancels others in a final written decision even though all claims were instituted.[81] However, mixed outcomes at the Board are relatively uncommon. While several factors impact a stay, district courts generally favor them, as shown in Figure 2.1.[82]

---

to advance its infringement claims"); Avago Techs. Fiber Ltd. v. IPtronics Inc., No. 10-CV-02863, 2011 WL 3267768, at *5 (N.D. Cal. July 28, 2011) ("Staying a case while [harm in the marketplace] is ongoing usually prejudices the patentee that seeks timely enforcement of its right to exclude."); Heraeus Electro-Nite Co. LLC v. Vesuvius USA Corp., 09-2417, 2010 WL 181375, at *1 (E.D. Pa. Jan. 11, 2010) ("[C]ourts have been reluctant to grant stays where, as here, the parties are direct competitors."); *VirtualAgility*, 2014 WL 94371, at *6.

79. SAS Inst., Inc. v. Iancu, 138 S. Ct. 1348 (2018).

80. *See, e.g.*, Qualcomm Inc. v. Apple Inc., No. 17-CV-2402, 2018 WL 4104951, at *2 (S.D. Cal. Aug. 29, 2018).

81. *See, e.g.*, Intell. Ventures I LLC v. T Mobile USA, Inc., No. 17-CV-577, Dkt. 255, 2018 WL 11363370, at *6 (E.D. Tex. Dec. 13, 2018).

82. Data obtained from Docket Navigator for Jan. 2012–May 2021.

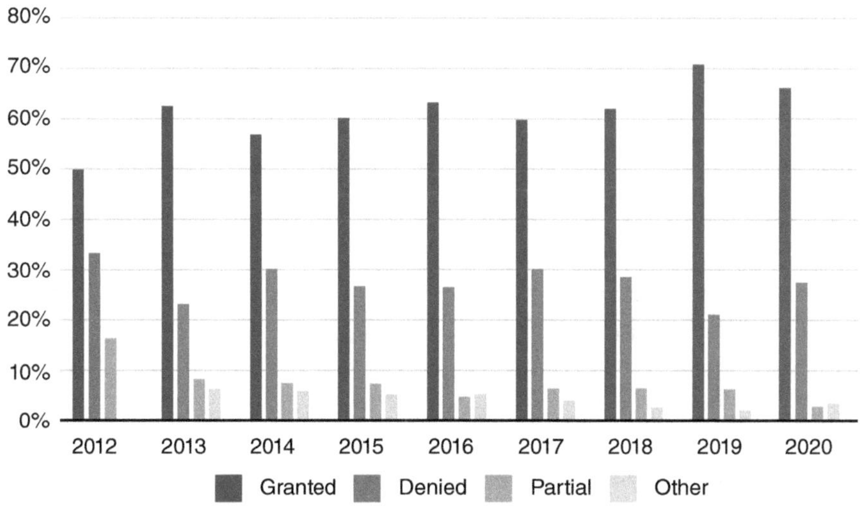

Figure 2.1
Motions to Stay Success Rate by Year: District Courts

2. ITC

The ITC traditionally weighs five factors in determining whether a stay is appropriate:

(1) the state of discovery and the hearing date;
(2) whether a stay will simplify the issues and hearing of the case;
(3) the undue prejudice or clear tactical disadvantage to any party;
(4) the stage of the PTAB proceedings; and
(5) the efficient use of Commission resources.[83]

These five factors are similar to those analyzed by district courts, but as shown in Figure 2.2, the ITC rarely grants a stay pending Board review.[84] The ITC has, however, exercised its discretion to suspend issuance of remedial orders if the Board issues a final written decision prior to the ITC's

83. Certain Automated Storage and Retrieval Systems, Robots, and Components Thereof, Inv. No. 337-TA-1228, Order No. 6, at 7 (Mar. 9, 2021); Certain Memory Modules and Components Thereof (Memory Modules), Inv. No. 337-TA-1089, Order No. 49, at 1–4 (Apr. 11, 2019).

84. Data obtained from Docket Navigator for Jan. 2016–May 2021.

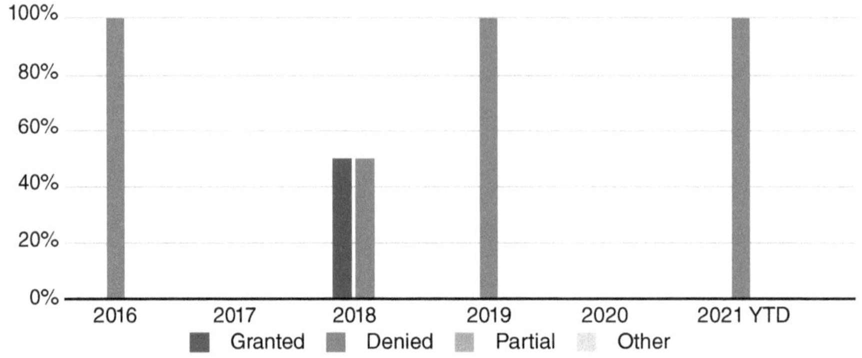

Figure 2.2
Motions to Stay Success Rate by Year: ITC

determination of a violation and issuance of remedial orders.[85] Such suspensions are generally limited to the claims canceled during the Board proceeding and, thus, have had little practical effect in cases involving additional patent claims.[86]

In at least one case, the ITC has extended these principles to suspend enforcement of its remedial orders *pending* the resolution of a Board proceeding.[87]

3. Other Considerations

District courts are less inclined to grant motions to stay in cases where fewer than all codefendants petition for IPR or PGR.[88] This is because defendants not involved in the proceeding will not be estopped from raising invalidity defenses that were raised or reasonably could have been raised in the

85. Certain Three-Dimensional Cinema Systems & Components Thereof, Inv. No. 337-TA-939, Comm'n Op., at 60–61 (Aug. 23, 2016); Certain Magnetic Tape Cartridges and Tape Components Thereof ("Magnetic Tape Cartridges"), Inv. No. 337-TA-1058, Comm'n Op., at 62–63 (Apr. 9, 2019).

86. *Id.*

87. Certain Unmanned Aerial Vehicles and Components Thereof (Unmanned Aerial Vehicles), Inv. No. 337-TA-1133, Comm'n Op. (Sept. 8, 2020).

88. Semiconductor Energy Lab. Co. v. Chimei Innolux Corp., No. SACV 12-21, 2012 WL 7170593, at *2 (C.D. Cal. Dec. 19, 2012) ("The estoppel effect of *inter partes* review carries less weight when there are several defendants that are not parties to, and thus are not bound by, the estoppel effects of the proceeding.").

post-grant proceeding, weighing against the simplification of the issues for trial.[89] As a result, district courts may condition the grant of a stay pending post-grant review on agreement from uninvolved codefendants to be bound by the outcome of the review.[90]

C. Claim Construction

Claim construction is a fundamental part of any patent proceeding and plays a significant role in the outcome of a patent litigation or post-grant challenge. But the applicable standard for claim construction and the effects of any proposed construction may vary based on the type of proceeding in which the claims are being construed.

1. Claim Construction Standards

District courts apply the familiar *Phillips* standard: claims are construed to have their "ordinary and customary meaning," which "is the meaning that the term would have to a person of ordinary skill in the art in question at the time of the invention."[91] The ITC similarly applies the *Phillips* standard.[92] In early post-grant proceedings, the Board applied the broadest reasonable interpretation standard, which is the standard applied for claim

89. *See* MPHJ Tech. Invs., LLC v. Rsch. Now, Inc., No. 13-CV-00962, 2014 WL 11514323, slip op., at *2 n.1 (E.D. Tex. June 10, 2014) (The fact that "[defendant] is not a party to the PTAB proceeding casts doubt on the extent, if any, a stay will simplify the issues in this case."); *see also* Evolutionary Intelligence, LLC v. Sprint Nextel Corp., No. 13-04513, 2014 WL 819277, at *5–6 (N.D. Cal. Feb. 28, 2014) ("[Defendant] represented to the court that it did not assist the IPR . . . . The court thus conditions the stay on [defendant's] agreement to be estopped only from asserting any invalidity contention that was actually raised and finally adjudicated in the IPR proceedings."); *but see* Intell. Ventures II, LLC v. Huntington Bancshares Inc., No. 13-CV-00785, 2014 WL 2589420, at *4 (S.D. Ohio June 10, 2014) ("[I]t would be unfair to condition a stay on Defendants' being bound by arguments raised in a proceeding over which they have no control.").

90. *Evolutionary Intelligence, LLC*, 2014 WL 819277, at *5–6.

91. Phillips v. AWH Corp., 415 F.3d 1303, 1313 (Fed. Cir. 2005).

92. *See, e.g.*, Kyocera Wireless Corp. v. ITC, 545 F.3d 1340, 1346 (Fed. Cir. 2008) (applying *Phillips* standard in review of ITC decision).

construction during prosecution[93] and ex parte reexamination,[94] but now, both IPRs and PGRs are subject to the *Phillips* standard applied in district court.[95] Thus, like the district courts and the ITC, the Board now focuses its claim construction inquiry on how one of ordinary skill, reviewing the claim terms in the context of the claims, specification, and prosecution history, that is, the intrinsic evidence, would read the claim term at issue.[96] Though so-called extrinsic evidence, such as dictionary definitions and expert testimony, may be helpful to this analysis, "it is less significant than the intrinsic record."[97] Applying the *Phillips* standard is generally considered to lead to a narrower interpretation of the claims when compared to the broadest reasonable interpretation standard.[98]

Accordingly, it may be easier to prove unpatentability in an ex parte reexamination, where the broadest reasonable interpretation applies to unexpired claims—a broader claim construction makes it easier to show any given limitation existed in the prior art. But it is important to remember that in reexamination, the patentee can freely amend the claims as long as the amendments do not broaden the scope of the claims and the reexamination requester's participation is limited to filing the request and responding to a patent owner's initial statement,[99] which are rarely filed. Thus, a reexamination may provide the patentee a better opportunity to amend the claims to avoid prior art while maintaining strong infringement positions as compared to an AIA postgrant proceeding. While the potential for amendments is an important consideration for IPR and PGR proceedings, patentees are constrained in the types of amendments that can be made in

---

93. MPEP, *supra* note 1, §§ 2258(I), 2258(G) (ex parte reexam).

94. *Id.* However, "[w]hen a patent expires during a reexamination proceeding, the PTO . . . thereafter appl[ies] the *Phillips* standard for claim construction." *In re* CSB-Sys. Int'l, Inc., 832 F.3d 1335, 1341 (Fed. Cir. 2016).

95. 37 C.F.R. §§ 42.100(b) (IPR), 42.200(b) (PGR).

96. *Phillips*, 415 F.3d at 1313–19.

97. *Id.* at 1317.

98. Facebook, Inc. v. Pragmatus AV, LLC, 582 F. App'x 864, 869 (Fed. Cir. 2014) (stating that the broadest reasonable interpretation standard "may be the same as or broader than the construction of a term under the *Phillips* standard. But it cannot be narrower.").

99. 35 U.S.C. § 305; *see* MPEP, *supra* note 1, § 2250.

those proceedings (and convincing the Board to grant a motion to amend, other than to cancel claims, has historically proven difficult).[100]

2. Impact of Claim Construction in and on Other Proceedings

Another consideration for both patent owners and potential petitioners is whether the claims at issue have previously been construed or may be construed in another proceeding.

If a claim term has already been formally construed, the parties to the first case may be collaterally estopped from relitigating that construction in subsequent actions.[101] Collateral estoppel (issue preclusion) "applies if: (1) the issue necessarily decided in the previous proceeding is identical to the one which is sought to be relitigated; (2) the first proceeding ended with a final judgment on the merits; and (3) the party against which collateral estoppel is asserted was a party or in privity with a party at the first proceeding."[102] Accordingly, the patent owner—generally the only repeat party—may be bound by a prior decision on claim construction. And even though the petitioner may be free to argue for another construction, it is nevertheless important to consider the impact of prior claim constructions on the grounds to be raised in a petition. Although a tribunal is not compelled to accept a prior district court or Board ruling on the construction of a term, it may nevertheless find a previous construction persuasive.[103] Indeed, the Board has explained that it "*will consider* any prior claim construction determinations from federal courts and the ITC that are timely made of record to enhance consistency."[104] The Federal Circuit has similarly instructed that "[g]iven 'the importance of uniformity in the treatment of a

100. *See* MasterImage 3D, Inc. v. RealD, Inc., IPR2015-00040, Paper 42 (July 15, 2015); REG Synthetic Fuels LLC v. Neste Oil Oyj, IPR2014-00192, Paper 48 (June 5, 2015); Riverbed Tech., Inc. v. Silver Peak Sys., Inc., IPR2013-00402, Paper 35 (Dec. 30, 2014).

101. *See, e.g.*, e.Digital Corp. v. Futurewei Techs., Inc., 772 F.3d 723, 726 (Fed. Cir. 2014) (ruling patentee collaterally estopped based on prior claim construction). *But see* RF Del., Inc. v. Pac. Keystone Techs., Inc., 326 F.3d 1255, 1262 (Fed. Cir. 2003) (ruling prior construction issued as part of summary judgment order without a formal Markman hearing was not entitled to preclusive effect).

102. *e.Digital*, 772 F.3d at 726 (citing Hydranautics v. FilmTec Corp., 204 F.3d 880, 885 (9th Cir. 2000)).

103. *See, e.g.*, IGT v. Bally Gaming Int'l, Inc., 659 F.3d 1109, 1117 n.1 (Fed. Cir. 2011).

104. 83 Fed. Reg. 51,340, 51,350 (Oct. 11, 2018) (emphasis added).

given patent,' . . . [any tribunal] would be remiss to overlook another district court's construction of the same claim terms."[105]

A prior claim construction under the *Phillips* standard, whether by a district court, the ITC, or the Board, may be less likely to persuade a reexamination examiner. A different claim construction standard is applied in reexamination, and the Federal Circuit has recognized (and even approved of) differing constructions of the same term as a result. For example, in *In re American Academy of Science Tech Center*,[106] the Federal Circuit considered the claim construction of "user computer." In reexamination, the examiner construed the term under the broadest reasonable interpretation standard and determined a "user computer" included mainframe computers.[107] Based on that construction, the examiner rejected the claims as unpatentable over the prior art, a conclusion that the Board affirmed.[108] Reviewing the decision, the Federal Circuit recognized that the examiner's construction was inconsistent with a district court's construction of the same term.[109] But the court still affirmed, noting "the Board is required to use a different standard for construing claims than that used by district courts. We have held that it is error for the Board to 'appl[y] the mode of claim interpretation that is used by courts in litigation.'"[110]

Parties should understand that a prior reexamination is less likely to impact other types of proceedings and, similarly, reexamination is less likely to be impacted by other types of prior proceedings. To the extent a prior *Phillips* construction makes an invalidity case untenable, petitioners may

105. Finisar Corp. v. DirecTV Grp., Inc., 523 F.3d 1323, 1329 (Fed. Cir. 2008) (quoting Markman v. Westview Instruments, Inc., 517 U.S. 370, 390 (1996)); *see also* Cisco Sys., Inc. v. Capella Photonics, Inc., No. 20-CV-01858, 2021 WL 1688307, at *6, *17 (N.D. Cal. Apr. 29, 2021) (stating "assuming the Federal Circuit has not construed the terms of a patent, district courts are to give more deference (stare decisis deference) to prior constructions from courts inside their district than to prior constructions from courts outside their district" and considering prior district court and Board constructions); Diebold Nixdorf, Inc. v. Hyosung TNS, Inc., No. 19-1695, 2021 WL 678672, at *3 (D. Del. Feb. 22, 2021) (considering prior ITC construction of claim terms).

106. 367 F.3d 1359, 1369 (Fed. Cir. 2004).

107. *Id.* at 1363.

108. *Id.*

109. *Id.* at 1369.

110. *Id.* (quoting *In re* Zletz, 893 F.2d 319, 321 (Fed. Cir. 1989)) (alteration in original).

wish to consider ex parte reexamination instead. Notably, however, the examiner may still consider prior *Phillips* constructions, and both patent owners and petitioners should address prior constructions explaining why that construction does or does not apply.[111]

Similar considerations apply when deciding how to argue claim construction in ongoing parallel proceedings. In two proceedings applying different claim construction standards, parties may fairly argue for different claim constructions. For example, in *Mike's Train House v. Broadway*,[112] a district court considered whether the defendant should be estopped from arguing noninfringement based on claim construction arguments presented in the defendant's petition for ex parte reexamination.[113] The defendant argued that prior art teaching a particular protocol—the same protocol used by the defendant in its accused product—met a claim limitation.[114] The patentee argued that this was "tantamount to an admission."[115] The court considered and rejected this contention. It explained that estoppel requires, among other elements, a factual incompatibility between two positions advanced by the same party.[116] The different standards for claim construction, the district court ruled, meant that the defendant's position in the reexamination was not inconsistent with its district court defense.[117] Other courts have similarly found that arguably inconsistent arguments between proceedings applying different standards are not inherently problematic.[118]

---

111. *See, e.g.*, Immunex Corp. v. Sanofi-Aventis U.S. LLC, 977 F.3d 1212, 1223 (Fed. Cir. 2020) (affirming construction under the broadest reasonable interpretation standard and noting that Board had considered district court's construction).

112. Mike's Train House, Inc. v. Broadway Ltd. Imports, LLC, No. 09-CV-02657, 2012 WL 664498, at *21 (D. Md. Feb. 27, 2012), *aff'd*, 500 F. App'x 958 (Fed. Cir. 2013).

113. *Id.*

114. *Id.*

115. *Id.*

116. *Id.* (explaining "the criteria for judicial estoppel: '(1) the party to be estopped must be asserting a position that is factually incompatible with a position taken in a prior judicial or administrative proceeding; (2) the prior inconsistent position must have been accepted by the tribunal; and (3) the party to be estopped must have taken inconsistent positions intentionally for the purpose of gaining unfair advantage'" (citation omitted)).

117. *Id.* at *22.

118. *See, e.g.*, GoPro, Inc. v. C&A Mktg., Inc., No. 16-CV-03590, 2017 WL 3131449, at *5 n.4 (N.D. Cal. July 24, 2017) ("The Court agrees with C&A that its arguments in its petition . . . that the claims required no construction do not constitute an admission for purposes of the claim construction in the district court litigation."); Rsch. Frontiers, Inc. v. E Ink Corp.,

But in presenting claim constructions in two proceedings applying the same claim construction standard, inconsistent positions may be problematic. A party that successfully argues for a particular construction may be estopped from arguing a different construction going forward, even before the end of the first proceeding.[119] And even in the absence of a binding position, taking inconsistent positions may pose credibility concerns. Parties to a post-grant proceeding must serve evidence of positions that may be considered inconsistent with those taken at the Board, including claim construction and infringement/noninfringement or validity/invalidity positions taken in district court.[120] Any claim construction positions to be considered by the Board must be set forth in an IPR or PGR petition and patent-owner response.[121] Regardless of which parallel proceeding reaches claim construction first, positions from one proceeding will likely be available for use in any and all parallel proceedings, and parties should keep that in mind as they finalize their claim construction positions and supporting evidence.

One final consideration is the Board's practice of announcing preliminary claim constructions in institution decisions. These preliminary constructions may be addressed during the course of the IPR or PGR, through and including oral argument.[122] Thus, depending on the perspective of the

No. 13-1231, 2016 WL 1169580, at *3 n.4 (D. Del. Mar. 24, 2016), *report and recommendation adopted*, No. CV 13-1231, 2016 WL 7217217 (D. Del. Dec. 13, 2016), *aff'd*, 706 F. App'x 685 (Fed. Cir. 2017) ("[T]he fact that [party] took certain claim construction positions during the . . . proceeding may well be relevant to the Court in resolving claim construction disputes here (as might the . . . analysis of a particular term). The point is just that [the party] should not be prohibited from arguing for the constructions it now puts forward.").

119. *See, e.g.*, FullView, Inc. v. Polycom, Inc., No. 18-CV-00510, 2021 WL 1253653, at *6 n.3 (N.D. Cal. Apr. 5, 2021) (noting collateral estoppel may bind parties following Board construction); Trs. of Columbia Univ. in City of N.Y. v. NortonLifeLock, Inc., No. 3:13CV808, 2019 WL 7040931, at *5 (E.D. Va. Dec. 20, 2019) (applying judicial estoppel based on prior claim construction statements, noting such estoppel applies where the party takes a position inconsistent with an earlier position that it successfully persuaded an earlier tribunal to accept and "the party seeking to assert an inconsistent position would derive an unfair advantage or impose an unfair detriment on the opposing party if not estopped" (quoting Trs. in Bankr. of N. Am. Rubber Thread Co., Inc. v. United States, 593 F.3d 1346, 1354 (Fed. Cir. 2010)).

120. 37 C.F.R. § 42.51.

121. *Id.* §§ 42.104, 42.204.

122. Rules of Practice for Trials before the Patent Trial and Appeal Board and Judicial Review of Patent Trial and Appeal Board Decisions, 77 Fed. Reg. 48,612, 48,627, Response to Comment 17 (Aug. 14, 2012).

party, all is not lost or gained if the Board initially construes a claim term in its decision to institute. Though the Board's initial analysis may be of interest to another tribunal, parties should remember that a construction at institution is subject to change.[123] Additional evidence—including constructions in another proceeding—may prove persuasive to the Board and may result in a different final claim construction.

D. Discretionary Denials

The statutory language setting requirements for instituting IPRs and PGRs is permissive, in that the statute sets out criteria that must be met to warrant institution.[124] These criteria include time bars for IPRs related to parallel litigation, limits on PGRs (relative to issue date), and the necessary showing of unpatentability (for at least one challenged claim). The threshold for instituting an IPR is a reasonable likelihood that at least one challenged claim is unpatentable;[125] the threshold for instituting a PGR is whether it is more likely than not that at least one challenged claim is unpatentable.[126] But institution is not required, even if these statutory criteria are met. The Board[127] always has discretion to deny institution. The Board may separately deny institution when a petitioner relies on "the same or substantially the same prior art arguments previously" considered by the Office, that is, when a petitioner raises grounds that were already overcome during prosecution,

123. *Id.*

124. Harmonic Inc. v. Avid Tech., Inc., 815 F.3d 1356, 1367 (Fed. Cir. 2016) ("[T]he PTO is permitted, but never compelled, to institute an IPR proceeding.").

125. 35 U.S.C. § 314(a).

126. *Id.* § 324(a).

127. The AIA authorizes the Director to institute IPRs and PGRs. *See* 35 U.S.C. §§ 314(a), 324(a). The Director has delegated this authority to the Board. *See, e.g.*, Ethicon Endo-Surgery, Inc. v. Covidien LP, 812 F.3d 1023, 1028, 1031–33 (Fed. Cir. 2016) ("[There is a] longstanding rule that agency heads have implied authority to delegate to officials within the agency, even without explicit statutory authority and even when agency officials have other statutory duties. . . . Before the AIA, the Director, as head of the PTO, regularly assigned tasks to subordinate officers. This carried over to the AIA, where Congress assigned the Director the decision to institute, necessarily assuming that the popularity of inter partes review and the short time frame to decide whether to institute inter partes review would mean that the Director could not herself review every petition. . . . We conclude that the Director has the inherent authority to delegate institution decisions to the Board."); 37 C.F.R. § 42.4(a).

reexamination, or another Board proceeding.[128] The Board may also deny institution to avoid serial attacks on a patent and to preserve resources.[129]

Discretionary denials have been increasing since the introduction of the AIA, especially after *SAS* prohibited the practice of partial institution (instituting some but not all claims and/or grounds).[130] And the Board has designated several precedential opinions, which outline factors that panels will consider when deciding whether to institute.

In 2017, the Board designated a portion of its *General Plastic v. Canon* decision precedential, which provides a seven-factor test to prevent inequities to patent owners facing serial IPR petitions challenging the same patent.[131] In 2019, the Board designated *Becton, Dickinson v. B. Braun* as precedential (after previously designating it informative in 2018), which provides a six-factor test for evaluating how close the proposed grounds are to challenges previously considered by the Office.[132] In 2020, the Board designated *Apple v. Fintiv* and *NHK Spring v. Intri-Plex* as precedential, which provide a six-factor test for evaluating when a parallel district court

---

128. 35 U.S.C. § 325(d).

129. *See, e.g.*, Gen. Plastic Indus. Co. v. Canon Kabushiki Kaisha, IPR2016-01357, Paper 19, at 16–17 (Sept. 6, 2017) (Precedential) (the Board recognizing the "potential for abuse of the review process by repeated attacks on patents"); PATENT TRIAL AND APPEAL BOARD CONSOLIDATED TRIAL PRACTICE GUIDE 59 (Nov. 2019) ("one petition should be sufficient to challenge the claims of a patent in most situations" and filing more than one petition in parallel against a single patent tends to place a "substantial and unnecessary burden on the Board and the patent owner and could raise fairness, timing, and efficiency concerns"); *see also, e.g.*, Comcast Cable Commc'ns, LLC v. Rovi Guides, Inc., IPR2020-00799, IPR2020-00812, Paper 8, at 8–11 (Oct. 21, 2020) (denying institution of second petition by party challenging same patent claims, noting: "Petitioner does not explain sufficiently how the two Petitions at issue here collectively challenge the claims in a materially different manner that justifies multiple proceedings. Moreover, the two Petitions at issue here create inefficiencies as compared to the single instituted petition in IPR2020-00798."); Ivantis, Inc. v. Glaukos Corp., IPR2019-00972, Paper 7, at 16–18 (Oct. 10, 2019).

130. SAS Inst. Inc. v. Iancu, 138 S. Ct. 1348 (2018) (holding that the Board's decision to institute is binary and that the Board must institute all or no grounds).

131. *Gen. Plastic Indus. Co.*, IPR2016-01357, Paper 19.

132. Becton, Dickinson & Co. v. B. Braun Melsungen AG, IPR2017-01586, Paper 8 (Dec. 15, 2017) (Precedential).

proceeding is at an advanced stage and Board review would be duplicative, redundant, or unnecessary.[133]

Institution decisions are "final and nonappealable."[134] While no estoppel applies to institution decisions and unsuccessful petitioners can raise or maintain invalidity positions in district court, several strategy considerations arise. For example, the likelihood of a stay is relevant to discretionary denial and impacts strategies for parallel litigations (district court or ITC). Court schedules and the timing of petition filing may also influence discretionary denial—for example, the earlier (more expeditiously) a petition is filed can weigh against discretionary denial.[135]

1. Previous Consideration by the Office—35 U.S.C. § 325(d)

Under 35 U.S.C. § 325(d), "[i]n determining whether to institute or order a proceeding under this chapter [PGRs], chapter 30 [ex parte reexaminations], or chapter 31 [IPRs], the Director may take into account whether, and reject the petition or request because, the same or substantially the same prior art or arguments were previously presented to the Office."[136] The Board laid out a number of factors in *Becton, Dickinson* for what constitutes "the same or substantially the same prior art or arguments."[137] Those factors include:

(a) the similarities and material differences between the asserted art and the prior art involved during examination;
(b) the cumulative nature of the asserted art and the prior art evaluated during examination;
(c) the extent to which the asserted art was evaluated during examination, including whether the prior art was the basis for rejection;

---

133. Apple Inc. v. Fintiv, Inc., IPR2020-00019, Paper 11 (Mar. 20, 2020) (Precedential); NHK Spring Co. v. Intri-Plex Techs., Inc., IPR2018-00752, Paper 8, at 20 (Sept. 12, 2018) (Precedential).

134. 35 U.S.C. § 314(d); Cuozzo Speed Techs. LLC v. Lee, 136 S. Ct. 2131 (2016).

135. *See, e.g.*, SK Hynix Inc. v. Netlist, Inc., IPR2020-01421, Paper 10, at 9, 13 (Mar. 16, 2021); Quantile Techs. Ltd. v. Trioptima AB, CBM2020-00011, Paper 12, at 19 (Sept. 23, 2020) ("We also note that Petitioner moved with speed in bringing this challenge—the Petition was filed less than four months after the complaint was filed and only about two months after the complaint was served. Thus, we weigh this factor against denial of institution.").

136. 35 U.S.C. § 325(d).

137. *Becton, Dickinson & Co.*, IPR2017-01586, Paper 8, at 16–28.

(d) the extent of the overlap between the arguments made during examination and the manner in which Petitioner relies on the prior art or Patent Owner distinguishes the prior art;
(e) whether Petitioner has pointed out sufficiently how the Examiner erred in its evaluation of the asserted prior art; and
(f) the extent to which additional evidence and facts presented in the Petition warrant reconsideration of the prior art or arguments.[138]

In applying these factors, the Board has highlighted the highly fact-specific nature of the inquiry. For example, when assessing factor (a) in *Becton, Dickinson* itself, the Board noted that the petitioner used the same primary reference applied during prosecution but relied on a different secondary reference and thus presented a facially different challenge than what the examiner considered.[139] But because, in the Board's view, the new secondary reference discloses something structurally similar to what the secondary reference applied during prosecution disclosed, the Board "g[a]ve little weight to" the facial difference and found it weighed in favor of denial.[140] For factor (b), the Board found the petitioner was seeking to use the secondary reference (though as part of a new combination in the petition) in the same way it was considered during prosecution.[141] The Board found this did not present "persuasive new evidence of unpatentability," was "cumulative in nature," and weighed in favor of denial.[142] And for factor (c), the Board noted both references were "considered by the Examiner, albeit in separate grounds of rejection," and found this distinct from situations where the petition's prior art is "simply listed in an [information disclosure statement] during prosecution."[143] After assessing all factors, the Board concluded:

> The same base reference, Woehr, as used in this obviousness ground was relied upon in the same manner during prosecution, and it is combined with a secondary reference, Tauschinski, which was

138. *Id.* at 17–18.
139. *Id.* at 18–21.
140. *Id.* at 21.
141. *Id.* at 21–22.
142. *Id.*
143. *Id.* at 22–23.

also applied in the same manner by the Examiner as it is here in the Petition. With only a nominally different combination of prior art and considering that Petitioner presents the same arguments as were meritoriously overcome by the Applicant during prosecution, based on our consideration of the non-exhaustive factors above, we are persuaded that exercising our discretion under 325(d) on this particular ground is appropriate.[144]

Since *Becton, Dickinson*, the Board has reallocated those six factors into a "two-part framework."[145] First, the Board will consider "whether the same or substantially the same art previously was presented to the Office or whether the same or substantially the same arguments previously were presented to the Office."[146] This part of the framework includes an inquiry into *Becton, Dickinson* factors (a), (b), and (d).[147] If this first part is satisfied, then the Board considers "whether the petitioner has demonstrated that the Office erred in a manner material to the patentability of challenged claims."[148] This includes an inquiry into factors (c), (e), and (f).[149] Examples of a "material error" include "misapprehending or overlooking specific teachings of the relevant prior art where those teachings impact patentability of the challenged claims" or "misconstruing a claim term, where the construction impacts patentability of the challenged claims."[150]

In view of these factors, petitioners should consider whether the prior art they plan to rely on in the petition was cited on an IDS or expressly considered by the examiner. If the latter, they should consider whether the prior art is being used in the same way in the petition, for the same limitations, or in the same combination. And they should be able to articulate meaningful differences between the challenge(s) presented in the petition

144. *Id.* at 28. This decision issued before *SAS*, when partial institution decisions were still permissible.

145. Advanced Bionics, LLC v. MED-EL Elektromedizinische Gerate GmbH, IPR2019-01469, Paper 6, at 6–22 (Feb. 13, 2020) (Precedential); Weatherford U.S., L.P. v. Enventure Global Tech., LLC, IPR2020-01661, Paper 19, at 14–35 (Apr. 15, 2021).

146. *Advanced Bionics*, IPR2019-01469, Paper 6, at 8.

147. *Id.* at 8–10.

148. *Id.* at 8.

149. *Id.* at 10–11.

150. *Id.* at 8–9 n.9.

and the challenge(s) overcome during prosecution, in particular identifying how an examiner may have overlooked or misapplied a reference. When filing a petition that has multiple grounds, petitioners should also be mindful that grounds that may warrant institution may nevertheless be denied if other grounds in the petition are deemed redundant or cumulative to one another.[151] The Board did just that in *Weatherford v. Enventure Global*, in view of the Supreme Court's mandate in *SAS* that petitions be denied or granted in their entirety.[152]

2. Procedural Denials—35 U.S.C. § 314

Under 35 U.S.C. § 314(a), the "Director may not authorize an inter partes review to be instituted unless the Director determines that the information presented in the petition . . . shows that there is a reasonable likelihood that the petitioner would prevail with respect to at least 1 of the claims challenged in the petition."[153] The Federal Circuit has explained that pursuant to this statutory directive, the PTO is "permitted, but never compelled, to institute an IPR."[154] "The Director bears the political responsibility of determining which cases should proceed. While he has the authority not to institute review on the merits of the petition, he could deny review for other reasons such as administrative efficiency . . . ."[155] This comports with 35 U.S.C. § 316(b), which provides that the Director is required to "consider the effect . . . on the economy, the integrity of the patent system, the efficient administration of the Office, and the ability of the Office to timely complete proceedings" when deciding whether to institute.[156]

151. Weatherford U.S., L.P. v. Enventure Global Tech., Inc., IPR2020-01661, Paper 19, at 14–35 (Apr. 15, 2021).

152. *Id.*

153. 35 U.S.C. § 314(a); Cuozzo Speed Techs., LLC v. Lee, 136 S. Ct. 2131, 2140 (2016) ("The Patent Office's decision to initiate inter partes review is 'preliminary,' not 'final.' And the agency's decision to deny a petition is a matter committed to the Patent Office's discretion.").

154. Harmonic Inc. v. Avid Tech., Inc., 815 F.3d 1356, 1367 (Fed. Cir. 2016).

155. Saint Regis Mohawk Tribe v. Mylan Pharms. Inc., 896 F.3d 1322, 1327 (Fed. Cir. 2018), *cert. denied*, 139 S. Ct. 1547 (2019) (citing Wi-Fi One, LLC v. Broadcom Corp., 878 F.3d 1364, 1372 (Fed. Cir. 2018) (en banc)).

156. 35 U.S.C. § 316(b); PATENT TRIAL AND APPEAL BOARD CONSOLIDATED TRIAL PRACTICE GUIDE 58 (Nov. 2019).

Before the Supreme Court's decision in *SAS*,[157] the Board had adopted a practice of issuing partial-institution decisions, where it would (in its discretion) not always institute all grounds against all claims, denying redundant or unsubstantiated grounds. The Supreme Court held that partial-institution practice conflicted with governing statutes and mandated that, if the Board elected to institute, it had to institute for all claims and grounds presented in a petition (a binary decision).[158] In view of that mandate, the Board began applying a holistic view when deciding whether to institute or deny petitions that presented numerous grounds, some with merit, some without.[159]

For example, in *EIK Engineering v. Wilco Marsh Buggies*, the Board explained that a "holistic view applies . . . to situations where some claims meet the requirements for instituting a trial and some do not. While we *consider* the number of claims that fail to meet the statutory and other requirements to institute an *inter partes* review, as well as the number of claims that meet these requirements, there is no fixed threshold or ratio of claims that meet the requirements compared to those that do not meet the requirements that controls our determination."[160] The Board then denied institution because four of the 20 grounds presented in the petition lacked sufficient particularity (as required by 35 U.S.C. § 312).[161] The Board also reasoned that the petitioner "chose to define the contours of this proceeding by presenting 20 separate, distinct, and admittedly repetitious grounds that both the Board, and Patent Owner, would need to address. This does not promote the efficient administration of the Office or of this proceeding."[162] This is consistent with guidance in the Consolidated Trial Practice Guide:

> If a panel determines that a petition meets the standards for institution in relation to fewer than all the challenges presented, or

157. SAS Inst. Inc. v. Iancu, 138 S. Ct. 1348 (2018).
158. *Id.*
159. *See, e.g.*, EIK Eng'g SDN, BHD. v. Wilco Marsh Buggies & Draglines, Inc., IPR2020-00344, Paper 12, at 18–23 (Mar. 4, 2021); *see also, e.g.*, Adaptics Ltd. v. Perfect Co., IPR2018-01596, Paper 20, at 17 (Mar. 6, 2019) (Informative); Chevron Oronite Co. v. Infineum USA L.P., IPR2018-00923, Paper 9, at 10–11 (Nov. 7, 2018) (Informative).
160. *EIK Eng'g SDN, BHD.*, IPR2020-00344, Paper 12, at 20.
161. *Id.* at 17–23.
162. *Id.* at 23.

> where deficiencies in the petition (such as a failure to provide a construction under 35 U.S.C. § 112(f)) affect only a portion of the challenges presented, the panel will evaluate all the challenges and determine whether, in the interests of efficient administration of the Office and integrity of the patent system, the entire petition should be denied.[163]

The Board has also identified a number of factors that inform its institution decision when multiple petitions are filed challenging the same patent claims, either by the same petitioner or by different petitioners. Those factors are provided in *General Plastic v. Canon* and include:

(1) whether the same petitioner previously filed a petition directed to the same claims of the same patent;
(2) whether at the time of filing of the first petition the petitioner knew of the prior art asserted in the second petition or should have known of it;
(3) whether at the time of filing of the second petition the petitioner already received the patent owner's preliminary response to the first petition or received the Board's decision on whether to institute review in the first petition;
(4) the length of time that elapsed between the time the petitioner learned of the prior art asserted in the second petition and the filing of the second petition;
(5) whether the petitioner provides adequate explanation for the time elapsed between the filings of multiple petitions directed to the same claims of the same patent;
(6) the finite resources of the Board; and
(7) the requirement under 35 U.S.C. § 316(a)(11) to issue a final determination not later than one year after the date on which the Director notices institution of review.[164]

---

163. PATENT TRIAL AND APPEAL BOARD CONSOLIDATED TRIAL PRACTICE GUIDE 64 (Nov. 2019); *see also, e.g., Adaptics Ltd.*, IPR2018-01596, Paper 20, at 17.

164. Gen. Plastic Indus. Co. Ltd. v. Canon Kabushiki Kaisha, IPR2016-01357, Paper 19, at 9–10 (Sept. 6, 2017) (Precedential); *see also id.* at 15–22.

These factors are designed to assess the burden placed on the patent owner and Board when serial or "follow-on" petitions are filed. In *General Plastics*, the Board denied institution because, among other things, (1) the same claims were challenged in the multiple petitions; (2) the follow-on petitions were filed nine months after the first set of petitions, at which point the petitioner had the chance to review the patent owner's preliminary response and the Board's prior institution decisions and make appropriate adjustments; and (3) the petitioner offered no meaningful reason for the delay.[165] The Board found unpersuasive the argument that prior art searching inspired the later petitions when that searching "did not commence until after the Board issued the Decisions Denying Institution in the proceedings based on the first-filed petitions."[166]

The Board has also outlined a number of factors that inform its decision to institute or deny a petition in view of an earlier trial date in a parallel proceeding in *Apple v. Fintiv.*[167] "These factors relate to whether efficiency, fairness, and the merits" support a denial.[168] The Board acknowledged that there is "some overlap among these factors" and explained that it will take a "holistic view of whether [the] efficiency and integrity of the system are best served by denying or instituting review."[169] The factors include:

(1) whether the court granted a stay or evidence exists that one may be granted if a proceeding is instituted;
(2) proximity of the court's trial date to the Board's projected statutory deadline for a final written decision;
(3) investment in the parallel proceeding by the court and parties;
(4) overlap between issues raised in the petition and in the parallel proceeding;
(5) whether the petitioner and the defendant in the parallel proceeding are the same party; and

165. *Id.* at 10–11, 19–22.
166. *Id.* at 10.
167. Apple Inc. v. Fintiv, Inc., IPR2020-00019, Paper 11 (Mar. 20, 2020) (Precedential).
168. *Id.* at 6.
169. *Id.*

(6) other circumstances that impact the Board's exercise of discretion, including the merits.[170]

As to the first factor, the Board has reasoned that when a district court stays litigation pending the resolution of an IPR proceeding, it allays any concerns regarding inefficiency and duplicated efforts. Generally, a stayed case has been "strongly weighed against" the Board exercising its authority to deny institution.[171] Similarly, cases where there is no stay but the court has indicated it will likely consider a stay should the Board institute "usually weigh[] against" denying institution.[172] Importantly, the court's trial date and the investment of time are also considered when weighing if the court might be willing to reconsider or grant a stay upon institution.[173] If a district court has denied a stay and has not indicated that it would consider a renewed motion to stay or reconsider a motion to stay if the Board instituted, then the Board has "sometimes weighed" this in favor of denying institution.[174] Similarly, an earlier ITC trial date may favor denial where the ITC is going to decide the same or substantially similar issues to those presented in the IPR petition. This is because, as noted earlier, the ITC rarely stays cases pending post-grant proceedings.[175]

For the second factor, the Board has reasoned that when the scheduled trial date is earlier than the projected statutory deadline to complete the post-grant proceeding (generally 18 months from when a petition is filed), this factor typically weighs in favor of denying institution.[176] If, however, the "trial date is at or around the same time as the projected statutory deadline," other factors, like investment in the proceedings, may come into

170. *Id.*

171. *Id.* (citing Precision Planting, LLC v. Deere & Co., IPR2019-01052, Paper 19, at 10 (Jan. 7, 2020); Apotex Inc. v. UCB Biopharma Sprl, IPR2019-00400, Paper 17, at 31–32 (July 15, 2019)).

172. *Id.* at 7 (citing Abbott Vascular, Inc. v. FlexStent, LLC, IPR2019-00882, Paper 11, at 30–31 (Oct. 7, 2019)).

173. *Id.* (citing DMF, Inc. v. AMP Plus, Inc., Case No. 2-18-CV-07090 (C.D. Cal. July 12, 2019)).

174. *Id.* at 8.

175. *See supra* Chapter 2, section B.2.

176. Apple Inc. v. Fintiv, Inc., IPR2020-00019, Paper 11, at 9 (Mar. 20, 2020) (Precedential).

play.[177] Ultimately, however, this factor is not dispositive. And depending on a holistic view of the remaining factors, the Board has instituted post-grant proceedings despite a trial date falling after the projected statutory deadline for a final written decision.[178]

For the third factor, the Board considers the amount and type of work already completed in the litigation by the parties and the court by the time of institution. If the court has already issued substantive orders related to the patent, the Board generally weighs this factor in favor of denial.[179] For example, claim construction hearings and similar substantive orders generally indicate there has been sufficient investment (by the parties and court) in the parallel proceeding to deny institution.[180] In contrast, where the court

177. *Id.*

178. *See, e.g.*, Micron Tech., Inc. v. Godo Kaisha IP Bridge 1, IPR2020-01007, Paper 15, at 12 (Dec. 7, 2020) (instituting review despite trial scheduled in W.D. Tex. two months before final written decision (FWD) deadline); Dish Network LLC v. Broadband iTV, Inc., IPR2020-01332, Paper 14, at 25–26 (Jan. 27, 2021) (instituting review despite parallel trial scheduled in W.D. Tex. two to three months before FWD deadline); Google LLC v. Parus Holdings, Inc., IPR2020-00846, Paper 9, at 12 (Oct. 21, 2020) (instituting review despite parallel trial scheduled in W.D. Tex. three months before FWD deadline); NanoCellect Biomed., Inc. v. Cytonome/ST, LLC, IPR2020-00551, Paper 19, at 16–17 (Aug. 27, 2020) (instituting review despite the parallel proceeding's scheduled trial date preceding the deadline for a FWD by four months and noting "[w]hen sued in a fast-moving district, this factor may often weigh toward denial, even if a petitioner files its petition very quickly. We note, however, that this factor is not considered in isolation, but holistically along with other factors[.]"); Quantile Techs. Ltd. v. TriOptima AB, CBM2020-00011, Paper 12, at 18 (Sept. 23, 2020) (instituting review despite parallel trial scheduled four months before deadline for FWD); Sand Revolution II, LLC v. Cont'l Intermodal Grp.—Trucking LLC, IPR2019-01393, Paper 24, at 8–10 (June 16, 2020) (Informative) (instituting review despite trial scheduled five months before FWD deadline, noting a "continuing degree of . . . uncertainty of the court's schedule"); Medtronic CoreValve LLC v. Colibri Heart Valve LLC, IPR2020-01454, Paper 11, at 12 (Mar. 10, 2021) (instituting review despite trial scheduled to begin nearly six months before FWD deadline); Peag LLC v. Varta Microbattery GmbH, IPR2020-01212, Paper 8, at 17 (Jan. 6, 2021) (instituting review despite trial scheduled to begin in the E.D. Tex. seven months before FWD deadline); Apple Inc. v. Maxell, Ltd., IPR2020-00204, Paper 11, at 13–14 (June 19, 2020) (instituting review although the parallel proceeding's trial date, while uncertain, was anywhere from five to nine months before FWD deadline).

179. *Apple Inc.*, IPR2020-00019, Paper 11, at 9–12 (citing E-One, Inc. v. Oshkosh Corp., IPR2019-00162, Paper 16, at 8, 13, 20 (June 5, 2019); Next Caller, Inc. v. TRUSTID, Inc., IRP2019-00963, Paper 8, at 13 (Oct. 28, 2019); Thermo Fisher Sci., Inc. v. Regents of the Univ. of Cal., IPR2018-01370, Paper 11, at 26 (Feb. 7, 2019)).

180. *Id.*

has not issued such orders at the time of institution, the Board weighs this factor against denying institution.[181]

As part of the third factor, the Board has also considered the expediency of a petitioner's filing.[182] The Board explained that even though petitioners have one year to file a petition, a patent owner may be prejudiced if a petitioner unreasonably delays filing a petition.[183] Petitions filed soon after learning which claims will be pursued in the district court (which may come several months after the complaint is filed) are less likely to be denied under this factor.[184] This factor implicates a predicament most defendants find themselves in: whether to file a petition early and challenge all of the patent claims, which can be costly and carries its own procedural hurdles, or wait until some of the claims drop out of the litigation. Waiting can save resources, but it may come at the cost of institution. Petitioners need to balance these factors (and others) when deciding when and how to challenge claims before the Board.

For the fourth factor, the Board has acknowledged that in cases where the same prior art arguments are being presented in court and before the Board, the "concerns of inefficiency and the possibility of conflicting decisions" are "particularly strong."[185] Because of this, if a petition includes the "same or substantially the same claims, grounds, arguments, and evidence as presented in the parallel proceeding," denial of institution is generally favored.[186] In contrast, if a petition includes "materially different grounds,

181. *Id.* (citing Facebook, Inc. v. Search & Social Media Partners, LLC, IPR2018-01620, Paper 8, at 24 (Mar. 1, 2019); Amazon.com, Inc. v. CustomPlay, LLC, IPR2018-01496, Paper 12, at 8–9 (Mar. 7, 2019)); *see also* SK Hynix Inc. v. Netlist, Inc., IPR2020-01421, Paper 10, at 8–10 (Mar. 16, 2021); Sotera Wireless, Inc. v. Masimo Corp., IPR2020-01019, Paper 12, at 18–19 (Dec. 1, 2020) (Precedential); Samsung Elecs. Am., Inc. v. Snik LLC, IPR2020-01325, Paper 10, at 9 (Mar. 9, 2021).

182. *Apple Inc.*, IPR2020-00019, Paper 11, at 9–12.

183. *Id.* at 11.

184. *Id.* at 11–12 (citing Intel Corp. v. VLSI Tech. LLC, IPR2019-01192, Paper 15, at 12–13 (Jan. 9, 2020)); *see also SK Hynix Inc.*, IPR2020-01421, Paper 10, at 9; *Sotera Wireless, Inc.*, IPR2020-01019, Paper 12, at 16–17; *Samsung Elecs. Am., Inc.*, IPR2020-01325, Paper 10, at 9.

185. *Id.* at 12.

186. *Id.* (citing Next Caller, Inc. v. TRUSTID, Inc., IPR2019-00963, Paper 8, at 11–12 (Oct. 28, 2019); ZTE (USA) Inc. v. Fractus, S.A., IPR2018-01451, Paper 12, at 20 (Feb. 19, 2019)).

arguments, and/or evidence" than those presented before the court, this factor weighs against the Board exercising its discretion to deny institution.[187]

This factor is highly fact specific and will be determined on a case-by-case basis. A petition that discusses the differences (including challenged claims, legal issues, and asserted prior art) between the grounds raised in the IPR and the contentions raised in the district court can increase chances of institution. One strategy that petitioners might consider (and patent owners should anticipate) is raising different grounds in the district court and in an IPR, though petitioners must also balance the possibility of estoppel if challenges before the Board are unsuccessful. Another strategy that has been well received by the Board is when a petitioner formally stipulates that it "will not pursue [in district court] any ground raised or that could have reasonably been raised in an IPR, i.e., any ground that could be raised under §§ 102 or 103 on the basis of prior art patents or printed publications."[188] The Board has found that this "address[es] concerns relating to overlapping issues."[189] The stipulation need not be entered in the district court before it can be considered by the Board.[190] But notably, the Board has consistently found that the language and breadth of the stipulation influence its decision as to how much weight to place upon this factor.[191]

For factor five, if the petitioner in an IPR is unrelated to the defendant in an earlier district court proceeding, the Board will weigh this factor against denying institution.[192] If the petitioner and defendant are not related to each other but the issues are nevertheless the same or substantially similar

187. *Id.* at 12–13 (citing Facebook, Inc. v. BlackBerry Ltd., IPR2019-00899, Paper 15, at 12 (Oct. 8, 2019); Chegg, Inc. v. NetSoc, LLC, IPR2019-01165, Paper 14, at 11–12 (Dec. 5, 2019)).

188. *SK Hynix Inc.*, IPR2020-01421, Paper 10, at 10; *Sotera Wireless, Inc.*, IPR2020-01019, Paper 12, at 13–14.

189. *SK Hynix, Inc.*, IPR2020-01421, Paper 10, at 10.

190. *Id.* at 11.

191. *Id.* at 9–12; *see Sotera Wireless, Inc.*, IPR2020-01019, Paper 12, at 18–19. *But see* Sand Revolution II, LLC v. Cont'l Intermodal Grp.—Trucking LLC, IPR2019-01393, Paper 24, at 12 (June 16, 2020) (Informative).

192. Apple Inc. v. Fintiv, Inc., IPR2020-00019, Paper 11, at 13–14 (Mar. 20, 2020) (Precedential) (citing Nalox-1 Pharms., LLC v. Opiant Pharms., Inc., IPR2019-00685, Paper 11, at 6 (Aug. 27, 2019)).

to the issues that were litigated, the Board may exercise its discretion to deny institution.[193]

For the last factor, factor six, the Board has explained that the remaining factors are balanced to consider all of the relevant circumstances, including the merits of the petition.[194] Where a petitioner raises strong arguments, institution may be favored.[195] In addition to the merits, factors like whether the petitioner has filed serial or parallel petitions challenging the same patent, or whether the grounds presented in the petition are the same or substantially similar to grounds previously considered by the Office, may also be considered.[196]

Ultimately, this last factor gives the Board a degree of flexibility. Because none of these factors is dispositive, the Board could institute where the merits are strong and clearly presented, even if the other factors weigh in favor of denial.[197]

E. Estoppel

Estoppel plays a significant role in deciding whether to challenge the validity of a patent. The Board's final written decision in an IPR or PGR triggers estoppel in all subsequent district court, PTAB, reexamination, and ITC proceedings.[198] The patent owner also faces estoppel following an adverse judgment in an IPR or PGR—it may not "tak[e] action inconsistent with the adverse judgment."[199]

---

193. *Id.* at 14 (citing Stryker Corp. v. KFx Med., LLC, IPR2019-00817, Paper 10, at 27–28 (Sept. 16, 2019)).

194. *Id.* (citing PATENT TRIAL AND APPEAL BOARD CONSOLIDATED TRIAL PRACTICE GUIDE 58 (Nov. 2019)).

195. *Id.* at 14–15 (referencing Illumina, Inc. v. Natera, Inc., IPR2019-01201, Paper 19, at 8 (Dec. 18, 2019); Facebook, Inc. v. Blackberry Ltd., IPR2019-00925, Paper 15, at 27 (Oct. 16, 2019); Abbott Vascular Inc. v. FlexStent, LLC, IPR2019-00882, Paper 11, at 29–30 (Oct. 7, 2019); Comcast Cable Commc'ns, LLC v. Rovi Guides, Inc., IPR2019-00231, Paper 14, at 11 (May 20, 2019)).

196. *Id.* at 16.

197. *See, e.g.*, Beckman Coulter, Inc. v. Sysmex Corp., IPR2020-01503, Paper 10, at 27–29 (Feb. 23, 2021); Samsung Elecs. Am., Inc. v. Snik LLC, IPR2020-01325, Paper 10, at 10 (Mar. 9, 2021).

198. 35 U.S.C. §§ 315(e), 325(e).

199. 37 C.F.R. § 42.73(d)(3) (2021).

These statutory and regulatory estoppels are specific to IPR and PGR proceedings. But even where there is no statutory or regulatory estoppel, as with ex parte reexamination, traditional estoppel principles—for example, collateral and assignor estoppel—may apply to limit available arguments.

1. Statutory and Regulatory Estoppel

a. Introduction

The AIA imposes statutory estoppel on petitioners following a final written decision in an IPR:

> (1) Proceedings before the office.—
>
> The petitioner in an inter partes review of a claim in a patent under this chapter that results in a final written decision under section 318(a), or the real party in interest or privy of the petitioner, may not request or maintain a proceeding before the Office with respect to that claim on any ground that the petitioner raised or reasonably could have raised during that inter partes review.
>
> (2) Civil actions and other proceedings.—
>
> The petitioner in an inter partes review of a claim in a patent under this chapter that results in a final written decision under section 318(a), or the real party in interest or privy of the petitioner, may not assert either in a civil action arising in whole or in part under section 1338 of title 28 or in a proceeding before the International Trade Commission under section 337 of the Tariff Act of 1930 that the claim is invalid on any ground that the petitioner raised or reasonably could have raised during that inter partes review.[200]

A virtually identical provision applies following a PGR.[201] In both proceedings, estoppel applies on a claim-by-claim basis.[202] Patent Office regulations implementing the AIA add a patent owner estoppel provision:

200. 35 U.S.C. § 315(e).
201. *Id.* § 325(e).
202. *Id.* §§ 315(e), 325(e); 37 C.F.R. §§ 42.73(d)(1), 1.510(a) (2021); MPEP, *supra* note 1, § 2212.

Patent applicant or owner. A patent applicant or owner is precluded from taking action inconsistent with the adverse judgment, including obtaining in any patent:

(i) A claim that is not patentably distinct from a finally refused or canceled claim; or

(ii) An amendment of a specification or of a drawing that was denied during the trial proceeding, but this provision does not apply to an application or patent that has a different written description.[203]

The impact of these provisions varies based on a party's role in the prior proceeding, the type of proceeding at issue, and the type of proceeding in which the estoppel is asserted to apply.

b. Statutory Estoppel in District Courts and the ITC

Statutory estoppel applies in the district courts and the ITC and applies to the party to the proceeding, its privies, and real parties in interest.[204] An important exception to note is that the staff attorneys (representing the public's interest) in an ITC case were not parties before the Board and are not bound by any estoppel.[205] Otherwise, estoppel at the ITC, though less commonly presented than in district court, generally follows the same analysis.[206] In either forum, the scope of the petitioner's estoppel may have a major impact on the petitioner's ability to present invalidity arguments in the case.

203. 37 C.F.R. § 42.73(d)(3) (2021).

204. *See* 35 U.S.C. §§ 315(e), 325(e).

205. *See, e.g.*, In the Matter of Certain Magnetic Tape Cartridges and Components Thereof, Inv. No. 337-TA-1058, USITC Pub. 4980, Initial Determination, at 106–07 (Aug. 17, 2018).

206. *See, e.g.*, In the Matter of Certain Memory Modules and Components Thereof, Inv. No. 337-TA-1089, Initial Determination at 104–12 (Oct. 21, 2019) (applying analysis similar to that discussed for district court cases).

i. Predicate Elements of Statutory Estoppel

By statute, the petitioner, as well as any real parties in interest or privies of the petitioner,[207] cannot petition for IPR or PGR "of a claim of a patent," receive a final written decision, and then "assert either in a civil action arising in whole or in part under section 1338 of title 28 or in a proceeding before the International Trade Commission under section 337 of the Tariff Act of 1930 that the claim is invalid on any ground that the petitioner raised or reasonably could have raised."[208]

Accordingly, on its face, estoppel attaches on a claim-by-claim basis for any claim addressed in a final written decision.[209] If the Board institutes review, it will address all challenged claims in a final written decision. Thus, a petitioner who challenges the validity of only some claims at the Board is not estopped from challenging the validity of other claims in the district court or at the ITC. There are, of course, considerations regarding the likelihood of a stay when challenging fewer than all asserted claims. Additionally, the one-year statutory time bar for petitioners served with a complaint applies on a patent-by-patent basis, and petitioners may consider forgoing IPR or PGR challenges for traditional invalidity claims in district court. Also, the Board has volume limits and practical limits on the number of grounds that petitioners can raise. Petitioners may consider using multiple petitions addressing different sets of claims and whether certain grounds are better presented in district court where there is more discovery.

In addition, "[b]y the statute's plain terms, for an IPR petition to create estoppel effect, the IPR must result in a final written decision."[210] Petitioners may accept an earlier estoppel—for example, to better argue

---

207. *See* Finjan, Inc. v. Cisco Sys. Inc., No. 17-CV-00072-BLF, 2020 WL 532991, at *3 (N.D. Cal. Feb. 3, 2020) ("The statute imposes IPR estoppel only to the petitioner and the 'real party in interest or privy of the petitioner' and no one else."); *see also infra* Chapter 2, section G, for a discussion of real parties in interest.

208. 35 U.S.C. § 315(e)(2); *accord* 35 U.S.C. § 325(e)(2).

209. 35 U.S.C. § 315(e); *accord* 35 U.S.C. § 325(e); *see also, e.g.*, Princeton Digit. Image Corp. v. Ubisoft Ent. SA, No. CV 13-335-LPS-CJB, 2019 WL 410432, at *3 (D. Del. Feb. 1, 2019) (under a pre-*SAS* framework, declining to apply estoppel to claims not addressed in the final written decision).

210. *Finjan*, 2020 WL 532991, at *3; *see also* Snyders Heart Valve LLC v. St. Jude Med., Inc., No. CV 18-2030 (JRT/DTS), 2020 WL 1445835, at *7 (D. Minn. Mar. 25, 2020).

against discretionary denial at the Board or better persuade the district court to stay a case[211]—but absent such an agreement, a petitioner faces no estoppel prior to the issuance of a final written decision. When that decision comes, however, estoppel applies—potentially even posttrial.[212] And estoppel likely attaches even where a final written decision is appealed[213] but may not apply if a final written decision is ultimately vacated.[214]

ii. Scope of Estoppel

District courts have been split on the scope of the estoppel and the correct interpretation of the statute.[215] This split stemmed from early Board

211. *See, e.g.*, Sotera Wireless, Inc. v. Masimo Corp., IPR2020-01019, Paper 12, at 19 (Dec. 1, 2020) (Precedential) (discussing such stipulations in the context of discretionary denials of institution).

212. *See* Novartis Pharms. Corp. v. Par Pharm. Inc., No. CV 14-1289-RGA, 2019 WL 9343055, at *3 (D. Del. Apr. 11, 2019) (finding estoppel applied to bar invalidity counterclaims even following trial); *but see* Intell. Ventures II LLC v. FedEx Corp., No. 2:16-CV-00980, 2019 WL 1434656, at *13 (E.D. Tex. Mar. 29, 2019) (declining to apply estoppel during posttrial briefing).

213. *See, e.g.*, Verinata Health, Inc. v. Ariosa Diagnostics, Inc., No. 12-CV-05501, 2017 WL 235048, at *5 (N.D. Cal. Jan. 19, 2017) (applying statutory estoppel despite pending appeal); *but see* Canfield Sci., Inc. v. Drugge, No. 16-CV-04636, 2020 WL 6375654, at *2 (D.N.J. Oct. 30, 2020) (denying motion to strike allegedly estopped IPR defenses without prejudice pending final decision on appeal). Notably, the existence of estoppel alone does not create standing on appeal and, accordingly, not all petitioners are able to appeal final written decisions. *See, e.g.*, Apple Inc. v. Qualcomm Inc., 992 F.3d 1378, 1381 (Fed. Cir. 2021).

214. *See, e.g.*, Power Integrations, Inc. v. ON Semiconductor Corp., 396 F. Supp. 3d 851, 880 (N.D. Cal. 2019); In the Matter of Certain Wireless Mesh Networking Products and Related Components Thereof, Inv. No. 337-TA-1131, Initial Determination, at 48 n.10 (Jan. 10, 2020).

215. In the early days of the AIA, district courts interpreted the statutory estoppel and Federal Circuit case law surrounding that estoppel in at least two different ways. Several courts applied estoppel to bar a petitioner from later raising grounds for invalidity that could have been included in the petition. *See, e.g.*, Biscotti Inc. v. Microsoft Corp., No. 2:13-CV-1015, 2017 WL 2526231, at *6 (E.D. Tex. May 11, 2017); Cobalt Boats, LLC v. Sea Ray Boats, Inc., No. 2:15-CV-21, 2017 WL 2605977, at *3 (E.D. Va. June 5, 2017); Douglas Dynamics, LLC v. Meyer Prods. LLC, No. 14-CV-886, 2017 WL 1382556, at *2–3 (W.D. Wis. Apr. 18, 2017); iLife Techs., Inc. v. Nintendo of Am. Inc., No. 3:13-CV-4987, 2017 U.S. Dist. LEXIS 87769, at *5–6 (N.D. Tex. May 30, 2017); Network-1 Techs., Inc. v. Alcatel-Lucent USA, Inc., No. 6:11-CV-00492, 2017 WL 4856473, at *1–2 (E.D. Tex. Oct. 27, 2017); Milwaukee Elec. Tool Corp. v. Snap-On Inc., 271 F. Supp. 3d 990, 1027 (E.D. Wis. 2017); Oil-Dri Corp. of Am. v. Nestle Purina Petcare Co., No. 15-CV-1067, 2017 WL 3278915, at *2 (N.D. Ill. Aug. 2, 2017); Parallel Networks Licensing, LLC v. Int'l Bus. Mach. Corp., No. 13-CV-2072, 2017 WL 1045912, at *11 (D. Del. Feb. 22, 2017); Precision Fabrics Grp., Inc. v. TieTex Int'l, Ltd., No. 1:13-CV-645, 2016 WL 6839394, at *9 (M.D.N.C. Nov. 21, 2016); *see also* Cellular Commc'ns Equip. LLC v. HTC Corp., No. 2:17-CV-78 (E.D. Tex. Sept. 13, 2017).

precedent and the Federal Circuit's early guidance on the issue.[216] Before the Supreme Court's decision in *SAS v. Iancu* (prohibiting partial institution),[217] the Federal Circuit held in *Shaw v. Automated Creel* that estoppel did not apply to claims or grounds that were not instituted.[218] *Shaw* led some district courts to narrowly apply estoppel (applying it only to those grounds that were actually instituted) and led others to broadly apply estoppel (exempting only those grounds not instituted).[219] *SAS*, which clarified that the Board must institute all grounds of unpatentability addressed in a petition and discuss those grounds in its final written decision or deny institution entirely,[220] indirectly resolved this split. And the Federal Circuit expressly overruled *Shaw* in *California Institute of Technology v. Broadcom*.[221] The Federal Circuit clarified "that estoppel applies not just to claims and grounds asserted in the petition and instituted for consideration by the Board, but to all grounds not stated in the petition but which reasonably could have been asserted against the claims included in the petition."[222]

In determining what arguments "reasonably could have [been] raised," the type of petition matters, and potential petitioners should carefully consider the scope of estoppel before filing. In an IPR, a party can raise invalidity grounds only "on the basis of prior art consisting of patents or printed publications."[223] Accordingly, following a final written decision in an IPR, petitioners are estopped from raising invalidity grounds based on prior art patents or printed publications that they raised (or reasonably could have

Others applied estoppel only to grounds raised (or that could have been raised) during the instituted proceeding. *See* Finjan, Inc. v. Blue Coat Sys., LLC, 283 F. Supp. 3d 839, 856 (N.D. Cal. 2017); Intell. Ventures I LLC v. Toshiba Corp., No. 13-453, 2017 WL 107980, at *1 (D. Del. Jan. 11, 2017); Verinata Health, Inc. v. Ariosa Diagnostics, Inc., No. 12-CV-05501, 2017 WL 235048, at *1 (N.D. Cal. Jan. 19, 2017). As discussed earlier, the Supreme Court's decision in *SAS* has largely resolved this dispute.

216. Shaw Indus. Grp., Inc. v. Automated Creel Sys., Inc., 817 F.3d 1293, 1299–1300 (Fed. Cir. 2016).

217. SAS Inst., Inc. v. Iancu, 138 S. Ct. 1348 (2018).

218. *Shaw Indus. Grp., Inc.*, 817 F.3d at 1299–1300; *see also* HP Inc. v. MPHJ Tech. Invs., LLC, 817 F.3d 1339, 1347 (Fed. Cir. 2016).

219. *See infra* note 215.

220. *SAS Inst., Inc.*, 138 S. Ct. at 1359–60.

221. Cal. Inst. of Tech. v. Broadcom Ltd., 25 F.4th 976 (Fed. Cir. 2022).

222. *Id.*

223. 35 U.S.C. § 311(b).

raised) in their petition.[224] But they are not barred from presenting art or arguments that could not have been raised in the IPR, such as subject matter or written description challenges or novelty and obviousness arguments based on prior art devices.[225] Notably, however, some courts have limited petitioners' ability to bring invalidity challenges based on prior art devices that are materially the same as patents or publications the petitioner is estopped from relying on.[226]

But in a PGR, a petitioner "may request to cancel as unpatentable 1 or more claims of a patent on any ground that could be raised under paragraph (2) or (3) of section 282(b) (relating to invalidity of the patent or any claim)."[227] Thus, PGR petitioners can argue for invalidity based on subject matter eligibility (under section 101), lack of utility, lack of novelty, obviousness, lack of written description or enablement, or even double patenting.[228] It is not unforeseeable that district courts or the Federal Circuit will consider estoppel to attach regardless of whether a petitioner actually raises each possible challenge in a PGR. For example, in *GREE v. Supercell Oy*,[229] the court considered the scope of estoppel following a final written decision in a PGR.[230] The petitioner had filed only a section 101 challenge

224. *See, e.g.*, Asetek Danmark A/S v. Coolit Sys. Inc., No. 19-CV-410, 2019 WL 7589209, at *9 (N.D. Cal. Dec. 12, 2019). A potential exception is where a petitioner files multiple petitions, some of which are not instituted. Courts have found that estoppel does not attach to such noninstituted grounds. *See, e.g.*, Fundamental Innovation Sys. Int'l, LLC v. ZTE Corp., No. 3:17-CV-1827, 2019 WL 6220895, at *2 (N.D. Tex. Nov. 20, 2019).

225. *See, e.g.*, *In re* Koninklijke Philips Pat. Litig., No. 18-CV-01885, 2020 WL 7392868, at *26–27 (N.D. Cal. Apr. 13, 2020).

226. *See, e.g.*, Wasica Fin. GmbH v. Schrader Int'l, Inc., 432 F. Supp. 3d 448, 455 (D. Del. 2020) (finding prior art device arguments estopped where device materially identical to a patent; collecting cases); Cal. Inst. of Tech. v. Broadcom Ltd., No. CV 16-3714-GW(AGRx), 2019 WL 8192255, at *8 (C.D. Cal. Aug. 9, 2019) (explaining "there must be some substantive difference between the two theories that is germane to the invalidity dispute at hand" to avoid estoppel); Medline Indus., Inc. v. C.R. Bard, Inc., No. 17 C 7216, 2020 WL 5512132, at *5 (N.D. Ill. Sept. 14, 2020) (adopting view that prior art devices are not estopped but noting such devices cannot simply be "publication-based invalidity theories in disguise," e.g., manuals or datasheets).

227. 35 U.S.C. § 321(b).

228. *See id.*; *see also* Olaplex, Inc. v. L'Oreal USA, Inc., 855 F. App'x 701, 715 (Fed. Cir. 2021) (noting PGR proceeding "is not limited to challenges based on prior art").

229. Gree, Inc. v. Supercell Oy, No. 2:19-CV-00071, 2020 WL 4999689 (E.D. Tex. July 9, 2020), *report and recommendation adopted*, No. 2:19-CV-00071, 2020 WL 4937111 (E.D. Tex. Aug. 24, 2020).

230. *Id.* at *1.

and had represented that it did not even conduct a prior art search before filing the petition.[231] The court ruled that because the petitioner could have raised art-based arguments in the petition, the petitioner was estopped from arguing anticipation or obviousness in district court.[232] As the court noted, "[a] petitioner can bring a broad number of grounds in its PGR petition in its attempt to invalidate another's patent. The counterbalance is that the resulting estoppel is proportionally broad in scope."[233]

In deciding what art-based grounds a petitioner "reasonably could have raised," courts generally apply a diligent searcher test, determining whether the petitioner knew of the art at issue or "a skilled searcher conducting a diligent search reasonably could have been expected to discover" the art at issue.[234] "The touchstone is reasonableness, not perfection."[235] Courts consider evidence on these issues, including whether the references were identified by the petitioner or other challengers in their searches[236] and whether actual searches failed to find a particular reference.[237] Other courts have considered proposed search strings that would reveal the prior art and expert testimony on why certain searches should be considered.[238] In sum, parties are expected to muster detailed evidence on these heavily factual points.[239]

---

231. *Id.*

232. *Id.* at *6.

233. *Id.* at *5.

234. SPEX Techs. Inc. v. Kingston Tech. Corp., No. SACV 16-01790-JVS (AGRx), 2020 WL 4342254, at *14 (C.D. Cal. June 16, 2020) (collecting cases).

235. Palomar Techs., Inc. v. MRSI Sys., LLC, No. 18-10236-FDS, 2020 WL 2115625, at *3 (D. Mass. May 4, 2020), *appeal withdrawn*, No. 2020-1913, 2020 WL 7382538 (Fed. Cir. Dec. 15, 2020).

236. *See, e.g.*, Wi-LAN Inc. v. LG Elecs., Inc., 421 F. Supp. 3d 911, 926 (S.D. Cal. 2019) (considering the presence of references in invalidity contentions, later search results); Gree, Inc. v. Supercell Oy, No. 2:19-CV-00071, 2020 WL 4999689, at *5 (E.D. Tex. July 9, 2020), *report and recommendation adopted*, No. 2:19-CV-00071, 2020 WL 4937111 (E.D. Tex. Aug. 24, 2020) ("[T]his Court holds that when a reference is found in a later prior art search, there is a reasonable inference that it could have been found earlier by a skilled searcher.").

237. *See* f'real Foods, LLC v. Hamilton Beach Brands, Inc., No. CV 16-41-CFC, 2019 WL 1558486, at *1 (D. Del. Apr. 10, 2019) (finding no estoppel where two searches provided sworn declarations that they had not found a reference).

238. *See* SiOnyx, LLC v. Hamamatsu Photonics K.K., 330 F. Supp. 3d 574, 603 (D. Mass. 2018) (discussing methods to make required showing).

239. *See, e.g.*, *Palomar Techs.*, 2020 WL 2115625, at *3 (holding full evidentiary hearing on estoppel).

For example, in *Ironburg Inventions v. Valve*,[240] the court considered the date of the references at issue and when they became accessible to the public.[241] It further discussed that another IPR petitioner had found and cited the references in their petition and that one of the references was cited during examination of the patent.[242] And it concluded the petitioner reasonably could have raised the references and was estopped.[243] Some courts have also acknowledged the difficulty of performing a fulsome prior art search before receiving claim construction orders or expert reports, and at least one has noted that there "could be a case" where a party's infringement analysis "is so outlandish that a court might decline to apply estoppel," but such decisions are rare.[244] Petitioners should carefully consider their search strategy and possible infringement and claim construction outcomes when selecting art to include in a petition.

iii. Joined Parties

Parties that are joined to an ongoing proceeding find themselves in an unusual position with respect to estoppel. Though they do not select the particular grounds included in a petition, joined parties are still bound by statutory estoppel. The scope of estoppel for a joined party, however, is less than for an original petitioner.

The Federal Circuit specifically addressed estoppel for a joined party in *Network-1 v. Hewlett-Packard*.[245] Following standard joinder procedure, HP filed a copycat petition and joined an IPR originally filed by another party.[246] The patent owner overcame the IPR, and in a district court proceeding, HP attempted to challenge the patent based on prior art.[247] The district court found HP estopped from doing so, ruling that HP could have raised

240. Ironburg Inventions Ltd. v. Valve Corp., 418 F. Supp. 3d 622 (W.D. Wash. 2019).
241. *Id.* at 630.
242. *Id.*
243. *Id.* at 631.
244. Microchip Tech. Inc. v. Aptiv Servs. US LLC, No. 1:17-CV-01194, 2020 WL 4335519, at *4 (D. Del. July 28, 2020).
245. Network-1 Techs., Inc. v. Hewlett-Packard Co., 981 F.3d 1015 (Fed. Cir. 2020).
246. *Id.* at 1020. Notably, HP was not permitted to include additional grounds—it attempted to do so, and the Board rejected its first request for joinder as a result. *Id.*
247. *Id.* at 1021.

its challenges in the IPR.[248] On appeal, the Federal Circuit reversed, explaining that because HP joined an existing IPR, and "the joinder provision does not permit a joining party to bring into the proceeding new grounds that were not already instituted,"[249] HP could not reasonably have raised additional challenges beyond those already instituted. The court ruled that "[b]ecause a joining party cannot bring with it grounds other than those already instituted, that party is not statutorily estopped from raising other invalidity grounds."[250] And it vacated the district court's contrary decision.[251] Petitioners presented with an opportunity for joinder may thus be able to benefit from a post-grant proceeding while minimizing the risk of estoppel.

iv. Burden of Proof

A final consideration regarding estoppel is the burden of proof. Most courts that have considered the issue have determined that a patent owner bears the burden of establishing that estoppel applies against a petitioner.[252] Some courts have considered a burden-shifting framework, such that "the initial burden to assert estoppel should be on the party seeking to invoke it (by raising it as a defense, and making a *prima facie* showing that it applies), after which the burden shifts to the responding party to show that the prior-art reference could not reasonably have been raised in the IPR proceeding."[253] Parties appearing in courts that have not yet adopted a framework should consider arguing for the approach best suited for their case.

248. *Id.*
249. *Id.* at 1027.
250. *Id.*
251. *Id.* at 1028.
252. *See, e.g.*, Asetek Danmark A/S v. Coolit Sys. Inc., No. 19-CV-410, 2019 WL 7589209, at *4 (N.D. Cal. Dec. 12, 2019) ("The party claiming estoppel has the burden of establishing it."); CliniComp Int'l, Inc. v. Athenahealth, Inc., No. A-18-CV-00425, 2020 WL 7011768, at *2 (W.D. Tex. Oct. 28, 2020) (placing burden on moving party); Medline Indus., Inc. v. C.R. Bard, Inc., No. 17 C 7216, 2020 WL 5512132, at *2 (N.D. Ill. Sept. 14, 2020) (same).
253. Palomar Techs., Inc. v. MRSI Sys., LLC, No. CV 18-10236-FDS, 2020 WL 2115625, at *4 (D. Mass. May 4, 2020), *appeal withdrawn*, No. 2020-1913, 2020 WL 7382538 (Fed. Cir. Dec. 15, 2020).

c. *Statutory and Regulatory Estoppel at the Patent Office*

At the Patent Office, both the patent owner and the petitioner may face estoppel due to an IPR or PGR. The triggering events and scope of the estoppel differ for patent owners and petitioners. Before the Board, the burden of proving estoppel generally rests with the party asserting estoppel.[254]

i. Patent Owner Estoppel

Patent owner estoppel applies following an "adverse judgment," and it precludes the patent owner from taking an action inconsistent with the adverse judgment.[255] The overarching regulations for IPRs and PGRs define "judgment" as a decision that "disposes of all issues that were, or by motion reasonably could have been, raised and decided."[256] The regulations also allow a party to request adverse judgment by

(1) disclaimer of the involved application or patent;
(2) cancellation or disclaimer of a claim such that the party has no remaining claim in the trial;
(3) concession of unpatentability or derivation of the contested subject matter; and
(4) abandonment of the contest.[257]

Thus, an "adverse judgment" is not limited to a final written decision that goes against the patent owner.[258] Cancelling all claims to avoid IPR or simply not contesting an IPR may trigger estoppel.[259] But a patent owner may generally cancel some claims without triggering estoppel. In *Daikin v.*

---

254. *See* 37 C.F.R. § 42.20(c) (2021); Illumina, Inc. v. Trs. of Columbia Univ. in City of N.Y., No. IPR2018-00385, Paper 20, at 16 n.8 (July 27, 2018) ("Although the burden for proving estoppel against Petitioner rests with Patent Owner, we are mindful that the ultimate burden for establishing reasonable likelihood of success on the merits remains with Petitioner.").

255. 37 C.F.R. § 42.73(d)(3) (2021).

256. *Id. § 42.73(a).*

257. *Id. § 42.73(b).*

258. At least one panel of the Board has noted that the use of "adverse judgment" in the estoppel provision of the regulation, though not defined expressly, "is best read as a reference to the earlier use of the term in 37 C.F.R. § 42.73(b)." SDI Techs., Inc., v. Bose Corp., No. IPR2014-00346, Paper 32, at 8 (June 11, 2015).

259. *Id.*

Chemours,[260] for example, the Board ruled that a preinstitution disclaimer of some, but not all, claims did not result in estoppel.[261] The Board noted, among other things, that a partial disclaimer did not meet the literal terms of the rule because it did not dispose of all the issues (and thus was not a judgment).[262]

When estoppel does attach, the patent owner is "precluded from taking action inconsistent with the adverse judgment" at the Patent Office, including obtaining a patent claim that "is not patentably distinct from a finally refused or canceled claim" or amending a specification or drawing (in a patent or application having the same written description as the patent involved in the IPR or PGR) that was denied during the IPR or PGR.[263] This estoppel impacts a patentee's ability to obtain additional patent claims[264] (i.e., in pending applications whether or not they have priority with the challenged patent) but also limits a patent owner's ability to amend claims in post-grant and reexamination proceedings.[265]

Patent owner estoppel can also limit a patent owner's ability to argue for patentability of related claims because the rule bars any "action inconsistent with the adverse judgment."[266] In *Alphatec v. NuVasive*,[267] for example, the Board considered whether a patent owner could advance certain arguments related to dependent claims following a final written decision in another

260. Daikin Indus., Ltd. v. The Chemours Co., IPR2018-00993, Paper 12 (Nov. 13, 2018).

261. *Id.* at 5–7.

262. *Id.*

263. 37 C.F.R. § 42.73(d)(3) (2021).

264. *See, e.g.*, Freshpoint Quality Assurance Ltd. v. JP Lab'ys Inc., IPR2017-00538, Paper 11, at 3–4 (Nov. 3, 2017) (noting duty of candor in pending applications following an adverse decision and noting pilot program for notifying examiners of postgrant proceedings related to applications pending on their dockets for initial examination).

265. *Id.*

266. *See, e.g.*, Ricoh Ams. Corp. v. MPHJ Tech. Invs., LLC, IPR2015-01178, Paper 22, at 32 (Oct. 25, 2016) (finding petitioner "persuasively argued" that patent owner arguments for patentability of dependent claims not challenged in earlier IPR were "the same material arguments" as made in the prior case and were "improper under 37 C.F.R. . . . § 42.73(d)(3)); *but see* Illumina, Inc. v. Trs. of Columbia Univ., IPR2018-00797, Paper 65, at 70–71 (Sept. 9, 2019) (ruling in a nonprecedential decision that the estoppel provision "does not apply to *inter partes* review proceedings because Patent Owner is not 'obtaining' a patent"); Gen. Elec. Co. v. United Techs. Corp., IPR2017-00428, Paper 38, at 6–9 (June 22, 2018) (ruling patent owner not estopped from arguing patentability).

267. Alphatec Holdings, Inc. v. NuVasive, Inc., IPR2019-00546, Paper 17 (July 9, 2019).

IPR that declared the independent claims invalid.[268] The Board ruled that the patent owner was "estopped from arguing that limitations of [the independent claim] render the challenged dependent claim patentable over [the references] because of the determination in [the prior IPR] that those references rendered claim 1 obvious."[269] Similarly, in *Ex parte Sunsdahl*,[270] the Board determined that a patent owner could not argue in a reexamination that a claim was patentable "based on the commercial success of a combination of elements already determined to be unpatentable" in an IPR.[271]

ii. Petitioner Estoppel

Petitioner estoppel before the Office is somewhat narrower than patent owner estoppel and effectively applies only after a "final written decision."[272] A petitioner may not, in any proceeding before the Office, "request or maintain a proceeding before the Office with respect to that claim on any ground that the petitioner raised or reasonably could have raised during that inter partes review."[273] As in district court, estoppel applies on a claim-by-claim basis at the Board.[274] And as in district court, "the Board has interpreted 'reasonably could have been raised' to encompass prior art other than the prior art instituted, if a 'skilled searcher conducting a diligent search reasonably could have been expected to discover' such prior art."[275] Note that the Board generally does not consider the page/word limits to alleviate estoppel and has found unpersuasive arguments that those limits prevent petitioners from reasonably raising a ground.[276] Also, petitioners are estopped from "maintaining" proceedings before the Office, which can

268. *Id.* at 20.
269. *Id.*
270. *Ex parte* Sunsdahl, Appeal 2018-000857, 2020 WL 2765696 (P.T.A.B. May 22, 2020).
271. *Id.* at *7.
272. 35 U.S.C. §§ 315(e), 325(e).
273. 35 U.S.C. §§ 315(e)(1), 325(e)(1).
274. *See* Westlake Servs., LLC v. Credit Acceptance Corp., CBM2014-00176, Paper 28, at 5 (May 14, 2015) (Precedential).
275. SK Hynix Inc. v. Netlist, Inc., IPR2018-00364, Paper 32, at 8–9 (Aug. 5, 2019) (citing Praxair Dist., Inc. v. INO Therapeutics LLC, IPR2016-00781, Paper 10, at 7 (Aug. 25, 2016)).
276. *See, e.g.*, *id.* at 9–10; *see also* Intuitive Surgical, Inc. v. Ethicon LLC, IPR2018-01248, Paper 34, at 10–11 (Feb. 6, 2020).

affect parallel proceedings, especially if those challenges are progressing at different paces (e.g., parallel IPRs).

Accordingly, after a final written decision, a petitioner cannot file another petition challenging the same claims, and the petitioner also cannot *maintain* a pending proceeding against those claims. For example, in *Kingston v. SPEX*,[277] the petitioner filed two petitions against the same claims.[278] After the first final written decision issued, the Board instructed the parties to brief whether the petitioner was estopped from maintaining the second IPR based on estoppel.[279] The Board determined that the petitioner could have raised the grounds presented in the second petition in the first proceeding—the petitioner admitted that it was aware of all the underlying references at the time the first petition was filed.[280] Accordingly, the Board determined that the petitioner was estopped from maintaining the second IPR and dismissed the proceeding.[281]

Petitioners considering filing multiple proceedings should consider the likely timing of any final written decisions, as well as the timing of their requests. Certain panels of the Board have expressed hesitancy in applying estoppel to dismiss a second petition that was filed at the same time as the first petition, but final written decisions are nevertheless staggered for reasons that are not a result of the petitioner's actions. In *SK Hynix v. Netlist*,[282] the Board considered whether to permit the petitioner to maintain an IPR filed five days after a first IPR that had already reached a final written decision.[283] The Board stated that "[p]etitions filed on the same day but at different times are not subject to subsection 315(e)(1)" but found the five-day difference estopped the petitioner and terminated the second IPR.[284] Other panels of the Board have been even less lenient. In *Intuitive Surgical v. Ethicon*,[285] the panel rejected the reasoning of *SK Hynix* and

277. Kingston Tech. Co. v. SPEX Techs. Inc., IPR2018-01002, Paper 12 (Nov. 6, 2018).
278. *Id.* at 3.
279. *Id.* at 4.
280. *Id.* at 8.
281. *Id.* at 8–9.
282. SK Hynix Inc. v. Netlist, Inc., IPR2018-00364, Paper 32 (Aug. 5, 2019).
283. *Id.* at 5–10.
284. *Id.* at 9, 13.
285. Intuitive Surgical, Inc. v. Ethicon LLC, IPR2018-01248, Paper 34 (Feb. 6, 2020).

ruled that "[t]here is no indication that the statute attempts to delineate between multiple petitions that are simultaneously filed or multiple petitions that are filed in some serial fashion."[286] The Board therefore found that although the petitioner had filed its petitions on the same day, after the first petition reached a final written decision, the petitioner was estopped from maintaining other proceedings.[287] The Board noted that if the petitioner wanted to avoid estoppel, it could have contacted the Board and asked to consolidate the various petitions prior to issuance of any final written decision or asked to coordinate the proceedings so that final written decisions would issue on the same day.[288] Having failed to do so, the petitioner was estopped from maintaining the second proceeding. These considerations impact appeal and overall case strategy, that is, which grounds and challenges may be preserved and terminated and how estoppel may apply in parallel (or subsequent) litigation.

An important distinction between estoppel before the Office and estoppel in district court is that the petitioner's estoppel does not necessarily end an invalidity challenge. Estoppel applies to the petitioner, not the Board. By statute, "[i]f no petitioner remains in the inter partes review, the Office may terminate the review or proceed to a final written decision."[289] In cases where the Board has already invested time in the case—such as having held oral argument—the Board may choose to proceed to a final written decision even where the petitioner drops out of the case.

Another noteworthy distinction is the ability to appeal the Board's estoppel decisions. Where the Board finds estoppel in a final written decision, its conclusion is generally reviewable, but where the Board declines to institute a proceeding because the petitioner is estopped, that decision is generally isolated from appeal.[290]

Finally, it should be noted that no statutory estoppel applies for either petitioners or patent owners just by filing a petition or receiving an institution

286. *Id.* at 14.
287. *Id.*
288. *Id.* at 12.
289. 35 U.S.C. § 317(a).
290. *See* Uniloc 2017 LLC v. Facebook Inc., 989 F.3d 1018, 1030 (Fed. Cir. 2021).

decision, and no statutory estoppel applies to an ex parte reexamination proceeding.[291] Accordingly, parties may seek to file additional petitions or reexamination requests even if other proceedings are pending, and parties may seek to file successive reexamination proceedings. Nevertheless, parties should be aware that the Board has discretion to grant and deny petitions and reexamination requests even if they warrant review, effectively providing the Office a de facto estoppel.[292]

2. Other Estoppels

Statute and regulation are not the only estoppels that impact patent proceedings. Judicial, collateral, and assignor estoppel also apply.

a. Judicial Estoppel

Judicial estoppel bars a party from later taking a position inconsistent with one that party previously convinced a court to accept.[293] The doctrine seeks to prevent unfair advantage and "prevent[] parties from playing fast and loose with the courts to suit the exigencies of self interest."[294] It remains unclear whether judicial estoppel applies to proceedings before the Board, whether originating in district court or before the Office. Few panels of the Board have considered the issue and are nonetheless split as to whether judicial estoppel applies.[295]

Judicial estoppel is unlikely to apply in reexamination. "Claims finally held invalid by a federal court, after all appeals, will be withdrawn from

291. *See, e.g.*, Google LLC v. Uniloc 2017 LLC, IPR2019-01584, Paper 7, at 11 (Mar. 24, 2020) (noting "the statutory estoppels provided by Congress are triggered by the issuance of a final written decision, and not by a decision to institute"); MPEP, *supra* note 1, § 2200. As discussed *infra*, however, nonstatutory estoppels may attach following reexamination proceedings.

292. 35 U.S.C. §§ 315(d), 325(d).

293. *See, e.g.*, Minn. Min. & Mfg. Co. v. Chemque, Inc., 303 F.3d 1294, 1303 (Fed. Cir. 2002).

294. *Id.* (quoting *In re* Coastal Plains, Inc., 179 F.3d 197, 205 (5th Cir. 1999)).

295. *Compare* Hendrickson USA LLC v. Trans Techs. Co., IPR2017-01510, Paper 61, at 18 (Feb. 14, 2019) ("In addition, Patent Owner does not cite authority indicating that judicial estoppel applies in an *inter partes* review."), *with* Merck Sharp & Dohme Corp. v. Microspherix LLC, IPR2018-00602, Paper 43, at 27–30 (July 8, 2019) (considering judicial estoppel argument on its merits).

consideration and not reexamined during a reexamination proceeding."[296] And a "rejection on the grounds of *res judicata* will not be appropriate in reexamination."[297] Because the Office does not participate in invalidity actions in the district courts, it is unlikely to be bound by a district court determination of no invalidity.[298]

b. Collateral Estoppel

Collateral estoppel (issue preclusion) applies in the administrative context and has been applied in postgrant proceedings before the Patent Office.[299] "[U]nder the doctrine of collateral estoppel, also known as issue preclusion, a judgment on the merits in a first proceeding precludes relitigation in a second proceeding 'of issues actually litigated and determined in the first [proceeding].'"[300] Collateral estoppel applies if "(1) the issue is identical to one decided in the first action; (2) the issue was actually litigated in the first action; (3) resolution of the issue was essential to a final judgment in the first action; and (4) the party against whom issue preclusion is asserted had a full and fair opportunity to litigate the issue in the first action."[301] For example, in *Amazon.com v. M2M Solutions*,[302] the Board applied collateral estoppel and ruled that a prior decision regarding whether a particular

296. MPEP, *supra* note 1, § 2259.

297. *Id.*

298. *See, e.g.*, *In re* Constr. Equip. Co., 665 F.3d 1254, 1256 n.3 (Fed. Cir. 2011) (declining to apply res judicata or issue preclusion to bar reexamination proceeding, noting the Office did not participate in prior action).

299. *See, e.g.*, Papst Licensing GMBH & Co. KG v. Samsung Elecs. Am., Inc., 924 F.3d 1243, 1250–51 (Fed. Cir. 2019) (noting applicability of issue preclusion following a Board decision); Google LLC v. Makor Issues & Rights Ltd., IPR2017-00818, Paper 25, at 44 n.7 (Sept. 7, 2018) (noting collateral estoppel applies and that "[i]t is well established that collateral estoppel, also known as issue preclusion, applies in the administrative context") (quoting MaxLinear, Inc. v. CF CRESPE LLC, 880 F.3d 1373, 1376 (Fed. Cir. 2018)); *see also* Grünenthal GmbH v. Antecip Bioventures II LLC, PGR2019-00003, Paper 22, at 48–50 (May 5, 2020) (noting applicability of collateral estoppel in PGR proceeding). Collateral estoppel, however, generally does not apply to determinations by the ITC. *See, e.g.*, Bio-Tech. Gen. Corp. v. Genentech, Inc., 80 F.3d 1553, 1564 (Fed. Cir. 1996) (stating that "it seems clear that any disposition of a Commission action by a Federal Court should not have a res judicata or collateral estoppel effect in cases before such courts").

300. Biodelivery Scis. Int'l, Inc. v. Monosol RX, LLC, IPR2015-00168, Paper 74, at 4 (Sept. 26, 2016) (citation omitted) (alteration in original).

301. *Id.* (citation omitted).

302. Amazon.com, Inc. v. M2M Sols. LLC, IPR2019-01205, Paper 43 (Jan. 25, 2021).

prior art reference taught a particular limitation controlled a subsequent proceeding, noting "that identical issues are involved, and Patent Owner had a full and fair opportunity to be heard."[303]

Collateral estoppel may also apply in reexamination proceedings. If a reexamination presents the same issues as a claim held invalid, for example, in a district court proceeding involving a patent in the same family, collateral estoppel may bar the patentee.[304] But following a successful defeat of an invalidity case in district court, collateral estoppel will not protect the patentee from a reexamination challenge—the Office is not a party to such proceedings, and it is not and cannot be estopped.[305]

c. *Assignor Estoppel*

Assignor estoppel had generally barred a party that assigned a patent to another from attacking that patent's validity.[306] Under current law, the doctrine does not apply in IPR or PGR proceedings.[307] Courts have reasoned that because, by statute, any person "not the owner of a patent" may file an IPR, the statute "unambiguously dictates that assignor estoppel has no place

303. *Id.* at 40.

304. *See, e.g.*, *In re* Arunachalam, 709 F. App'x 699, 703 (Fed. Cir. 2017) ("As noted, where a patentee has had a full and fair opportunity to litigate the validity of a patent in one proceeding, but is ultimately unsuccessful, the patentee is collaterally estopped from relitigating the validity or patentability of the patent in a later proceeding.").

305. *See, e.g.*, *In re* Trans Tex. Holdings Corp., 498 F.3d 1290, 1297 (Fed. Cir. 2007) ("Issue preclusion is not warranted in this case because the PTO was not a party to the earlier litigation. Our case law has identified four prerequisites to the application of issue preclusion: '(1) identity of the issues in a prior proceeding; (2) the issues were actually litigated; (3) the determination of the issues was necessary to the resulting judgment; and, (4) *the party defending against preclusion had a full and fair opportunity to litigate the issues*.'" (quoting Jet, Inc. v. Sewage Aeration Sys., 223 F.3d 1360, 1365–66 (Fed. Cir. 2000)).

306. *See, e.g.*, Scott Paper Co. v. Marcalus Mfg. Co., 326 U.S. 249, 252 (1945) ("[A]n assignor of a patent right is estopped to attack the utility, novelty or validity of a patented invention which he has assigned or granted as against any one claiming the right under his assignment or grant. As to the rest of the world, the patent may have no efficacy and create no right of monopoly; but the assignor can not be heard to question the right of his assignee to exclude him from its use." (quoting Westinghouse Elec.c & Mfg. Co. v. Formica Insulation Co., 266 U.S. 342, 349 (1924))).

307. *See, e.g.*, Athena Automation Ltd. v. Husky Injection Molding Sys. Ltd., IPR2013-00290, Paper 18, at 12–13 (Oct. 25, 2013) (Precedential); *see also* Hologic, Inc. v. Minerva Surgical, Inc., 957 F.3d 1256, 1266 (Fed. Cir. 2020) ("This court has held that the doctrine of assignor estoppel does not bar an assignor from filing a petition for IPR.").

in IPR proceedings."[308] Applying similar reasoning, courts have concluded assignor estoppel similarly does not apply in reexamination.[309] The Supreme Court directly addressed this question in *Minerva Surgical v. Hologic*.[310] The Court noted that assignor estoppel was a "bounded doctrine designed to prevent an inventor from first selling a patent and then contending that the thing sold is worthless."[311] But the Court recognized that the doctrine has limits and held it "applies only when an inventor says one thing (explicitly or implicitly) in assigning a patent and the opposite in litigating against the patent's owner."[312] The Court explained that "[a]ssignor estoppel should apply only when its underlying principle of fair dealing comes into play."[313] And absent an "inconsistency, an invalidity defense raises no concern of fair dealing—so assignor estoppel has no place."[314]

F. Joinder

Under 35 U.S.C. § 315(c), the Board may join as a party to an instituted IPR any person who properly files a petition that the Board determines warrants institution.[315] Under 35 U.S.C. § 325(c), the Board may consolidate multiple PGRs into a single review if more than one petition is properly filed against the same patent and more than one of the petitions warrants institution.[316] For both IPR and PGR proceedings, either the patent owner or the petitioner can request joinder.[317] The deadline for requesting joinder is one month after institution of the proceeding for which joinder is

308. Arista Networks, Inc. v. Cisco Sys., Inc., 908 F.3d 792, 804 (Fed. Cir. 2018).
309. *See, e.g.*, Ralph Gonnocci Revocable Living Tr. v. Three M Tool & Mach., Inc., No. 02-74796, 2003 WL 22870902, at *5 (E.D. Mich. Oct. 7, 2003) (collecting cases).
310. Minerva Surgical Inc. v. Hologic, Inc., 141 S. Ct. 2298 (2021).
311. *Id.* at 2308.
312. *Id.* at 2304.
313. *Id.* at 2309–10.
314. *Id.* at 2311.
315. 35 U.S.C. § 315(c).
316. 35 U.S.C. § 325(c).
317. 37 C.F.R. §§ 42.122(b), 42.222(b) (2021).

requested.[318] The request must be in the form of a motion that has been authorized by the Board.[319]

Under 35 U.S.C. § 315(b), a petitioner, real party in interest, or privy must file a petition for IPR within one year after being served with a complaint for infringement.[320] This requirement does not apply to requests for joinder.[321] Under 35 U.S.C. § 321(c), a petitioner must file a petition for PGR within nine months after the grant of a patent or issuance of a reissue patent.[322] Unlike the IPR statute, there is no exception to this requirement for consolidation.

The scope of IPR joinder has been the subject of several (sometimes inconsistent) decisions from the Board. In some historical cases, the Board found that the statute permitted same-party joinder and new-issue joinder, that is, an original petitioner or a third party could file a second petition with new grounds and "join" the second petition to the first petition.[323] The Board separately held the opposite.[324] In 2018, the Precedential Opinion Panel (POP) issued a precedential decision in *Proppant v. Oren* to address the inconsistent decisions.[325] In *Proppant*, the POP held that a petitioner may be joined to a proceeding to which it is already a party (same-party joinder) and that the Board has discretion to allow joinder of new issues to a proceeding (new-issue joinder).[326]

---

318. *Id.*

319. *See* Kyocera Corp. v. SoftView LLC, IPR2013-00004, Paper 15, at 4 (Apr. 24, 2013), *aff'd sub nom.* Softview LLC v. Kyocera Corp., 592 F. App'x 949 (Fed. Cir. 2015) (Mem.).

320. 35 U.S.C. § 315(b)–(c); *see* Microsoft Corp. v. Proxyconn, Inc., IPR2013-00109, Paper 15, at 4 (Feb. 25, 2013) (Representative); Target Corp. v. Destination Maternity Corp., IPR2014-00508, Paper 18, at 9–10 (Sept. 28, 2014) (expanded panel), *rev'd on other grounds*, IPR2014-00508, Paper 28 (Feb. 12, 2015) (further expanded panel).

321. 35 U.S.C. § 315(b)–(c); *see also* 37 C.F.R. § 42.122(b) (2021).

322. 35 U.S.C. § 321(c).

323. *See Microsoft Corp.*, IPR2013-00109, Paper 15; *Target Corp.*, IPR2014-00508, Paper 18; Zhongshan Broad Ocean Motor Co., Ltd. v. Nidec Motor Corp., IPR2015-00762, Paper 16 (Oct. 5, 2015).

324. SkyHawke Techs., LLC v. L&H Concepts, LLC, IPR2014-01485, Paper 13, at 3–4 (Mar. 20, 2015); Micro Motion, Inc. v. Invensys Sys., Inc., IPR2014-01409, Paper 14, at 14 (Feb. 18, 2015); Medtronic, Inc. v. Endotach LLC, IPR2014-00695, Paper 18 (May 28, 2014).

325. Proppant Express Invs., LLC v. Oren Techs., LLC, IPR2018-00914, Paper 38 (Mar. 13, 2019) (Precedential).

326. *Id.* at 10–11, 15–16.

In an unrelated case, however, the Federal Circuit addressed the rationale in *Proppant*, abrogating it by holding the statute does not authorize same-party joinder or new-issue joinder.[327] The Federal Circuit explained that 35 U.S.C. § 315(c) is limited to joining a "new party" to an instituted and pending IPR proceeding.[328] Accordingly, a petitioner cannot file a second petition and "join" the second petition to an instituted first petition (i.e., no same-party joinder); nor can a third party join a proceeding and introduce issues that were not raised in the original petition (i.e., no new-issue joinder). Effectively, third parties seeking to join an instituted petition must file a copycat petition and join the instituted proceeding at whatever stage that proceeding is at, which can be after much of the substantive case. For example, a patent owner has a statutory right to file a preliminary response to any petition, which can be filed three months after the petition, and the Board has three months to issue a decision on institution. Considering that a petition and motion for joinder can be filed one month after a first petition is instituted, a third party may not join a proceeding until seven months after institution, which, depending on schedules, may be after patent owner discovery, patent owner response, petitioner discovery, and petitioner reply.

Addressing same-party joinder, the Federal Circuit explained the statute allows joinder of "a party" to an existing proceeding and allowing the same party to file a second petition and join it to a first petition is joining proceedings, not parties.[329] The Federal Circuit contrasted 35 U.S.C. § 315(c) (IPR joinder) with 35 U.S.C. § 315(d) (IPR consolidation), explaining that the latter, not the former, provides the Director's statutory authority to put two proceedings together,[330] which given proceeding schedules and timing relative to parallel litigation (time-bar exception applies to joinder but not consolidation) is a significant distinction.

327. Facebook, Inc. v. Windy City Innovations, LLC, 973 F.3d 1321, 1335 (Fed. Cir. 2020).

328. *Id.* at 1333–35.

329. *Id.* at 1328.

330. *Id.* at 1336. Notably, section 315(d) (consolidation) is not exempt from the one-year time bar on filing IPR petitions. *See* 35 U.S.C. § 315(b) (limiting the time-bar exception to "request[s] for joinder under subsection (c)").

Addressing new-issue joinder, the Federal Circuit noted that the lack of express prohibition does not create an affirmative right or an ambiguity.[331] It reasoned that the statute is limited to joining parties and simply allows just that—joinder of parties.[332] That is, the statute does not authorize "joining" issues.[333] Thus, even if a new party can be joined to an existing IPR, the new petitioner is not permitted to introduce new issues, that is, no new grounds.[334] Effectively, a party can be joined but must adopt the challenges already raised.

Notably, however, a joined party is not estopped from raising grounds that it could not have raised under 35 U.S.C. § 315(e), that is, new grounds that an original petitioner did not raise.[335] Because a joining party cannot introduce new grounds into the proceeding, it is estopped only for the grounds already instituted.[336] While the statutory effect of estoppel may be limited for joined parties, those parties may enter the already instituted proceeding well into the schedule and have little opportunity to further develop evidence or arguments to support them. Joined parties, however, can maintain already instituted proceedings if the original petitioner drops out of the proceeding (like when the first petitioner settles with the patent owner).

G. Real Parties in Interest

A petitioner is required to identify in the petition any privy or real party in interest (RPI) that may benefit from the outcome of the proceedings.[337] The Board has explained that this requirement "serves important notice functions to patent owners, to identify whether the petitioner is barred from bringing an IPR due to an RPI that is time-barred or otherwise estopped, and to the Board, to identify conflicts of interests that are not readily apparent. . . ."[338]

331. *Facebook, Inc.*, 973 F.3d at 1335.
332. *Id.* at 1335–36 (internal citation omitted).
333. *Id.*
334. *Id.*
335. *See supra* Chapter 2, section E.1.b.iii.
336. *Id.*
337. 35 U.S.C. § 312(a)(2); 37 C.F.R. § 42.8(b)(1) (2021).
338. SharkNinja Operating LLC v. iRobot Corp., IPR2020-00734, Paper 11, at 17 (Oct. 6, 2020) (Precedential); NOF Corp. v. Nektar Therapeutics, Inc., IPR2019-01397, Paper 25, at

The statutory time bar and estoppel provisions each implicate privies and real parties in interest:

> (b) **Patent Owner's Action**—An inter partes review may not be instituted if the petition requesting the proceeding is filed more than 1 year after the date on which the petitioner, real party in interest, or privy of the petitioner is served with a complaint alleging infringement of the patent. . . .
>
> (e)(1) **Proceedings before the Office**—The petitioner in an inter partes review of a claim in a patent under this chapter that results in a final written decision under section 318(a), or the real party in interest or privy of the petitioner, may not request or maintain a proceeding before the Office with respect to that claim on any ground that the petitioner raised or reasonably could have raised during that inter partes review.[339]

Whether a nonparty is considered a privy or an RPI is a "highly fact-dependent question" that must be considered on a case-by-case basis.[340] As the Federal Circuit explained (invoking the Trial Practice Guide), "the two questions lying at [the] heart [of this inquiry] are [1] whether a non-party 'desires review of the patent' and [2] whether a petition has been filed at a nonparty's 'behest.'"[341] A number of factors are relevant to this determination, such as whether the nonparty exercised or could have exercised control over a petitioner in filing a petition and/or the proceedings; the extent to which the nonparty funded a petition or proceeding; the nonparty's relationship to the petitioner; and the nature of the entity filing the petition.[342]

---

6 (Feb. 10, 2020); PATENT TRIAL AND APPEAL BOARD CONSOLIDATED TRIAL PRACTICE GUIDE 12 (Nov. 2019); *see also* Applications in Internet Time, LLC v. RPX Corp., 897 F.3d 1336, 1350 (Fed. Cir. 2018) (two related purposes for RPI are "(1) to ensure that third parties who have sufficiently close relationships with IPR petitioners would be bound by the outcome of instituted IPRs under § 315(e), the related IPR estoppel provision; and (2) to safeguard patent owners from having to defend their patents against belated administrative attacks by related parties via § 315(b)").

339. 35 U.S.C. §§ 315(b), 315(e)(1).

340. Ventex Co. v. Columbia Sportswear N. Am., Inc., IPR2017-00651, Paper 148, at 6 (Jan. 24, 2019) (Precedential); *see also Applications in Internet Time, LLC*, 897 F.3d at 1342.

341. *Applications in Internet Time, LLC*, 897 F.3d at 1351.

342. *Ventex Co.*, IPR2017-00651, Paper 148, at 12.

Ultimately, the inquiry "demands a flexible approach that takes into account both equitable and practical considerations, with an eye toward determining whether the non-party is a clear beneficiary that has a preexisting, established relationship with the petitioner."[343]

In *Ventex Co. v. Columbia Sportswear North America, Inc.*, the Board found a nonparty to the petition to be an RPI, in part because the nonparty was time barred from filing its own petition.[344] The Board noted that the nonparty "would not receive a merely generalized benefit from [petitioner's] filing of the Petition, but rather, the direct benefit of a finding of unpatentability of claims of the [challenged] patents for which [patent owner] had accused [the nonparty] of infringing."[345] It also found persuasive that the petitioner and nonparty "had a specially structured, preexisting, and well established business relationship with one another, including indemnification and exclusivity arrangements."[346]

Although RPIs must be identified, the Board has explained that its jurisdiction to consider a petition does not require a "correct" identification of all RPIs.[347] If a petition fails to identify all real parties in interest, the Board allows a petitioner to correct its petition and add a real party in interest, provided that the addition does not trigger the § 315(b) time bar.[348] Because the Board does not consider this requirement to impact jurisdiction, it may not need to specifically address questions, even when raised by patent owners. For example, in *SharkNinja Operating LLC v. iRobot Corp.*, the Board held that it did not need to address whether an unnamed third party was an RPI "because, even if it were, it would not create a time bar or estoppel

343. *Applications in Internet Time, LLC*, 897 F.3d at 1351.

344. *Ventex Co.*, IPR2017-00651, Paper 148, at 7–11.

345. *Id.* at 10.

346. *Id.*

347. Lumentum Holdings, Inc. v. Capella Phonotics, Inc., IPR2015-00739, Paper 38, at 6 (Mar. 4, 2016) (Precedential); *see also* Blue Coat Sys., Inc. v. Finjan, Inc., IPR2016-01444, Paper 11, at 10 (July 18, 2017) ("[E]vidence [of failure to identify all RPIs] is, at best, suggestive regarding an issue that is not jurisdictional.").

348. Mayne Pharma Int'l Pty. Ltd. v. Merck Sharp & Dohme Corp., 927 F.3d 1232, 1238 (Fed. Cir. 2019) (quoting Wi-Fi One, LLC v. Broadcom Corp., 878 F.3d 1364, 1374 n.9 (Fed. Cir. 2018) (en banc)); *see also, e.g.*, SharkNinja Operating LLC v. iRobot Corp., IPR2020-00734, Paper 11, at 16–20 (Oct. 6, 2020) (Precedential).

[issue] under 35 U.S.C. § 315."[349] Although there were "at least twenty pages of pre-institution briefing" on whether the nonparty should have been listed as an RPI because it was allegedly "intertwined with Petitioner's business and was in a position to fund and exercise control over the Petition," there was "no allegation that Petitioner's failure to name [the nonparty] as an RPI should result in termination of the proceeding or denial of institution for any reason other than for the alleged failure of a procedural requirement that can be corrected under our precedent."[350] Nonetheless, patent owners should consider the impact of raising RPI and privy arguments before the Board, especially in view of past, ongoing, or future parallel litigation.

349. *SharkNinja Operating LLC*, IPR2020-00734, Paper 11, at 18.
350. *Id.*

Chapter 3

Petition Preparation

This chapter explores the requirements for and preparation of a petition for inter partes review and post-grant review.

A. Petition Requirements

1. Anyone but the Patent Owner May File

To request institution of a trial for inter partes review (IPR) or post-grant review (PGR), any "person who is not the owner of a patent"—a petitioner—may file a petition to institute review.[1] Identifying the petitioner(s) and patent owner(s) in a petition also allows the Board to identify any potential conflicts when assigning administrative patent judges.

2. Based on Patents or Printed Publications

An IPR petitioner may request to cancel as unpatentable one or more claims of a patent only on a ground that could be raised under section 102 (anticipation) or 103 (obviousness) and only based on prior art patents or printed publications.[2] A petitioner may find prior art in a variety of ways, including from (1) a professional prior art searcher; (2) experts in the field;

1. 35 U.S.C. §§ 311(a), 321(a); Leahy-Smith America Invents Act, Pub. L. No. 112-29, § 18(a)(1)(B) (2011) [hereinafter AIA].
2. 35 U.S.C. § 311(b).

(3) in-house personnel, for example, scientists and counsel familiar with the subject matter; and (4) the prosecution history of the challenged patent.

Sometimes, prior art will be published in a foreign language. Because PTAB proceedings are conducted in English, the Board requires translations of such documents into English.[3] The petitioner's translation may be filed as an exhibit, along with an accompanying declaration or certification by the translator. It is possible that the translator may be deposed regarding the translation and/or that an opposing party may file a competing translation.

A PGR petitioner, in contrast to IPR proceedings, may request to cancel as unpatentable one or more claims of a patent on any ground that could be raised under paragraph (2) or (3) of section 282(b), including anticipation, obviousness, lack of written description, lack of enablement, and indefiniteness, as well as patent ineligibility under section 101.[4]

3. Standing and Timing for Filing

The petition must set forth grounds for standing. The petitioner has to certify that the challenged patent is available for the type of review sought and that the petitioner is not barred or estopped from requesting review of the challenged claims on the grounds identified in the petition.[5]

For AIA patents, an IPR petition may be filed after the later of either (1) nine months after the grant of a patent or issuance of a reissue patent or (2) if the patent is currently the subject of a PGR proceeding, the termination of that proceeding.[6] These deadlines, however, are not applicable to pre-AIA patents, which are immediately available for IPR.[7] Related litigation may also affect when a petitioner must file an IPR. If a petitioner has been sued for infringement, an IPR must be requested within one year of service of the complaint.[8] Also, if the petitioner filed a civil action challenging the validity of a claim of the patent before filing the petition, then IPR is unavailable.[9]

---

3. PATENT TRIAL AND APPEAL BOARD CONSOLIDATED TRIAL PRACTICE GUIDE 24 (NOV. 2019).
4. 35 U.S.C. § 321(b); AIA § 18(a)(1)(A).
5. 37 C.F.R. §§ 42.104(a), 42.204(a).
6. 35 U.S.C. § 311(c).
7. AIA § 6(f)(2)(A).
8. 35 U.S.C. § 315(b).
9. *Id.* § 315(a)(1). If the petitioner or real party in interest files a civil action on or after

A petition for PGR, in which the petitioner may assert grounds of unpatentability expanding beyond anticipation and obviousness, must be filed within nine months after the grant of a patent or issuance of a reissue patent.[10]

4. Page-Length and Formatting Requirements

Petitioners must comply with the page-length and formatting requirements for petitions. IPR petitions have a limit of 14,000 words and PGR petitions have a limit of 18,700 words.[11] Mandatory notices (*infra* section A.5), tables of contents, tables of authorities, certificates of service, certificates of word count, and claim listings are excluded from this requirement and thus may be omitted when calculating the word count.[12] The Board generally accepts a petitioner's word count calculation based on the word processing software used to prepare the petition.[13] But the patent owner may raise a dispute and obtain relief from the Board if the petitioner appears to have improperly circumvented the word count requirement, such as by using unusually formatted citations or excessive figures containing text.[14]

Petitioners may also seek to waive the word limit for a petition by filing a petition accompanied by a motion seeking relief.[15] The Board may authorize additional words in the interests of justice.[16] But if the motion is not granted, the petition may be expunged or returned.[17]

5. Petitioner's Mandatory Notices

The petitioner must file mandatory notices as part of the petition, which identify the real party in interest, any related matters, lead and backup

the date on which the petitioner files a petition, the civil action is automatically stayed. *See* 35 U.S.C. § 315(a)(2).

10. 35 U.S.C. § 321(c).

11. 37 C.F.R. § 42.24(a)(1).

12. *Id.*

13. 37 C.F.R. § 42.24(d); Patent Trial and Appeal Board Consolidated Trial Practice Guide 38–39 (Nov. 2019).

14. *See, e.g.*, EMC Corp. v. Intell. Ventures I LLC, IPR2017-00429, Paper 11, at 27–29 (July 5, 2017) (granting patent owner an expanded word count for responding to petitioner's overlength petition).

15. 37 C.F.R. § 42.24(a)(2).

16. *Id.*

17. *Id.*

counsel (if the party is represented by counsel), and service information.[18] If there are any changes to this required information, the petitioner must file updated notices within 21 days.[19]

a. Identify All Real Parties in Interest

A petition must identify all real parties in interest (RPI).[20] A patent owner must identify RPIs in the mandatory notices due within 21 days after service of the petition.[21] The RPI requirement exists so that the Board can quickly deny petitions that are legally barred from institution under 35 U.S.C. § 315(b) and because an RPI will face the same principles of estoppel and preclusion that apply to the petitioner.[22] The naming of RPIs also assists the Board in identifying potential conflicts when assigning administrative patent judges to a proceeding.

There is a rebuttable presumption that the petitioner's identification of RPIs complies with the requirement.[23] If a dispute requires the Board to determine who is an RPI, it will look at evidence of the relationship between the nonparty and petitioner and the nature and/or degree of involvement between the nonparty and the petitioner.[24] No bright-line test exists to determine when a party, other than the petitioner, is an RPI; rather, the inquiry "is a highly fact-dependent question."[25] The Trial Practice Guide states that multiple factors guide the analysis of whether a party qualifies as an RPI, citing the Supreme Court case of *Taylor v. Sturgell* as a guide.[26]

Merely having a relationship with the petitioner may not be enough to make a nonparty an RPI. For example, codefendants in a lawsuit with shared counsel may not be sufficiently related to establish that a nonparty defen-

18. *Id.* § 42.8(b).
19. *Id.* § 42.8(a).
20. 35 U.S.C. § 312(a)(2).
21. 37 C.F.R. § 42.8(a)–(b).
22. PATENT TRIAL AND APPEAL BOARD CONSOLIDATED TRIAL PRACTICE GUIDE 12 (Nov. 2019).
23. *See* Galderma S.A. v. Allergan Industrie, SAS, IPR2014-01422, Paper 14, at 6 (Mar. 5, 2015).
24. Office Patent Trial Practice Guide, 77 Fed. Reg. 48,756, 48,759 (Aug. 14, 2012).
25. *Id.*
26. *Id.*; Taylor v. Sturgell, 553 U.S. 880, 893–96 (2008).

dant was an RPI.[27] In addition, the existence of an indemnity agreement between parties,[28] a joint venture relationship,[29] or a simple parent–subsidy relationship, without more, may not be sufficient.[30] Rather, the Board looks to the relationship between the party and the proceeding. One key factor is whether a nonparty has control or the opportunity to exercise control over the proceeding. For example, the Board has found a parent company that could have controlled (or did control) the filing and conduct during the proceeding to be an RPI.[31] And if a named RPI is only a "nominal plaintiff" with no substantial interest in the IPR but rather acts as a proxy for a nonparty, that nonparty has been held to be an RPI.[32] A representative order on RPIs was provided in *Intellectual Ventures Management, LLC v. Xilinx*.[33]

b. Related Matters

A petitioner's mandatory notices must identify any judicial or administrative matters that would affect, or be affected by, a decision in the proceeding.[34] Judicial matters include any actions involving the patent in federal court.[35] Administrative matters include applications and patents that claim priority to the patent involved in the IPR proceeding.[36] Administrative matters

27. Syntroleum Corp. v. Nestle Oil Oyj, IPR2013-00178, Paper 22, at 7 (Sept. 4, 2013).

28. Mercedes-Benz USA, LLC v. Proximity Monitoring Innovations LLC, IPR2015-00397, Paper 18, at 5 (July 17, 2015); Nissan N. Am., Inc. v. Diamond Coating Tech., LLC, IPR2014-01546, Paper 18, at 7–9 (Apr. 21, 2015).

29. *See* PATENT TRIAL AND APPEAL BOARD CONSOLIDATED TRIAL PRACTICE GUIDE 17 (Nov. 2019).

30. Par Pharm., Inc. v. Jazz Pharm. Inc., IPR2015-00551, Paper 19, at 11–19 (July 28, 2015).

31. Zoll Lifecor Corp. v. Philips Elec. N. Am. Corp., IPR2013-00606, Paper 13, at 9–10 (Mar. 20, 2014); Galderma S.A. v. Allergan Industrie, SAS, IPR2014-01422, Paper 14, at 8–13 (Mar. 5, 2015).

32. RPX Corp. v. Virnetx Inc., IPR2014-00171, Paper 51, at 9–10 (June 5, 2014); Taylor v. Sturgell, 553 U.S. 880, 895 (2008).

33. Intell. Ventures Mgmt., LLC v. Xilinx, Inc., IPR2012-00018, Paper 12 (Jan. 24, 2013) (Representative).

34. PATENT TRIAL AND APPEAL BOARD CONSOLIDATED TRIAL PRACTICE GUIDE 18 (Nov. 2019).

35. *Id.*

36. *Id.*

also include other PTAB trials and any ex parte or inter partes reexamination proceedings.[37]

c. Lead and Backup Counsel

The petitioner must identify lead and backup counsel for each proceeding.[38] At least one backup counsel must be named, but additional backup counsel are permitted.[39] A power of attorney must be filed designating counsel, unless patent owner's counsel is already of record in the challenged patent.[40] The Office expects that lead counsel will participate in all hearings and conference calls with the Board and will sign all papers submitted in the proceeding.[41] Backup counsel may conduct business with the Board on behalf of lead counsel when lead counsel is not available.[42]

Lead counsel must be a registered practitioner.[43] The Board may recognize counsel pro hac vice upon a showing of good cause.[44] As proceedings before the Office can be technically complex, the Board requires counsel filing a motion to appear pro hac vice to have an established familiarity with the subject matter at issue in the proceeding.[45] A motion for pro hac vice must be accompanied by an affidavit or declaration from the individual seeking to appear.[46]

6. Requirements of Sections 312 and 42.104

a. Identify Each Claim Challenged and the Statutory Ground for Each Challenge

The petition must identify, for each challenged claim, the specific statutory grounds under 35 U.S.C. § 102 or 103 and the prior art patents or printed

37. *Id.*
38. 37 C.F.R. § 42.10(a).
39. 80 Fed. Reg. 28,561, 28,563 (May 19, 2015).
40. 37 C.F.R. § 42.10(b).
41. *See* PATENT TRIAL AND APPEAL BOARD CONSOLIDATED TRIAL PRACTICE GUIDE 11 (Nov. 2019).
42. *Id.*
43. 37 C.F.R. § 42.10(c).
44. *Id.*
45. PATENT TRIAL AND APPEAL BOARD CONSOLIDATED TRIAL PRACTICE GUIDE 11 (Nov. 2019); 37 C.F.R. § 42.10.
46. Unified Patents, Inc. v. Parallel Iron, LLC, IPR2013-00639, Paper 7, at 3 (Oct. 15, 2013).

publications relied upon for each ground.[47] PGR petitions can challenge claims under any of the statutory invalidity defenses available to an accused infringer.[48] The petition must identify, for each challenged claim, the specific statutory grounds permitted under 35 U.S.C. § 282(b)(2) or (3) the claim is challenged under, except as modified by section 18(a)(1)(C) of the Leahy-Smith America Invents Act (Pub. L. No. 112–29, 125 Stat. 284 (2011)).[49]

b. Identify How the Claim Should Be Construed

For all petitions, the statement of precise relief requested must identify how the challenged claims are to be construed.[50] In general, however, the petitioner need not define every claim term.[51] The Board generally only construes terms disputed by the parties and only to the extent necessary to resolve the proceeding.[52]

If the claim contains a means-plus-function or step-plus-function limitation, the construction must identify the portions of the specification that describe the structure, material, or acts corresponding to each claimed function.[53] A difficulty may arise when construing means-plus-function terms that may not be supported by the specification. In some instances, the Board has construed an indefinite term to be any hardware or software for performing the claimed function.[54] In other instances, the Board has found the term could not be construed.[55] And where means-plus-function terms were

47. 37 C.F.R. § 42.104(b)(2).

48. 35 U.S.C. § 321(b); *see also id.* § 282(b)(2), (3).

49. 37 C.F.R. § 42.304(b)(2).

50. *Id.* §§ 42.104(b)(3), 42.204(b)(3), 42.304(b)(3).

51. 77 Fed. Reg. 48,680, 48,699–700, Response to Comment 35 (Aug. 14, 2012).

52. *See, e.g.*, Realtime Data, LLC v. Iancu, 912 F.3d 1368, 1375 (Fed. Cir. 2019) ("The Board is required to construe 'only those terms . . . that are in controversy, and only to the extent necessary to resolve the controversy.'" (quoting Vivid Techs., Inc. v. Am. Sci. & Eng'g, Inc., 200 F.3d 795, 803 (Fed. Cir. 1999)); Patent Trial and Appeal Board Consolidated Trial Practice Guide 49 (Nov. 2019).

53. 37 C.F.R. §§ 42.104(b)(3), 42.204(b)(3), 42.304(b)(3).

54. *See, e.g.*, Sony Comp. Entm't of Am. v. Grobler, IPR2013-00076, Paper 12, at 8 (July 22, 2013).

55. *See, e.g.*, Universal Remote Control, Inc. v. Universal Elecs., Inc., IPR2013-00152, Paper 8, at 20 (Aug. 19, 2013).

unsupported in the specification, the Board has concluded that those claim terms could not be construed and, as a result, denied institution.[56]

c. Identify the Statutory Grounds and Evidence Supporting the Challenge

The petition must also identify how the construed claim is unpatentable under the identified statutory grounds and provide the exhibit number of any supporting evidence along with an identification of the portions of the evidence that support the challenge.[57] Where the grounds for unpatentability are based on prior art, the petition must specify where each element of the claim is found in the prior art.[58] The petitioner also bears the initial burden of establishing that a reference qualifies as prior art (*infra* section C.1).[59] For all other grounds of unpatentability (e.g., in PGRs), the petition must identify the part of the claim that fails to comply with the statutory grounds raised and state how the identified subject matter fails to comply with the statute.[60]

7. Service of Petition

The petitioner must serve the petition, and the accompanying evidence, on the patent owner at the correspondence address of record for the challenged patent.[61] The petitioner may also serve the materials "at any other address known to the petitioner as likely to effect service."[62]

8. Incomplete Petition

When an incomplete petition is filed, the petitioner will not be accorded a filing date.[63] The Board will give the petitioner one month to resolve any

---

56. *See* Space Expl. Techs. Corp. v. Blue Origin LLC, IPR2014-01378, Paper 6, at 4–9 (Mar. 3, 2015) (refusing to institute trial because it could not conduct the requisite validity analysis).
57. 37 C.F.R. §§ 42.104(b)(4)–(5), 42.204(b)(4)–(5), 42.304(b).
58. *Id.* §§ 42.104(b)(4), 42.204(b)(4), 42.304(b)(4).
59. *See, e.g.*, Dynamic Drinkware, LLC, v. Nat'l Graphics, Inc., 800 F.3d 1375, 1378–79 (Fed. Cir. 2015).
60. 37 C.F.R. §§ 42.204(b)(4), 42.304(b)(4).
61. *Id.* § 42.105(a).
62. *Id.*
63. *Id.* § 42.106(b).

deficiencies.[64] If the petitioner does not resolve the deficiencies in the allotted time, the Board will dismiss the petition.[65] If one month is not sufficient time to correct the deficiencies, the Board suggests filing a separate, complete petition.[66] This will not affect the filing date because one was not accorded for the initial petition.[67]

The Board is primarily concerned with major deficiencies.[68] Thus, it will accord a filing date even if minor deficiencies are present that do not affect its ability to determine whether to institute review or the patent owner's ability to file a preliminary response.[69] An example of a major deficiency is when a petitioner fails to include a statement for the precise relief requested for each claim challenged.[70]

B. Confidential Information and Protective Orders

1. Petition and Supporting Evidence Generally Made Public (Section 312(b))

The Director shall make the petition public "[a]s soon as practicable."[71] And "the record of a proceeding, including documents and things, shall be made available to the public, except as otherwise ordered."[72]

2. Motion to Seal and Protective Order (Sections 42.14, 42.54)

A petitioner may, however, file a motion to seal and a proposed protective order concurrent with the petition.[73] The petitioner must file, but need not serve, the confidential information.[74] The institution of a trial will constitute

64. *Id.*
65. *Id.*
66. 77 Fed. Reg. 48,680, 48,701, Response to Comment 48 (Aug. 14, 2012).
67. *Id.*
68. *See id.* at 48,700–01, Response to Comment 45 (explaining that the Board generally will "accept minor deficiencies that do not impact the Board's ability to determine whether to institute review or the patent owner's ability to file a preliminary response").
69. *Id.*
70. *Id.* at 48,701, Response to Comment 47.
71. 35 U.S.C. § 312(b).
72. 37 C.F.R. § 42.14.
73. *Id.* § 42.55.
74. *Id.* § 42.55(a).

a grant of the motion unless the Board orders otherwise.[75] Where a petitioner requests entry of the default protective order, the patent owner may access the confidential information before the trial is instituted only if the patent owner agrees to the terms of the default order or obtains relief from the Board. If the petitioner requests entry of another proposed protective order, the patent owner may access the confidential information before the trial is instituted only if the patent owner agrees to the terms of the proposed order; agrees to the terms of a jointly filed order; or obtains entry of another order, for example, the default protective order.

3. Default Protective Order in Trial Practice Guide and Potential Modifications

The Office's Trial Practice Guide contains a default protective order that the parties may adopt.[76] It requires that the parties mark documents containing confidential information as "PROTECTIVE ORDER MATERIAL."[77] It also restricts access to confidential information to (1) parties, (2) party representatives, (3) experts, (4) in-house counsel of the parties, (5) support personnel (e.g., clerical staff and court reporters), and (6) the Board and other employees or representatives of the Office who have a need to review the confidential information.[78] Experts are required to sign an acknowledgment certifying that they are not a competitor of any party or an employee of or consultant for a competitor to any party.[79] The default protective order also requires persons receiving confidential information to take reasonable measures to maintain confidentiality, including maintaining the information in a secure location to which unauthorized persons shall not have access.[80] Within 60 days of a final disposition of the proceeding, the parties must return or certify destruction of all copies of confidential information received from another party.[81]

75. *Id.* § 42.55.
76. PATENT TRIAL AND APPEAL BOARD CONSOLIDATED TRIAL PRACTICE GUIDE App'x B (Nov. 2019).
77. *Id.*
78. *Id.*
79. *Id.*
80. *Id.*
81. *Id.*

The default protective order permits a party to file documents containing confidential information accompanied by a motion to seal.[82] In general, a party should redact confidential information from such documents filed with the Board, and the motion to seal should explain the reasons why the information is confidential. A party may also oppose an opponent's motion to seal.[83] The documents or information filed will remain under seal unless the Board determines that some or all of the information does not qualify for confidential treatment.[84]

Parties may propose modifications to the Board's default protective order. For example, they may propose multiple tiers of confidentiality.[85] If certain information is particularly sensitive, the parties may also agree to eliminate access to certain individuals (e.g., in-house counsel). The Board will consider proposed modifications to the default protective order and will generally accept such modifications if they are consistent with the integrity and efficient administration of the proceedings.[86]

C. Demonstrating Prior Art Status

Prior art for IPRs is limited to patents and printed publications, each of which must be qualified as prior art, following procedures and requirements unique to each.

1. Qualifying Nonpatent Literature as Prior Art

Any printed reference that is not a patent or patent publication is nonpatent literature (NPL). Common examples of NPL include

- pharmaceutical drug labels;
- websites;
- technical publications (e.g., Institute of Electrical and Electronics Engineers (IEEE) documentation);

82. *Id.*
83. *Id.*
84. *Id.*
85. *Id.*
86. *Id.*

- conference presentations and papers;
- dissertations and theses; and
- textbooks.

The determination of whether a document qualifies as a "printed publication" under 35 U.S.C. § 102 "involves a case-by-case inquiry into the facts and circumstances surrounding the reference's disclosure to members of the public."[87] In certain situations, particularly for manuscripts or dissertations stored in libraries, courts may inquire whether a reference was sufficiently indexed, cataloged, and shelved.[88] In other situations, such as for information displayed at meetings and trade shows, courts have explained that indexing is not required if it was sufficiently disseminated.[89]

While cataloging and indexing have "played a significant role" in cases involving library references, "neither cataloging nor indexing is a necessary condition for a reference to be publicly accessible."[90] Meaningful indexing requires some coherent organization that allows a skilled and interested artisan to narrow the universe of possible references to a manageable number, allowing the skilled artisan to exercise reasonable diligence to access the reference.[91]

To demonstrate that NPL, such as textbooks, dissertations, or technical publications, was meaningfully indexed before the earliest priority date of a challenged patent, a petitioner may file a librarian declaration showing when the library would have obtained the reference and how the library ordinarily

87. Medtronic, Inc. v. Barry, 891 F.3d 1368, 1380 (Fed. Cir. 2018) (citing *In re* Klopfenstein, 380 F.3d 1345, 1350 (Fed. Cir. 2004)).

88. *See, e.g.*, *In re* Hall, 781 F.2d 897, 898–99 (Fed. Cir. 1986); *In re* Lister, 583 F.3d 1307, 1315 (Fed. Cir. 2009) (finding that a manuscript became publicly accessible once it was placed in a searchable database).

89. *See Medtronic*, 891 F.3d at 1381 (citing Suffolk Techs., LLC v. AOL Inc., 752 F.3d 1358, 1365 (Fed. Cir. 2014)).

90. *Lister*, 583 F.3d at 1312 (citing *Klopfenstein*, 380 F.3d at 1348); *see also* Samsung Elecs. Co., Ltd. v. Infobridge Pte. Ltd., 929 F.3d 1363, 1369 (Fed. Cir. 2019) ("[W]hile indexing is not required to show that a work is publicly accessible, some evidence that a person of ordinary skill could have reasonably found the website and then found the reference on that website is critical.").

91. *See* Microsoft Corp. v. Uniloc 2017 LLC, IPR2019-01116, Paper 22, at 37–38 (Oct. 26, 2020) (explaining that a website "index" that was not text searchable, was not organized by subject matter, and did not contain the full names of uploads did not enable a skilled artisan, exercising reasonable diligence, to find one of hundreds of articles).

indexes materials. For a website, the petition may explain (potentially with a supporting declaration) how the website was meaningfully indexed and accessible (i.e., by subject matter or title, not just by date). Even without "meaningful indexing," a reference may be found publicly accessible if the petitioner demonstrates that a skilled and interested artisan "would have been independently aware of" the website where the reference is found and the interested artisan would have found the reference using the website's search functions.[92]

If a reference is not indexed or distributed (e.g., conference presentations and any other temporary NPL references), courts should consider the *Klopfenstein* factors to determine "whether or not [the reference] was sufficiently publicly accessible in order to be considered a 'printed publication' under § 102(b)."[93] Those factors are (1) "the length of time the display was exhibited"; (2) "the expertise of the target audience"; (3) "the existence (or lack thereof) of reasonable expectations that the material displayed would not be copied"; and (4) "the simplicity or ease with which the material displayed could have been copied."[94]

2. Qualifying Patents or Published Applications as Prior Art as of an Earlier Filing Date

Under pre-AIA section 102(e), a patent or published application is prior art as of the filing date of an earlier-filed application, such as a provisional application, if (1) the subject matter relied upon in the patent is described in the provisional application and (2) at least one of the issued claims is supported under section 112 by the disclosure of the provisional application.[95] The Federal Circuit has also extended this principle to published patent applications filed under the Patent Cooperation Treaty (PCT).[96]

92. *See* Voter Verified, Inc. v. Premier Election Sols., Inc., 698 F.3d 1374, 1381 (Fed. Cir. 2012).

93. *See Klopfenstein*, 380 F.3d at 1350.

94. *Id.*

95. Dynamic Drinkware, LLC, v. Nat'l Graphics, Inc., 800 F.3d 1375, 1378 (Fed. Cir. 2015); *see also* Manual of Patent Examining Procedure § 2136.03 (rev. Jan. 2018).

96. Amgen v. Sanofi, 872 F.3d 1367 (Fed. Cir. 2017); *see also* Manual of Patent Examining Procedure § 2136.03 (rev. Apr. 5, 2018).

AIA section 102(d) provides that a patent or published application shall be considered to have been effectively filed (and thus qualify as prior art) as of the filing date of an earlier application if it is entitled to claim a right of priority to such earlier-filed application. The Federal Circuit has not analyzed this AIA provision, and thus it remains undetermined whether, and to what extent, this standard will differ from the pre-AIA section 102(e) standard.

D. Expert Declarations

While a petitioner is not required to support its petition with expert testimony, many petitioners elect to do so. Such testimony must be submitted in the form of an affidavit or declaration.[97] Expert declarations may assist the Board and help a petitioner present its case by explaining the technological background and the patents at issue, defining the general meaning of claim terms, outlining the teachings of prior art, and explaining how the prior art compares to challenged claims. Qualified experts may be identified in many different ways, including through (1) research by counsel, (2) professional expert searchers, (3) recommendations by in-house or outside counsel, and (4) authorship of relevant publications or prior art.

E. Addressing Potential Bases for Discretionary Denial of Institution

Under 35 U.S.C. § 314(a), the Board has broad discretion to deny institution. The Board, for example, has denied institution if the same issues have been presented in a parallel district court proceeding that has reached an advanced stage.[98] The Board has also exercised its discretion under section 314(a) to deny institution based on the serial filing of multiple petitions against a patent.[99] In addition, 35 U.S.C. § 325(d) gives the Board specific

97. 37 C.F.R. § 42.53(a).

98. Apple Inc. v. Fintiv, Inc., IPR2020-00019, Paper 11 (Mar. 20, 2020) (Precedential).

99. Gen. Plastic Indus. Co. v. Canon Kabushiki Kaisha, IPR2016-01357, Paper 19 (Sept. 6, 2017) (Precedential).

discretion to deny institution where "the same or substantially the same prior art or arguments previously were presented to the Office."

If there is potential for a discretionary denial of institution, the Board encourages petitioners to address the relevant facts in the petition. For example, in evaluating its discretion under section 325(d), the Board may consider "whether Petitioner has pointed out sufficiently how the Examiner erred in its evaluation of the asserted prior art" and "the extent to which additional evidence and facts in the Petition warrant reconsideration of prior art or arguments."[100] While the Board does not require petitioners to preemptively address potential discretionary bases for denying institution, failure to do so could jeopardize a petitioner's chances of success at institution.

F. Multiple Petitions

1. Challenging Related Patents

When a patent owner obtains two or more related patents or patents covering related subject matter, a petitioner may have reason to file petitions against multiple patents. Under its standard operating procedures, the Board seeks to facilitate efficiency and consistency of results by assigning such petitions to the fewest total administrative patent judges (APJs) as practicable.[101] For example, it is preferred (but not required) that the lead APJ also serve as lead APJ on a related case. It is also preferred that related cases be paneled with the same three APJs, if practicable, or that there be at least some overlap between the panels of APJs for related cases. The requirement that a petitioner identify related matters in the mandatory notices portion of the petition assists the Board in making these assignments.[102]

100. Oticon Med. AB v. Cochlear Ltd., IPR2019-00975, Paper 15, at 10 (Oct. 16, 2019) (Precedential) (citing Becton, Dickinson & Co. v. B. Braun Melsungen AG, IPR2017-01586, Paper 8 (Dec. 15, 2017) (Precedential)).

101. PATENT TRIAL AND APPEAL BOARD STANDARD OPERATING PROCEDURE 1, § III(G)(3) (Rev. 15, 2018).

102. 37 C.F.R. § 42.8(b).

2. Challenging a Single Patent

The Board generally discourages a petitioner from filing multiple petitions against a single patent, explaining that "one petition should be sufficient to challenge the claims of a patent in most situations."[103] The Board has further stated that receiving multiple challenges to the same patent can hinder its ability "to complete proceedings in a timely manner and may place an unfair burden on the patent owner."[104]

While the Board has recognized "that there may be circumstances in which more than one petition may be necessary, including, for example, when the patent owner has asserted a large number of claims in litigation or when there is a dispute about priority date requiring arguments under multiple prior art references," the Board has identified these circumstances as outliers.[105]

If a petitioner does elect to file multiple petitions against the same patent, the Office's November 2019 Trial Practice Guide Update clarifies that the petitioner should provide "(1) a ranking of the petitions in the order in which it wishes the Board to consider the merits, if the Board uses its discretion to institute any of the petitions, and (2) a succinct explanation of the differences between the petitions, why the issues addressed by the differences are material, and why the Board should exercise its discretion to institute additional petitions if it identifies one petition that satisfies petitioner's burden under 35 U.S.C. § 314(a)."[106]

3. Multiple Petitioners

A single patent may be the subject of multiple petitions from separate petitioners. For example, this can occur when a patent owner has asserted the patent against multiple defendants and at least two or more of those

103. PATENT TRIAL AND APPEAL BOARD CONSOLIDATED TRIAL PRACTICE GUIDE 59 (Nov. 2019).

104. Comcast Cable Commc'ns, LLC v. Rovi Guides, Inc., IPR2019-00224, Paper 10, at 3 (April 3, 2019); *Trial Practice Guide Update*, USPTO (July 2019), https://www.uspto.gov/sites/default/files/documents/trial-practice-guide-update3.pdf.

105. *See* PATENT TRIAL AND APPEAL BOARD CONSOLIDATED TRIAL PRACTICE GUIDE 59 (Nov. 2019).

106. *See id.* at 59–60.

defendants independently file IPR or PGR petitions. As detailed earlier in section D.2, the Board aims to assign the same panel of APJs to IPRs involving the same patent. The Board also often seeks to coordinate briefing and oral hearing schedules among the multiple petitioners, for example, having one petitioner act as the lead.[107]

4. Serial Petitions—*General Plastic* Factors

The Board has expressed concerns about the potential harassment of patent owners through the filing of multiple, successive challenges to a single patent, using filings and decisions from previous IPR or PGR proceedings as a "guide" for future challenges. Counterbalancing these concerns is the Board's interest in affording unique petitioners their day at the Board. Thus, it may be necessary for a petitioner to evaluate past proceedings involving an asserted patent to determine whether the Board could potentially exercise its discretion to deny a follow-on petition. In *General Plastic Industrial Co., Ltd. v. Canon Kabushiki Kaisha*,[108] the Board set forth seven nonexhaustive factors that it considers in these situations:

(1) whether the same petitioner previously filed a petition directed to the same claims of the same patent;
(2) whether at the time of filing of the first petition the petitioner knew of the prior art asserted in the second petition or should have known of it;
(3) whether at the time of filing of the second petition the petitioner already received the patent owner's preliminary response to the first petition or received the Board's decision on whether to institute review in the first petition;
(4) the length of time between when the petitioner learned of the prior art asserted in the second petition and the filing of the second petition;

107. David P. Ruschke & William V. Saindon, *An Analysis of Multiple Petitions in AIA Trials* 41, USPTO (Oct. 24, 2017), https://www.uspto.gov/sites/default/files/documents/Chat_with_the_Chief_Boardside_Chat_Multiple_Petition_Study_20171024.pdf.

108. Gen. Plastic Indus. Co., Ltd. v. Canon Kabushiki Kaisha, IPR2016-01357, Paper 19, at 9 (Sept. 6, 2017) (Precedential).

(5) whether the petitioner provides adequate explanation for the time elapsed between the filings of multiple petitions directed to the same claims of the same patent;
(6) the finite resources of the Board; and
(7) the requirement under 35 U.S.C. § 316(a)(11) to issue a final determination not later than one year after the date on which the Director notices institution of review.

The Board explained that these factors serve as a baseline "formulation of relevant considerations," noting that there may be other considerations that can be assessed to promote "efficiency . . . and the fundamental fairness of the process for all parties."[109]

5. Joinder of Multiple Proceedings

The Board can join multiple IPR or PGR proceedings.[110] For both IPR and PGR proceedings, either the patent owner or a petitioner can request joinder.[111] The deadline for requesting joinder comes up quickly: it is just one month after institution of the proceeding for which joinder is requested.[112] The request must be in the form of a motion that has been authorized by the Board.[113]

For IPR proceedings, joinder is only possible if (1) the Board has instituted an IPR, (2) the party requesting joinder files a proper IPR petition, (3) the patent owner files a preliminary response or the time period for a preliminary response expires, and (4) the Board determines the petition filed by the party requesting joinder warrants institution.[114] For PGR proceedings, joinder is possible when multiple petitions have been filed on the same patent and the Board has determined that more than one petition warrants institution.[115] Thus, IPR proceedings can be joined with other

109. *Id.* at 18.
110. 35 U.S.C. §§ 315(c), 325(c).
111. 37 C.F.R. §§ 42.122(b), 42.222(b).
112. *Id.*
113. *See* Kyocera Corp. v. Softview LLC, IPR2013-00004, Paper 15 (Apr. 24, 2013), *aff'd sub nom.* Softview LLC v. Kyocera Corp., 592 F. App'x 949 (Fed. Cir. 2015) (Mem.).
114. 35 U.S.C. § 315(c).
115. *Id.* § 325(c).

IPR proceedings, and likewise, PGR proceedings can be joined with other PGR proceedings.[116]

The requirement that a petitioner must file an IPR within one year after being served with a complaint for infringement does not apply to requests for joinder.[117] Thus, if an IPR proceeding is already instituted based on a petition that was filed within one year, a separate petitioner can file another IPR petition and request that it be joined to the first proceeding.[118]

When considering a joinder motion, "the Office will consider the particular facts of each case including how the consolidation of the reviews impacts the Office's ability to complete reviews timely."[119] In particular, the Board considers whether (1) the two proceedings are substantially related (e.g., same parties, same patent, substantially the same prior art), (2) the petitioner was diligent, and (3) the joinder will not cause undue delay in the first proceeding.[120] The Board has been amenable to joining cases where both parties consent to joinder[121] and where the cases to be joined are directed to the same claims and the same grounds of unpatentability.[122] The Board has, however, denied joinder where it may substantially affect the schedule of the proceeding[123] or where the cases have different prior art issues.[124] And it has denied joinder where the same petitioner proposed grounds it could have raised in the first petition[125] or where the same petitioner created its own bar date.[126]

---

116. Microsoft Corp. v. Proxyconn, IPR2013-00109, Paper 15 (Feb. 25, 2013) (Representative), *rev'd on other grounds*, 789 F.3d 1292 (Fed. Cir. 2015).

117. 35 U.S.C. § 315(c); *see Microsoft Corp.*, IPR2013-00109, Paper 15, at 2; Target Corp. v. Destination Maternity Corp., IPR2014-00508, Paper 18 (Sept. 25, 2014) (expanded panel), *rev'd on other grounds*, Target Corp. v. Destination Maternity Corp., IPR2014-00508, Paper 28 (Feb. 12, 2015) (further expanded panel).

118. *Microsoft Corp*, IPR2013-00109, Paper 15.

119. 77 Fed. Reg. 48,680, 48,707, Response to Comment 88 (Aug. 14, 2012).

120. *Microsoft Corp.*, IPR2013-00109, Paper 15.

121. *Id.*

122. Motorola Mobility LLC v. Softview LLC, IPR2013-00256, Paper 10, at 2 (June 20, 2013).

123. NetApp, Inc. v. Pers. Web Techs., LLC, IPR2013-00319, Paper 18 (July 22, 2013).

124. Liberty Mut. Ins. Co. v. Progressive Cas. Ins. Co., CBM2012-00002, Paper 16 (Feb. 22, 2013).

125. Reloaded Games, Inc. v. Parallel Networks LLC, IPR2014-00950, Paper 12, at 4 (Oct. 22, 2014).

126. Medtronic, Inc. v. Endotach LLC, IPR2014-00695, Paper 18, at 3 (Sept. 25, 2014).

G. Potential Authorization for a Petitioner Reply to Patent Owner's Preliminary Response

While a petition must meet the requirements detailed in section A earlier, a petitioner may have an opportunity to file an additional preinstitution paper to reply to possible deficiencies identified in a patent owner's preliminary response. Such replies are not granted as of right. Instead, a petitioner must request authorization to file a reply and establish good cause.[127]

In considering whether a petitioner has satisfied the good-cause standard, the Board may evaluate whether the petitioner seeks to reply to an argument that the petitioner could not have reasonably foreseen at the time the petition was filed.[128] The Board may also grant authorization if it believes that further briefing would be helpful on the issue petitioner identified in the request.[129] Issues for which the Board has occasionally (but not always) granted authorization for a petitioner reply include patent owner's claim construction positions, arguments for discretionary denial of institution, and potential inconsistent statements (e.g., compared to patent owner's arguments in prosecution or litigation).[130]

127. 37 C.F.R. § 42.108(c).

128. Intel Corp. v. VLSI Tech., LLC, IPR2018-01038, Paper 13, at 2 (Sept. 28, 2018).

129. 37 C.F.R. § 42.20(d) ("The Board may order briefing on any issue involved in the trial."); Runway Safe Grp. AB v. Earthstone Int'l LLC, IPR2019-01490, Paper 11 (Dec. 9, 2019).

130. *Runway*, IPR2019-01490, Paper 11; *Intel Corp.*, IPR2018-01038, Paper 13; Roku, Inc. v. Universal Elecs. Inc., IPR2019-01620, Paper 8 (Mar. 11, 2020).

Chapter 4

Preliminary Response to a Petition

This chapter explores patent owner preliminary responses to petitions, including the requirements for a preliminary response and strategy considerations for when to file and what to include in a preliminary response.

A. Optional to File

After a petition has been filed, and before the Board makes its institution determination, the patent owner has a statutory right to file a preliminary response within three months after the petition is granted a filing date.[1] However, patent owners should be aware that the Board may shorten the time to file a preliminary response.[2] If filed, the preliminary response may present arguments and evidence, including testimonial evidence such as declarations, to demonstrate that no review should be instituted.[3]

1. 35 U.S.C. §§ 313, 323; 37 C.F.R. §§ 42.107(b), 42.207(b). The Board may contact a patent owner to determine whether the patent owner intends to file a preliminary response.

2. SAP Am., Inc. v. Versata Dev. Grp., Inc., CBM2012-00001, Paper 10, at 6 (Oct. 17, 2012), *aff'd*, Versata Dev. Grp., Inc. v. SAP, Inc., 793 F.3d 1306 (Fed. Cir. 2015).

3. 37 C.F.R. §§ 42.107(a), 42.207(a).

B. Who Can File

An owner of the entire right, title, and interest in the patent may file a preliminary response, to the exclusion of the inventor.[4] An owner of only a partial interest in the patent, however, must file a motion to act without the inventor or co-owner.[5] Such a motion must show the inability or refusal of an inventor or co-owner to participate in the proceeding or show why it is in the interests of justice to permit the partial owner to act.[6]

C. Requirements for Filing

The preliminary response (and accompanying exhibits, if any) must be filed electronically unless otherwise authorized.[7] It must also be served on each opposing party at the time of filing along with any exhibits that were not previously served.[8] Any preliminary response must be filed no later than three months after a Notice of Filing Date is issued for the petition.[9] However, the Board may require the preliminary response to be filed before the three-month deadline.[10] A preliminary response has the same word limit as the corresponding petition.[11] Thus, for an IPR, the patent owner's preliminary response is limited to 14,000 words, and for a PGR, it is limited to 18,700 words.[12]

4. *Id.* § 42.9(a).
5. *Id.* § 42.9(b).
6. *Id.*
7. *Id.* § 42.6(b), (c), (e).
8. *Id.*
9. *Id.* §§ 42.107(b), 42.207(b).
10. SAP Am., Inc. v. Versata Dev. Grp., Inc., CBM2012-00001, Paper 10, at 6 (Oct. 17, 2012), *aff'd*, Versata Dev. Grp., Inc. v. SAP, Inc., 793 F.3d 1306 (Fed. Cir. 2015).
11. 37 C.F.R. § 42.24(b)(2).
12. *Id.* § 42.24(a)(1); *see also* PATENT TRIAL AND APPEAL BOARD CONSOLIDATED TRIAL PRACTICE GUIDE 38–40 (Nov. 2019).

D. Types of Arguments

The preliminary response is limited to addressing why the Board should not institute a review under 35 U.S.C. § 314 or § 324.[13] It can include claim-construction arguments,[14] but it cannot present any claim amendments.[15] The preliminary response can include evidence supporting the patent owner's contentions,[16] including new testimonial evidence[17] prepared for the proceeding, but there is no right of cross-examination of a declarant prior to institution.[18]

Alternatively, or in addition to a preliminary response, the patent owner may file a motion to dismiss after obtaining authorization to do so.[19] Patent owners should note, however, that arguments cannot take the place of factually supported objective evidence, and the patent owner will have the burden of proof to establish that dismissal is appropriate.[20] Furthermore, depending on the complexity of the issues involved, the Board may order additional briefing on the motion.[21]

1. Arguments against Institution

a. Section 325(d) (Substantially the Same Arguments)

Under 35 U.S.C. § 314(a), the Board has broad discretion to deny institution. In addition, 35 U.S.C. § 325(d) gives the Board specific discretion to deny institution when "the same or substantially the same prior art or arguments previously were presented to the Office." The Board has denied petitions under section 325(d) that presented the same or substantially the same prior art and arguments presented in an earlier petition or during the original examination or reexamination.[22] The Board has also exercised its

13. 35 U.S.C. §§ 313, 323; 37 C.F.R. §§ 42.107(a), 42.207(a); *see also* Patent Trial and Appeal Board Consolidated Trial Practice Guide 49–52 (Nov. 2019).
14. 77 Fed. Reg. 48,680, 48,700, Response to Comment 38 (Aug. 14, 2012).
15. 37 C.F.R. §§ 42.107(d), 42.207(d).
16. *Id.* §§ 42.107(a), 42.207(a).
17. 81 Fed. Reg. 18,750, 18,755, Response to Comment 1 (Apr. 1, 2016).
18. *Id.* at 18,756, Response to Comment 2.
19. 77 Fed. Reg. 48,680, 48,702, Response to Comment 53 (Aug. 14, 2012).
20. *Id.*; *see also* 37 C.F.R. § 42.20(c).
21. 37 C.F.R. § 42.20(d).
22. Medtronic, Inc. v. Nuvasive, Inc., IPR2014-00487, Paper 8, at 2, 7 (Sept. 11, 2014)

discretion under section 325(d) to deny petitions even when the petitioner has raised different prior art.[23]

In early 2020, the Board clarified that section 325(d) presents two distinct issues: first, whether the petition presents the same or substantially the same prior art as previously presented to the Office; and second, whether the petition presents the same or substantially the same arguments as previously presented to the Office.[24] Each inquiry is separate and highly factual.[25] If the Board finds that the same prior art or arguments were previously presented, it must then consider whether the petition has demonstrated that the Office "erred in a manner material to the patentability of challenged claims."[26] The error must be clear: if "reasonable minds can disagree," the Office cannot have materially erred.[27] Thus, even if the Board determines that the same art or arguments were previously presented under the first prong of section 325(d), it may nonetheless institute review under the second prong if it determines that the Office materially erred in its earlier analysis.[28]

Several factors from *Becton, Dickinson & Co. v. B. Braun Melsungen AG*[29] guide this two-part analysis:[30]

(Informative) (denying institution as redundant over two previously filed IPRs, one of which was instituted and one of which was not); Unified Patents, Inc. v. Pers. Web Techs., LLC, IPR2014-00702, Paper 13, at 2–3, 7–9 (July 24, 2014) (Informative) (denying institution as redundant over three prior IPRs filed by third parties, one of which was on appeal before the Federal Circuit); Prism Pharma Co., Ltd. v. Choongwae Pharma Corp., IPR2014-00315, Paper 14, at 2, 12–13 (July 8, 2014) (Informative) (denying institution as redundant over same prior art and arguments made during prosecution); ZTE Corp. v. Contentguard Holdings Inc., IPR2013-00454, Paper 12, at 4–5 (Sept. 25, 2013) (Informative) (denying institution as redundant over a previously filed but not initiated IPR on the same patent and claims).

23. Unilever, Inc. v. Procter & Gamble Co., IPR2014-00506, Paper 17, at 2, 6–8 (July 7, 2014) (Informative); Intelligent Bio-Sys., Inc. v. Illumina Cambridge Ltd., IPR2013-00324, Paper 19, at 5–7 (Nov. 21, 2013) (Informative) (reasoning that petitioner failed to explain how additional art than that previously relied upon was any different).

24. Advanced Bionics, LLC v. MED-EL Elektromedizinische Geräte GmbH, IPR2019-01469, Paper 6 (Feb. 13, 2020) (Precedential).

25. *Id.* at 7–9.

26. *Id.* at 8.

27. *Id.* at 9.

28. *Id.* at 7–9.

29. Becton, Dickinson & Co. v. B. Braun Melsungen AG, IPR2017-01586, Paper 8, at 17–18 (Dec. 15, 2017) (Precedential as to § III.C.5, first paragraph).

30. *Advanced Bionics*, IPR2019-01469, Paper 6, at 9–11 (citing *Becton, Dickinson & Co.*, IPR2017-01586, Paper 8, at 17–18).

(a) the similarities and material differences between the asserted art and the prior art involved during examination;
(b) the cumulative nature of the asserted art and the prior art evaluated during examination;
(c) the extent to which the asserted art was evaluated during examination, including whether the prior art was the basis for rejection;
(d) the extent of the overlap between the arguments made during examination and the manner in which petitioner relies on the prior art or patent owner distinguishes the prior art;
(e) whether petitioner has pointed out sufficiently how the examiner erred in its evaluation of the asserted prior art; and
(f) the extent to which additional evidence and facts presented in the petition warrant reconsideration of the prior art or arguments.

Factors (a), (b), and (d) guide consideration of the first prong of the section 325(d) test in determining whether the same prior art or arguments were previously presented.[31] And factors (c), (e), and (f) guide consideration of the second prong in determining whether the petitioner has demonstrated a material error by the Office.[32]

Patent owners should thus consider whether the asserted prior art references and arguments raised in the petition are similar to, cumulative to, or exactly the same as references and arguments considered by the Office during prosecution. If so, the patent owner may argue in its preliminary response that the Board should exercise its discretion to deny the petition under section 325(d).

In some cases, the Board's analysis of whether to exercise its discretion to institute trial under section 325(d) may be influenced by considerations regarding 35 U.S.C. § 314, discussed next.[33]

31. *Advanced Bionics*, IPR2019-01469, Paper 6, at 9–10.
32. *Id.* at 10–11.
33. *See, e.g.*, Oticon Med. AB v. Cochlear Ltd., IPR2019-00975, Paper 15 (Oct. 16, 2019) (Precedential as to §§ II.B, II.C). For more information regarding 35 U.S.C. § 314, see section D.1.b, *infra*.

*b. Section 314 (*Fintiv *and* General Plastic*)*

Under 35 U.S.C. § 314, review cannot be instituted "unless . . . the information presented in the petition . . . shows that there is a reasonable likelihood that the petitioner would prevail with respect to at least 1 of the claims challenged in the petition."[34] The Board has cited this statutory section in two important precedential decisions that examine when and under what circumstances it will exercise its discretion not to institute review.

In the first decision, *General Plastic Industrial Co., Ltd. v. Canon Kabushiki Kaisha*,[35] the Board addressed the issue of serial IPR petitions challenging the same patents.[36] It identified seven factors intended to prevent unfairness to the patent owner while ensuring efficiency of the IPR (or PGR) process:[37]

(a) whether the same petitioner previously filed a petition directed to the same claims of the same patent;
(b) whether at the time of filing the first petition the petitioner knew of the prior art asserted in the second petition or should have known of it;
(c) whether at the time of filing the second petition the petitioner already received the patent owner's preliminary response to the first petition or the Board's decision on whether to institute review in the first petition;
(d) the length of time that elapsed between when the petitioner learned of the prior art asserted in the second petition and the filing of the second petition;
(e) whether the petitioner has adequately explained the time elapsed between the filings of multiple petitions directed to the same claims of the same patent;
(f) the finite resources of the Board; and

34. 35 U.S.C. § 314(a).

35. Gen. Plastic Indus. Co., Ltd. v. Canon Kabushiki Kaisha, IPR2016-01357, Paper 19 (Sept. 6, 2017) (Precedential).

36. *Id.* at 2–3.

37. *Id.* at 9–10.

(g) the requirement under 35 U.S.C. § 316(a)(11) to issue a final determination not later than one year after the Director notices institution of review.

Although the Board in *General Plastic* denied institution of the serial petition in that case, it did not create a per se rule against follow-on petitions. Rather, it stated that "there may be circumstances where multiple petitions by the same petitioner against the same claims of a patent should be permitted, and that such a determination is dependent on the facts at issue in the case."[38]

The first factor mentions "the *same* petitioner,"[39] but the *General Plastic* factors have also been applied to prevent institution of follow-on petitions filed by related petitioners.[40] The Board has specified that a *General Plastic* denial "is not limited solely to instances when multiple petitions are filed by the same petitioner."[41] For example, where two petitioners are similarly situated and share a "significant relationship . . . with respect to Patent Owner's assertion" of the challenged patent, one or more *General Plastic* factors may weigh against institution.[42] Petitioners may have a "significant relationship," for example, when they are indemnitor and indemnitee.[43]

Thus, if the petition is not the first time the patent has been challenged, the patent owner should consider whether an analysis of the *General Plastic* factors may support a denial of institution. For example, if the petition is a follow-on filing by the same petitioner, or if it appears to be a copycat of a petition filed by a different petitioner, it may be ripe for a *General Plastic* challenge. Patent owners should also consider whether the petitioner has

38. *Id.* at 18.

39. *Id.* at 9 (emphasis added).

40. *See, e.g.*, Apple Inc. v. Uniloc 2017 LLC, IPR2020-00854, Paper 9 (Oct. 28, 2020) (Precedential) (denying both institution and a motion for joinder of a follow-on copycat petition).

41. Valve Corp. v. Elec. Scripting Prods., Inc., IPR2019-00062, Paper 11, at 2 (Apr. 2, 2019) (Precedential).

42. *Id.* at 10.

43. *See, e.g.*, Choirock Contents Factory Co. v. Spin Master Ltd., IPR2019-00901, Paper 17, at 16–17 (Sept. 26, 2019); *see also Valve Corp.*, IPR2019-00062, Paper 11, at 9–10 ("significant relationship" found where the petitioners, one a licensee and one a licensor of relevant technology, were codefendants in the same lawsuit brought by the owner of the challenged patent).

a sufficiently close relationship to a prior petitioner such that the petition may be challenged under *General Plastic*.

In the second major decision, *Apple Inc. v. Fintiv, Inc.*,[44] the Board identified six nondispositive factors it may consider under section 314(a) in determining whether to institute an IPR or PGR that involves an ongoing parallel district court proceeding:[45]

(a) whether the court granted a stay or evidence exists that a stay may be granted if a proceeding is instituted;
(b) proximity of the court's trial date to the Board's projected statutory deadline for a final written decision;
(c) investment in the parallel proceeding by the court and the parties;
(d) overlap between issues raised in the petition and in the parallel proceeding;
(e) whether the petitioner and the defendant in the parallel proceeding are the same party; and
(f) other circumstances that impact the Board's exercise of discretion, including the merits.

Because these factors often overlap, the Board will take a holistic view of overarching concerns including judicial efficiency, fairness, and patent quality.[46]

With regard to the first factor, if the district court in a parallel proceeding has stayed the case, that fact may weigh heavily against denying institution.[47] So too would the fact that the district court has expressed on the record that it would reconsider a previously denied motion to stay upon institution.[48] These considerations remain important even if the district court case was stayed pending resolution of an International Trade Commission investigation, despite the fact that neither the Board nor the district court would be bound by the Commission's final determinations.[49]

---

44. Apple Inc. v. Fintiv, Inc., IPR2020-00019, Paper 11 (Mar. 20, 2020) (Precedential).
45. *Id.* at 5–6.
46. *Id.* at 6.
47. *Id.* at 6–9.
48. *Id.* at 7–8.
49. *Id.* at 8–9.

The timing of a petition's filing is also relevant.[50] If the petitioner filed the petition soon after learning which claims would be asserted in the district court proceeding, that would weigh against denying institution.[51] But if the petitioner waited to file its petition, for example, until after the patent owner responded to invalidity contentions, that fact would favor denial.[52] Further, if a district court trial has been scheduled to begin before the statutory deadline for the Board's final written decision, that fact weighs in favor of denying institution.[53]

Thus, if the petition is related to a parallel district court or ITC proceeding,[54] the patent owner should consider whether a *Fintiv* attack may prove effective. For example, if the parallel district court case has significantly advanced, the *Fintiv* factors may weigh in favor of the Board using its discretion to deny institution.

In sum, both *General Plastic* and *Fintiv* provide compelling avenues for patent owners to challenge petitions under section 314. Depending on the circumstances, either or both cases may support a strong challenge.

c. Failure to Identify Real Party in Interest

Under 35 U.S.C. § 312(a)(2), a petition for inter partes review must identify all real parties in interest (RPIs), and the Board may address this issue if there is a time bar or estoppel allegation based on an unnamed RPI.[55] Determining whether a nonparty is an RPI is a fact-dependent inquiry that considers both equitable and practical considerations. The Board generally considers whether the nonparty is a clear beneficiary to the proceeding and has a preexisting, established relationship with the petitioner. While the identity of the RPIs is often a topic of frequent debate between parties

50. *Id.* at 11–12.
51. *Id.* at 11.
52. *Id.* at 11–12.
53. *Id.* at 9.
54. *See* Patent Trial and Appeal Board Consolidated Trial Practice Guide 58 (Nov. 2019) (contemplating challenges based on not just district court proceedings but also ITC proceedings).
55. 35 U.S.C. § 312(a)(2); SharkNinja Operating LLC v. iRobot Corp., IPR2020-00734, Paper 11 (Oct. 6, 2020) (Precedential).

before the Board, several decisions help define an RPI, most notably *RPX Corp. v. Applications in Real Time.*[56]

In *RPX Corp.*, the Board highlighted that IPR and PGR petitioners have the burden to show the petition is not time barred under section 315(b), which states that "an inter partes review may not be instituted if the petition requesting the proceeding is filed more than 1 year after the date on which the petitioner, real party in interest, or privy of the petitioner is served with a complaint alleging infringement of the patent."[57] The Board further noted that the RPI determination is a "highly fact-dependent question."[58] To make that determination, the Board considered two questions:[59]

(a) "who, from a 'practical and equitable' standpoint, will benefit from the redress" that the IPR or PGR might provide; and
(b) "whether [the petitioner] can be said to be representing [the unnamed party's] interest after examining [their] relationship."

To answer these questions, the Board analyzed several factors relating to the relationship between the alleged unnamed RPI and the petitioner, including the following notable considerations:[60]

(a) the petitioner's business model;
(b) the petitioner's interest in filing the IPR or PGR;
(c) whether, under the circumstances, the petitioner takes a particular client's interests into account when determining whether to file IPR or PGR petitions;
(d) the alleged RPI's relationship with the petitioner;
(e) the alleged RPI's interest in and benefit from the IPRs or PGRs;
(f) whether the petitioner can be said to "represent the alleged RPI's interest";
(g) whether the alleged RPI desired institution of the IPR or PGR; and
(h) the relevance of the overlap in Board members between the alleged RPI and the petitioner.

56. RPX Corp. v. Applications in Real Time, IPR2015-01750, Paper 128 (Oct. 2, 2020).
57. 35 U.S.C. § 315(b) (emphasis added).
58. *See RPX Corp.*, IPR2015-01750, Paper 128, at 7.
59. *Id.* at 8.
60. *See generally id.* at 11–30.

In *RPX Corp.*, consideration of these factors, and communications between the two parties, resulted in a finding that the unnamed party should have been named as an RPI. The Board found that the petitioner's core business involved "patent aggregation, licensing, and filing IPRs to protect its clients," which "work together to protect its members from the threat of patent litigation."[61] It also found that the petitioner had an interest to challenge patents "to reduce risk to existing clients," including the unnamed party.[62]

Under petitioner's own Best Practices Guide, it would not discuss validity challenges with a member who would not agree to be named as an RPI, take suggestions from the member whether to file, or otherwise allow the member to exercise control over the IPR.[63] The Board, however, was not convinced by this practice, stating that "intentionally avoiding discussion about a forthcoming IPR against its client for the sole purpose of avoiding having to name the client as an RPI, yet challenging patents asserted against its client, suggests a 'willful blindness' strategy."[64] The petitioner also argued that the unnamed party subscribed solely to the petitioner's patent aggregation services and not for validity challenges. Once again, however, the Board was not swayed, finding that one of the "most important benefits of [the unnamed party's] membership" was for petitioner to assist the unnamed party with obtaining or clearing patent rights.[65] Also, the evidence showed that petitioner and the unnamed party had communicated about the asserted patents.

The Board concluded that the pending litigation supported a finding that the unnamed party was an RPI because invalidation of the challenged patents would provide a benefit to the unnamed party.[66] The fact that the petitioner was a member organization that existed in part to file IPR petitions against patents being potentially asserted against its members was indicative of an RPI relationship between the organization and its members.[67]

61. *Id.* at 15.
62. *Id.* at 16–17.
63. *Id.* at 18–20.
64. *Id.* at 20.
65. *Id.* at 22.
66. *Id.* at 24.
67. *Id.* at 26.

Given the analysis in *RPX*, the Board seems to have undergone a paradigm shift in its determination of RPI issues. For the first six years of Board trial practice, the RPI analysis focused on whether an unnamed party exerted sufficient "control" over the petition and relied on factors such as whether the unnamed party had input into whether a Board challenge was filed, paid for Board-related attorney/filing fees, and/or selected prior art. However, *RPX* suggests that while "control" of an IPR or PGR filing continues to be considered in RPI inquiries, the Board will take a more flexible approach that may result in parties being deemed RPIs, despite no explicit evidence of control.

d. One-Year Time Bar

After being sued for patent infringement, defendants seeking to challenge the asserted patent at the Board have a one-year time limit in which to file their petition. Under 35 U.S.C. § 315, review "may not be instituted if the petition requesting the proceeding is filed more than 1 year after the date on which the petitioner, real party in interest, or privy of the petitioner is served with a complaint alleging infringement of the patent."[68] Petitions filed after the one-year time limit are time barred and will be dismissed.[69] The time bar does not apply, however, when another party joins an existing IPR.[70]

Patent owners should consider when the petitioner—or a real party in interest, or a party in privy with the petitioner—was served with a complaint alleging infringement of the challenged patent. If service occurred over a year prior to filing the petition, it may be time barred under section 315. And once the Board has determined that a petition is time barred under section 315(b), that determination cannot be judicially reviewed.[71] Thus, if

68. 35 U.S.C. § 315(b).
69. *Id.*
70. 35 U.S.C. § 315(c).
71. 35 U.S.C. §§ 314(d), 315(b); *see* Thryv Inc. v. Click-to-Call Techs. LP, 140 S. Ct. 1367 (2020).

a patent owner shows that the petition is time barred, the petitioner cannot appeal that decision to the Federal Circuit.[72]

2. Arguments against the Merits

a. Pointing Out Nonpatent Literature Is Not Prior Art

Any printed reference that is not a published patent or patent application is nonpatent literature (NPL). Common examples of NPL include:

- Drug labels
- Websites
- Technical publications (e.g., Institute of Electrical and Electronics Engineers (IEEE) documentation, scientific articles, etc.)
- Conference presentations and papers
- Dissertations
- Textbooks

Determining whether a document is a "printed publication" under 35 U.S.C. § 102 "involves a case-by-case inquiry into the facts and circumstances surrounding the reference's disclosure to members of the public."[73] In certain situations, particularly for manuscripts or dissertations stored in libraries, courts may inquire whether a reference was sufficiently indexed, cataloged, and shelved in determining whether it qualifies as a printed publication.[74] In other situations, such as for information displayed at meetings and trade shows, indexing is not required for a reference to qualify as a printed publication, if it was sufficiently disseminated.[75] While cataloging and indexing have "played a significant role" in cases involving library

72. Note that petitioners may still be able to seek relief from time-bar determinations through a writ of mandamus to the Federal Circuit, although that standard may be difficult to meet.

73. Medtronic, Inc. v. Barry, 891 F.3d 1368, 1380 (Fed. Cir. 2018) (citing *In re* Klopfenstein, 380 F.3d 1345, 1350 (Fed. Cir. 2004)).

74. *See, e.g.*, *In re* Hall, 781 F.2d 897, 898–99 (Fed. Cir. 1986); *In re* Lister, 583 F.3d 1307, 1315 (Fed. Cir. 2009) (manuscript became publicly accessible once it was placed in a searchable database).

75. *See Medtronic*, 891 F.3d at 1381 (citing Suffolk Techs., LLC v. AOL Inc., 752 F.3d 1358, 1365 (Fed. Cir. 2014)).

references, "neither cataloging nor indexing is a necessary condition for a reference to be publicly accessible."[76]

Meaningful indexing requires some coherent organization that allows a skilled and interested artisan to narrow the universe of possible references to a manageable number, allowing a skilled artisan to exercise reasonable diligence to access the reference. For example, in *Acceleration Bay v. Activision Blizzard*,[77] the Federal Circuit affirmed the Board's finding that the primary cited reference did not qualify as a printed publication.[78] There, the disputed reference had been posted to a university library's website before the critical date.[79] But the Board concluded (and the Federal Circuit affirmed) that the site was not meaningfully indexed because it indexed reports by author and year only, not by subject matter, and there was no evidence regarding how the website's search functions worked (if at all) or whether they had been maintained.[80]

Demonstrating that NPL, such as textbooks, dissertations, or technical publications, was meaningfully indexed may require the petitioner to submit a librarian declaration showing when the library obtained the reference and how the library ordinarily indexes materials. Specifically, the petitioner may need to demonstrate that the indexing included the subject matter or title of the reference, not just the date. Preferably, the petitioner should demonstrate that the website index was keyword searchable, if applicable. It should also demonstrate that the indexing existed before the earliest priority date of the challenged patent. Absent such evidence, a patent owner may challenge the prior art status of the NPL in its preliminary response as a basis for denying institution.

Even without meaningful indexing, a reference may be publicly accessible if a skilled and interested artisan would have been independently aware of

76. *Lister*, 583 F.3d at 1312 (citing *Klopfenstein*, 380 F.3d at 1348); *see also* Samsung Elecs. Co., Ltd. v. Infobridge Pte. Ltd., 929 F.3d 1363, 1369 (Fed. Cir. 2019) ("[W]hile indexing is not required to show that a work is publicly accessible, some evidence that a person of ordinary skill could have reasonably found the website and then found the reference on that website is critical.").

77. Acceleration Bay v. Activision Blizzard, 908 F.3d 765 (Fed. Cir. 2018).

78. *Id.* at 768.

79. *Id.* at 772–73.

80. *Id.* at 773–74.

the website where the reference is found and the artisan would have found the reference using the website's search functions.[81] If a reference is not indexed or publicly distributed, the Board will consider the *Klopfenstein* factors to determine whether the reference was sufficiently publicly accessible to be considered a printed publication under section 102(b).[82] Those factors are (1) "the length of time the display was exhibited"; (2) "the expertise of the target audience"; (3) "the existence (or lack thereof) of reasonable expectations that the material displayed would not be copied"; and (4) "the simplicity or ease with which the material displayed could have been copied."[83]

For nonindexed references found on a website, the petition should first demonstrate that a skilled artisan would have accessed the website before the earliest priority date of the challenged patent. An expert declaration can demonstrate that skilled artisans frequented a website at a given time. Second, the petitioner should consider using the Wayback Machine to prove that the website's search function existed before the earliest priority date of the challenged patent. Again, if the petition omits such evidence, a patent owner may challenge the prior art status of the reference in its preliminary response as a basis for denying institution.

For example, in *Microsoft Corp. v. Uniloc 2017 LLC*, the petitioner cited a reference that was archived on the IEEE website but that was not published by IEEE Explore.[84] The IEEE website stored this reference on what the website termed an "index," along with hundreds of other references listed only by date, not by subject matter or title. In addition, the index did not include the full names of the references listed.[85] Because the petitioner did not demonstrate that the "index" was text searchable or otherwise allowed a skilled artisan to narrow the field of possible references to only relevant references, the Board found that the "index" did not enable a skilled artisan,

81. *See* Voter Verified, Inc. v. Premier Election Sols., Inc., 698 F.3d 1374, 1381 (Fed. Cir. 2012).
82. *In re* Klopfenstein, 380 F.3d 1345, 1350 (Fed. Cir. 2004).
83. *Id.*
84. Microsoft Corp. v. Uniloc 2017 LLC, IPR2019-01116, Paper 22, at 37–38 (Oct. 26, 2020).
85. *Id.*

exercising reasonable diligence, to find one of hundreds of articles.[86] As a result, the Board found the reference was not publicly accessible and denied institution.[87]

b. Claim Construction Arguments

Petitions must address any claim terms that require construction. As stated in 37 C.F.R. § 42.104(b)(2), "[t]he statement must identify . . . [h]ow the challenged claim is to be construed." And the Board has rejected petitions that set forth only conclusory allegations, reiterating that petitioners must specifically point out the claim limitations in the prior art.[88] Despite this requirement, many petitions include only generalized claim construction arguments or assert that all terms in the challenged claims should be construed using their plain and ordinary meaning without providing those plain and ordinary meanings. In addition, petitioners often construe only some claim limitations in a petition while avoiding construction of others, ostensibly to provide a blank canvas for applying the prior art to the challenged claims. In such situations, patent owners may challenge the lack of any meaningful claim constructions as a proposed basis for denying institution.

A patent owner's preliminary response could address any missing or weak claim constructions, especially those that affect the petition's unpatentability arguments. For example, in *ASM IP Holding B.V. v. Kokusai Semiconductor Equipment Corp.*, the petitioner offered no specific construction for any term, instead stating that each term should be construed using its plain and ordinary meaning.[89] The patent owner Kokusai, on the other hand, offered constructions for several claim terms.[90] The Board found that only one claim term needed to be construed in order to reach a determination on institution, construed the term consistent with the patent owner's proposal, and

86. *Id.*
87. *Id.*
88. *See, e.g.*, Tasco, Inc. v. David Pagnani, IPR2013-00103, Paper 6, at 11, 19, 22 (May 23, 2013).
89. ASM IP Holding B.V. v. Kokusai Semiconductor Equip. Corp., IPR2018-01582, Paper 11, at 7 (Feb. 25, 2019).
90. *Id.*

denied institution because the prior art did not disclose this element using the correct construction.[91]

c. Missing Claim Element(s)

A patent owner's preliminary response could also challenge any failure by the petition to specify where all of the elements of the challenged claims are found in the prior art. IPR and PGR petitions must specify "where each element of the claim is found in the prior art patents or printed publications relied upon."[92]

The Board has indicated that it will strictly enforce the requirements for a petition. For example, it has rejected anticipation and obviousness contentions based on a failure to include an analysis in the petition of how the prior art discloses every limitation in a challenged claim.[93] It has also declined to adopt any of the proposed grounds of unpatentability when a petitioner has failed to clearly explain or identify where the claim elements are found in the prior art references.[94]

Therefore, if a petition contains only vague, conclusory allegations concerning the content of the prior art or how it pertains to the challenged claims, a patent owner should consider addressing this deficiency in its preliminary response as a proposed basis for denying institution. When a petition fails to apply the teachings of the cited references to the claim elements, it may be denied under 37 C.F.R. § 42.104(b)(4).

d. Legally Insufficient Motivation to Combine

Petitions must identify, "with particularity, each claim challenged, the grounds on which the challenge to each claim is based, and the evidence that supports the grounds for the challenge to each claim."[95] As part of that requirement, a petition asserting that the challenged claims are obvious is

91. *Id.* at 8–9, 18–19.
92. 37 C.F.R. § 42.104(b)(4).
93. *See, e.g.*, Sony Corp. of Am. v. Network-1 Security Sols., Inc., IPR2013-00092, Paper 21, at 19–21, 27–28 (May 24, 2013).
94. *See, e.g.*, Synopsys, Inc. v. Mentor Graphics Corp., IPR2012-00041, Paper 16 (Feb. 22, 2013).
95. 35 U.S.C. § 314(a)(3).

required to adequately set forth its ground(s) of obviousness, including establishing that a skilled artisan would have been motivated to combine the asserted references.[96]

The Board has held that the failure to provide detailed evidence of motivation to combine references asserted as part of an obviousness challenge can doom a petition before institution.[97] A petitioner must not merely make conclusory statements that a skilled artisan would have combined the references; rather, the petition must articulate both why and how the skilled artisan would have combined or modified the teachings of the asserted references to arrive at the claimed invention.[98] For example, a petition that does not include reasons to substitute compositions in one reference with those of another does not provide sufficient evidence of motivation to combine.[99] Similarly, unsupported, conclusory expert testimony is not enough to establish a motivation to combine.[100]

Thus, even if all elements of the claims are met by the combined asserted references, the patent owner should consider making a detailed attack on the factual bases for the alleged motivation to combine the references relied upon in the petition. If appropriate, the patent owner may also consider arguing that the petitioner's expert testimony is conclusory or unsupported and thus cannot support a motivation to combine. Such challenges may potentially preclude institution.

96. 35 U.S.C. § 103.

97. *See, e.g.*, Manville Corp. v. Knauf Insulation, Inc., IPR2018-00827, Paper 9 (Oct. 16, 2018); Adaptics Ltd. v. Perfect Co., IPR2018-01596, Paper 20 (Mar. 6, 2019) (denying institution for failure to identify grounds with particularity); Facebook, Inc. v. Sound View Innovations, LLC, IPR2017-00985, Paper 17, at 13–14 (Sept. 5, 2017) ("We will not make arguments for Petitioner.").

98. *See, e.g.*, *Manville Corp.*, IPR2018-00827, Paper 9, at 10–13; Kingston Tech. Co. v. SPEX Techs., Inc., IPR2017-00824, Paper 8, at 18–19 (Aug. 17, 2017); Ubisoft, Inc. v. Guitar Apprentice, Inc., IPR2015-00298, Paper 24, at 15–18 (Apr. 1, 2016).

99. *Manville Corp.*, IPR2018-00827, Paper 9, at 10–13, 18.

100. *See, e.g.*, TQ Delta, LLC v. Cisco Sys., Inc., 942 F.3d 1352 (Fed. Cir. 2019).

e. New Testimonial Evidence (e.g., Declaration)

The Office allows new testimonial evidence to be submitted with a patent owner's preliminary response.[101] For example, a patent owner may submit expert testimony in support of its preliminary response.[102] Such testimony could potentially rebut the testimony of the petitioner's expert, strengthening the patent owner's challenge to the petition.

Before submitting a declaration, however, the patent owner should carefully consider any relevant updates to the Board's practice to determine whether such testimonial evidence will be advantageous. For example, in 2016, the Office amended its rules to provide a presumption in favor of the petitioner for any genuine issues of material fact that were created by testimonial evidence submitted with the patent owner's preliminary response for purposes of deciding whether to institute review.[103] This rule caused some confusion regarding when the presumption should be applied.[104] In 2020, the Office again amended the rule to eliminate the presumption.[105] Under the new rule, "any testimonial evidence submitted with a patent owner's preliminary response will be taken into account as part of the totality of the evidence."[106]

Nevertheless, some Board panels have expressed doubt about meaningfully relying on testimonial evidence submitted by the patent owner in the preliminary response, because such testimony cannot be cross-examined or challenged by the petitioner as a matter of right.[107] In an effort to balance the rights of the parties, the Board allows petitioners to seek leave to file a preliminary, preinstitution reply addressing expert testimony submitted with

---

101. 37 C.F.R. §§ 42.108, 42.208 ("The Board's decision will take into account a patent owner preliminary response where such a response is filed, including any testimonial evidence.").

102. *Id.*

103. *See* Amendments to Rules of Practice for Trials before the Patent Trial and Appeal Board, 81 Fed. Reg. 18,750, 18,755–57 (Apr. 1, 2016).

104. *See, e.g.*, Hulu, LLC v. Sound View Innovations, LLC, IPR2019-01039, Paper 15 (Apr. 3, 2019) (granting Precedential Opinion Panel review).

105. PTAB Rules of Practice for Instituting on All Challenged Patent Claims and All Grounds and Eliminating the Presumption at Institution Favoring Petitioner as to Testimonial Evidence, 85 Fed. Reg. 79,120 (Dec. 9, 2020).

106. *Id.*

107. *See, e.g.*, OSI Pharms., LLC v. Arch Dev. Corp., IPR2016-01034, Paper 7, at 2–3 (June 30, 2016).

the preliminary response,[108] but the reply may only respond to arguments raised in the preliminary response.[109] The patent owner may then request a sur-reply, which itself may only address arguments made in the reply.[110]

f. Strategic Disclaimer of Challenged Claims

Another tactic to preclude institution is to disclaim certain challenged claims, since no review will be instituted on disclaimed claims.[111] If the patent owner disclaims all challenged claims, "such that [it] has no remaining claim in the trial," that request, if granted by the Board, may moot the petition.[112] As a less drastic measure, the patent owner's choice to disclaim some, but not all, challenged claims may also weigh against institution.[113] Patent owners should be aware that claims must be disclaimed in their entirety and that claims may not be amended in the patent owner preliminary response.[114]

E. Practice Tips

1. Whether to File a Patent Owner Preliminary Response

Once a petition for IPR or PGR has been filed, the patent owner has three options: (1) file a preliminary response to the petition within three months; (2) file no response and wait to see whether the Board grants the petition and institutes a trial; or (3) affirmatively waive filing a preliminary response. Note that a patent owner's waiver of a preliminary response does not trigger any adverse inference by the Board.[115]

A number of benefits come with filing a preliminary response. For example, filing a response allows a patent owner to present arguments about why

108. 37 C.F.R. § 42.108(c) ("A petitioner may seek leave to file a reply to the preliminary response.").

109. *Id.* § 42.23(b).

110. *Id.*

111. *Id.* §§ 42.73(b), 42.107(e).

112. *Id.* § 42.73(b).

113. *Id.* § 42.107(e); *see also* Google LLC v. Personalized Media Commcn's, LLC, IPR2020-00724, Paper 16, at 8–9 (Aug. 31, 2020); ZTE (USA) Inc. v. Fractus, S.A., IPR2018-01451, Paper 12, at 8 (Feb. 19, 2019).

114. 37 C.F.R. § 42.107(d) ("The preliminary response shall not include any amendment.").

115. *Id.* § 42.107(a) (clarifying that there is "no negative inference on [a] patent owner's choice to forgo an opportunity to file a preliminary response").

institution should be denied. Considering the likelihood of receiving a decision holding at least some of the claims unpatentable once an IPR or PGR is instituted, the preliminary response can work as a powerful preventative measure for stopping institution in the first place. Additionally, because institution of an IPR or PGR is not appealable, the preliminary response becomes the patent owner's first and only chance to prevent institution. It also provides a unique opportunity for patent owners to address easily attackable positions in the petition without the petitioner having a statutory right to reply. One ripe area of attack can be whether the petition is statutorily barred from institution. For instance, as discussed earlier, if the petitioner files a declaratory judgment action challenging the validity of the patent at issue before seeking review, the Board will not initiate IPR or PGR.[116] Similarly, the Board will not institute an IPR if the petition is filed more than one year after the petitioner was served with a complaint alleging infringement of the patent.[117] The petitioner may also be estopped from presenting certain unpatentability arguments if it already raised those arguments in a previous proceeding.[118]

Of course, there may also be advantages to waiving the right to file a preliminary response. For example, forgoing a preliminary response will provide the patent owner with up to nine months to develop and buttress its arguments before committing them to the record in a full patent owner response. This time could also be spent on seeking alternative resolutions, such as settlement with the petitioner. In addition, this keeps the petitioner in the dark regarding patent owner's positions for an additional six months compared to a scenario in which the patent owner files a preliminary response. This may help to even the playing field, since the petitioner likely spent several months preparing the petition before the patent owner ever saw those arguments.

2. Which Arguments to Include or Hold Back

When filing a patent owner preliminary response, it is important to consider whether to lay all of your cards on the table or instead take a more

116. 35 U.S.C. § 315(a)(1).
117. *Id.* § 315(b).
118. *Id.* § 315(a).

targeted approach by, for example, selecting arguments that have had a high rate of success with the Board in other cases. At the institution phase, less technically complex arguments may prove more successful for the patent owner. Instead of making every possible argument, patent owners should consider focusing on a few straightforward arguments that affect all challenged claims. The benefits of crafting such a focused brief are twofold.

First, even if you can clearly show that some claims are patentable, there is little reason to point this out unless you can show that all claims are patentable. This is because the Supreme Court ruled that the Board does not have the ability to partially institute an IPR or PGR.[119] If an IPR or PGR is instituted against one challenged claim, it must be instituted against all challenged claims. Unless you can show that an independent claim is patentable, arguments related to its dependent claims may be irrelevant to whether the Board will institute the IPR or PGR and should be withheld.

Second, by holding back many of the more specific patentability theories, the patent owner is able to leave the petitioner mostly in the dark regarding what potential rebuttals or counterarguments the patent owner may make later in the proceeding. Because the petition must lay out the entire roadmap of the petitioner's arguments, patent owners are able to obtain a good grasp of the petitioner's arguments from that document. On the other hand, by holding back the more specific arguments from the preliminary response, the patent owner can enjoy the benefits of an additional three months for preparing those arguments with full knowledge of the petitioner's positions, including deposing the petitioner's witnesses, while the petitioner remains unadvised of the patent owner's positions.

3. Increase in Section 325(d) Denials (Substantially the Same Arguments)

As discussed earlier, section 325(d) allows the USPTO Director to reject a petition or request because "the same or substantially the same prior art or arguments previously were presented to the Office." This determination to institute or deny an IPR or PGR is nonappealable.

119. SAS Inst., Inc. v. Iancu, 138 S. Ct. 1348 (2018).

Section 325(d) has been cited in an increasing number of institution denials. It has become a strong defense in the right circumstances. Given the rise of section 325(d) as a reason for noninstitution, it is imperative for petitioners to select and use the best prior art at the outset—and for patent owners, where appropriate, to challenge asserted prior art references as cumulative of art considered during prosecution.[120]

Based on the factors of the *Advanced Bionics* and *Becton* cases,[121] patent owners now have more guidance regarding the types of arguments that the Board may find persuasive to deny institution under section 325(d). Three forms of prior art that had been commonly used in petitions are now ripe for challenge by patent owners: (1) prior art that was relied upon in the original examination; (2) prior art that has a similar disclosure or covers substantially the same technology as prior art that was relied upon in the original examination; and (3) prior art that was only cited on the face of the patent but was not relied upon in the original examination.

The first category of prior art can often form the basis for a strong patent owner challenge in the preliminary response. The Board has made it clear that reliance on prior art that has already been considered during prosecution is risky, even if the old prior art is now supported with "new" expert testimony. For example, the Board has denied institution based on previously reviewed prior art, despite new expert testimony, because it was not persuaded that petitioner's expert testimony meaningfully distinguished the record before the examiner.[122]

Similarly, the second category of prior art may provide a strong basis for a section 325(d) challenge if the petitioner's arguments for unpatentability are similar to the positions that the examiner took during prosecution. For example, the Board denied institution when a petition relied on a reference

120. *See, e.g.*, Kevin J. Spinella, *Recent PTAB Decisions Further Illuminate Denial of Review under 35 U.S.C. § 325(d)*, Finnegan: At the PTAB Blog (Jan. 27, 2017), https://www.finnegan.com/en/insights/blogs/at-the-ptab-blog/recent-ptab-decisions-illuminate-denial-review-35-u-s-c-%C2%A7-325d.html; Virginia L. Carron & Ashley M. Winkler, *Trends in IPR Institution: Part 1—Ex Parte Art or Arguments*, Finnegan (Jan. 11, 2017), https://www.finnegan.com/en/insights/articles/trends-in-ipr-institution-part-1-ex-parte-art-or-arguments.html.

121. *See supra* notes 29, 30.

122. Telebrands Corp. v. Tinnus Enters., LLC, PGR2017-00015, Paper 16 (Oct. 11, 2017).

that was similar to one filed with a third-party submission during prosecution. The third-party submission cited reference X for teaching a claim element. In the IPR petition, petitioner cited new reference Y for teaching the same element. The Board denied institution under section 325(d) because the petitioner's arguments were too similar to the arguments from the third-party submission that the examiner had already considered.[123]

Finally, although patent owners can challenge the third category of prior art under section 325(d), the challenge may be more difficult. For example, the Board granted institution based on references listed in an Information Disclosure Statement (IDS) during an ex parte reexamination of the challenged patent but that were not relied on by the examiner in any rejection.[124] The Board found that the references were "not applied against the claims" and there was "no evidence that the examiner considered the particular disclosures" cited by the petition.[125] Thus, patent owners should identify any similarities between the cited prior art and references made of record during prosecution and emphasize those similarities in the preliminary response to bolster the chances of securing a denial of institution under section 325(d).

4. Increase in Section 314 Denials (*Fintiv* and *General Plastic*)

As section 325(d) denials have increased, so too have denials under section 314 based on *Fintiv* and *General Plastic.*[126] In fact, *Fintiv* denials have become so common that petitioners often go to great lengths to avoid them, including, for example, stipulations that they will not raise certain invalidity grounds in parallel district court proceedings.[127] Several large technology

123. Cultec Inc. v. StormTech LLC, IPR2017-00777, Paper 7 (Aug. 22, 2017).

124. Microsoft Corp. v. Parallel Networks Licensing LLC, IPR2015-00486, Paper 10 (July 15, 2015).

125. *Id.*

126. These cases are discussed in further detail *supra*, section D.1.b; *see also, e.g.*, Muireann Bolger, *NHK-Fintiv: As PTAB Denials Mount, Petitioners Seek a Remedy*, WORLD INTELL. PROP. REV. (Mar. 23, 2021), https://www.worldipreview.com/news/nhk-fintiv-as-ptab-denials-mount-petitioners-seek-a-remedy-21171; Gracie K. Mills et al., *After* Fintiv*: The Continuing Evolution of Discretionary Denial at the PTAB*, IP LITIGATOR (Mar./Apr. 2021), https://www.finnegan.com/a/web/bLytJLtsx8GGqkg7RA8mXe/published-ip-litigator-after-fintiv_the-continuing-evolution-of-discretionary-denial-at-the-ptab-gkm-jdm-dcc-march-april-2021.pdf.

127. *See, e.g.*, Sotera Wireless, Inc. v. Masimo Corp., IPR2020-01019, Paper 12 (Dec. 1, 2020) (noting that the petitioner stipulated that, if IPR was instituted, it "will not pursue in the District Court . . . any [] ground that was raised or could have been reasonably raised in an IPR under §§ 102 or 103 on the basis of prior art patent or printed publications").

companies, frustrated with the rise of *Fintiv* denials, filed a lawsuit against the U.S. Patent and Trademark Office in the Northern District of California, seeking a declaratory judgment that the *Fintiv* rule is unlawful.[128] The lawsuit alleges that the *Fintiv* rule violates the AIA, is arbitrary and capricious, and is procedurally invalid.[129]

Thus, patent owners should seriously consider whether a procedural challenge based on *General Plastic* or *Fintiv* may be appropriate in their case. Given the rise of denials under both cases, such a challenge could have a high likelihood of success. And in cases where the parallel proceeding is in a court with a quick schedule, for example the Western District of Texas or the Eastern District of Virginia, a *Fintiv* challenge may be even stronger, especially if trial is set to occur before the Board's statutory deadline to issue a final written decision.

5. Be Careful of Preinstitution Replies

Before filing a preliminary response, the patent owner should consider the possibility that the Board will allow the petitioner to file a preinstitution reply. Indeed, the petitioner has the right to seek leave to file a reply to the preliminary response for "good cause."[130] In many cases, petitioners have been granted leave to file preinstitution replies when those replies sought to respond to arguments related to 35 U.S.C. § 314(a),[131] claim interpretation of challenged claims, alleged mischaracterization of petitioner's arguments, real party in interest, or time-bar issues under 25 U.S.C. § 315(a).[132] Certain patent owner actions can provide such "good cause," for example the inclusion of new testimonial evidence from an expert.[133]

128. Apple Inc. et al. v. Iancu, No. 5:20-cv-6128, Complaint, Dkt. 1 (N.D. Cal. Aug. 31, 2020).

129. *Id.* at 3.

130. 37 C.F.R. § 42.108(c).

131. *See, e.g.*, Gen. Plastic Indus. Co. v. Canon Kabushiki Kaisha, No. IPR2016-01357, Paper 19 (Sept. 6, 2017).

132. *See* Han-Wei Chen et al., *What Qualifies as a Good "Good Cause" When Responding to Patent Owners' Preliminary Responses*, JD SUPRA (Mar. 15, 2021), https://www.jdsupra.com/legalnews/what-qualifies-as-a-good-good-cause-4439601/.

133. *See, e.g.*, OSI Pharms., LLC v. Arch Dev. Corp., IPR2016-01034, Paper 7, at 2–3 (June 30, 2016).

Chapter 5

Postinstitution: Briefing and Discovery

This chapter explores the briefing and discovery that takes place following institution. Motions to amend are explored in Chapter 6. Oral argument and requests for rehearing on institution decisions and final written decisions are discussed in Chapter 7.

A. Schedule

1. Timing and Extensions of Time

The general framework for inter partes review (IPR) and post-grant review (PGR) trials and certain deadlines, including the timing for the Board to issue an institution decision[1,2] and issue a final written decision,[3] are set by statute. All other deadlines and timing are set by the Board.[4,5] Before institution, the due date for the patent owner preliminary response is typically

1. 35 U.S.C. §§ 314(b), 324(c).
2. All citations to Title 35 of the U.S. Code are to the 2006 edition, Supplement 5 (2011), in effect as of January 3, 2012, as amended by the Leahy-Smith America Invents Act, Pub. L. No. 112-29 (2011), and the AIA Technical Corrections Act, Pub. L. No. 112-274 (2013), unless noted otherwise.
3. 35 U.S.C. §§ 316(a)(11), 326(a)(11).
4. 37 C.F.R. § 42.5(c)(1).
5. All citations to Title 37 of the Code of Federal Regulations refer to rules in effect as of June 19, 2016, unless noted otherwise.

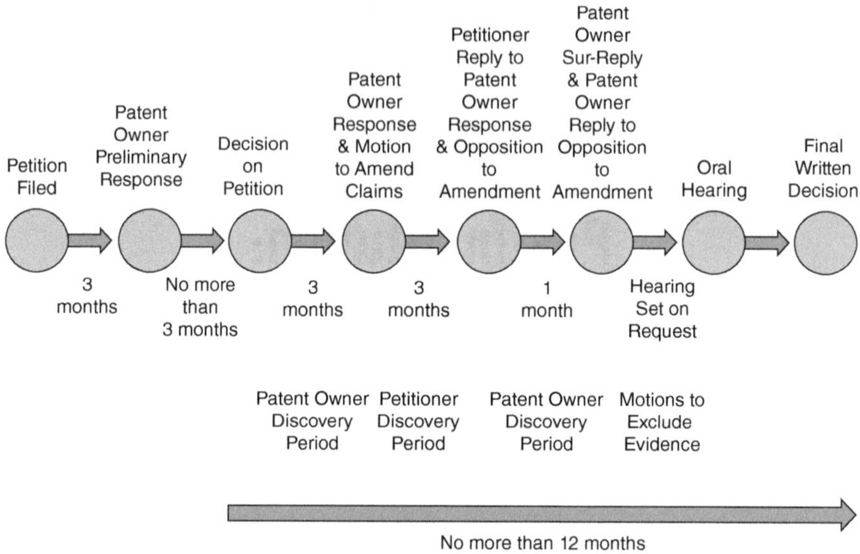

Figure 5.1

three months from the notice indicating that the petition was granted a filing date.[6] After institution, the timeline for a trial varies and is determined by a scheduling order entered concurrently with the Board's decision to institute trial.[7] The Office has provided a representative timeline for trials (Figure 5.1),[8] which is also reflected in its representative scheduling order.[9]

After an IPR or PGR is instituted, the Board issues a scheduling order that sets out the default due dates for the proceeding.[10] The Patent Trial and Appeal Board Consolidated Trial Practice Guide provides an exemplary scheduling order.[11] The Board may modify nonstatutory deadlines by

6. 37 C.F.R. §§ 42.107(b), 42.207(b).

7. 77 Fed. Reg. 48,680, 48,705–07, Responses to Comments 76, 85 (Aug. 14, 2012); PATENT TRIAL AND APPEAL BOARD CONSOLIDATED TRIAL PRACTICE GUIDE App'x A-1 (Nov. 2019).

8. PATENT TRIAL AND APPEAL BOARD CONSOLIDATED TRIAL PRACTICE GUIDE 7 (Nov. 2019).

9. *Id.* at App'x A-1.

10. 37 C.F.R. § 42.5(c)(1).

11. PATENT TRIAL AND APPEAL BOARD CONSOLIDATED TRIAL PRACTICE GUIDE App'x A-1 (Nov. 2019).

order and may determine any deadline not covered by the existing rules.[12] A party seeking adjustments to the scheduling order may request an initial conference call to discuss changes to the schedule.[13] Scheduling orders generally permit the parties to stipulate to changes of certain due dates, such as dates for the patent owner response, petitioner's reply, patent owner's sur-reply, motions to exclude evidence, and oppositions to motions to exclude evidence.[14] At the same time, scheduling orders generally prohibit the parties from stipulating to extensions of the oral argument date and the date for replies to motions to exclude evidence.[15] A party may also request an extension of time[16] or permission for a late action by filing a motion and supporting it with a showing of good cause or that consideration on the merits would be in the interest of justice.[17]

2. Telephone Conferences with the Board

Most of the business of a PTAB trial is conducted via telephone conferences with the Board. The Board uses conference calls to resolve issues raised during trial, such as scheduling and motions.[18] Before requesting a conference call, the parties should meet and confer to resolve any disputes.[19] During these calls, a party should be prepared to address their specific issues concisely and have an understanding of relevant patent trial rules.[20] A party to a conference call with the Board may arrange to have a court reporter present. When contacting the Board to arrange the conference call, the party should inform the Board that it intends to provide a court reporter.[21]

---

12. 37 C.F.R. § 42.5(c)(1); 77 Fed. Reg. 48,612, 48,628, Response to Comment 20 (Aug. 14, 2012).

13. PATENT TRIAL AND APPEAL BOARD CONSOLIDATED TRIAL PRACTICE GUIDE 8, App'x A-1 (Nov. 2019).

14. *Id.* at App'x A-1.

15. *Id.*

16. 37 C.F.R. § 42.5(c)(2).

17. 37 C.F.R. § 42.5(c)(3).

18. PATENT TRIAL AND APPEAL BOARD CONSOLIDATED TRIAL PRACTICE GUIDE 9–10 (Nov. 2019).

19. *Id.*

20. *See id.*

21. *Id.*

All substantive communications with the Board must include all parties.[22] Ex parte communications generally are not permitted.[23] The Board expects that lead counsel will, and backup counsel may, participate in all conference calls with the Board.[24] The Board also expects that counsel attending a conference call has the authority to participate on behalf of the respective party.[25] Any counsel who does not have power of attorney, or who has not appeared pro hac vice, may not be able to attend or participate in discussions with the Board.[26]

B. Merits Briefing and Strategy

1. Patent Owner Response

After institution of an IPR or PGR, a patent owner can file a response to the petition addressing grounds of unpatentability raised in the petition.[27] The due date for filing the response is typically set in the Board's scheduling order, which is issued at the time the Board institutes the trial. Otherwise, the default due date for the response is three months from the date the review is instituted.[28] The word limit for the patent owner response to the petition is the same as the word limit for the petition (IPR: 14,000 words; PGR: 18,700 words).[29] The Board may authorize additional words in the interests of justice.[30] Any motion to waive word limits must be granted before filing a patent owner response.[31]

In the response, the patent owner should identify all claims that the patent owner believes to be patentable and state the basis for that belief.[32]

---

22. *Id.* at 9.
23. *Id.*
24. *Id.* at 11.
25. *Id.*
26. *See* 37 C.F.R. § 42.10(c).
27. 35 U.S.C. §§ 316(a)(8), 326(a)(8); 37 C.F.R. §§ 42.120(a), 42.220(a).
28. 37 C.F.R. §§ 42.120(b), 42.220(b).
29. *Id.* § 42.24(b).
30. *Id.* § 42.24(a)(2).
31. *Id.*
32. PATENT TRIAL AND APPEAL BOARD CONSOLIDATED TRIAL PRACTICE GUIDE 66 (Nov. 2019).

And the patent owner must file any additional factual evidence and expert opinions on which the patent owner relies in support of the response and should explain the relevance of such evidence.[33] Typically, a patent owner will include testimony of an expert in support of a patent owner response. In addition, a patent owner may include additional testimony obtained through cross-examination of any declarant used to support the petition.[34] Cross-examination is discussed in more detail in section D.1 of this chapter, including strategy considerations on whether to cross-examine a declarant.

If the patent owner intends to challenge the petitioner's claim construction or the level of one of ordinary skill in the art, the patent owner should include such arguments in the patent owner response. And if the petition includes a listing of material facts, the response must include a listing of facts admitted, denied, or that otherwise cannot be admitted or denied.[35] Issues that are not addressed in the patent owner response may be waived even if they were included in a preliminary response to the petition filed before institution.[36]

In addition to the response, the patent owner can file a motion to amend the patent by canceling a challenged claim or proposing a reasonable number of substitute claims.[37] Motions to amend are discussed in more detail in Chapter 6.

If the patent owner elects not to file a patent owner response, then the patent owner should contact the Board to schedule a conference call to discuss whether a request for adverse judgment should be filed.[38]

33. 35 U.S.C. § 316(a)(8); PATENT TRIAL AND APPEAL BOARD CONSOLIDATED TRIAL PRACTICE GUIDE 66 (Nov. 2019).

34. PATENT TRIAL AND APPEAL BOARD CONSOLIDATED TRIAL PRACTICE GUIDE 51 (Nov. 2019); 37 C.F.R. § 42.51(b)(1)(ii).

35. 37 C.F.R. § 42.23(a).

36. *See id.*; SAP Am., Inc. v. Versata Dev. Grp., Inc., CBM2012-00001, Paper 81 (Sept. 13, 2013).

37. 35 U.S.C. §§ 316(d), 326(d); 37 C.F.R. §§ 42.121, 42.221.

38. PATENT TRIAL AND APPEAL BOARD CONSOLIDATED TRIAL PRACTICE GUIDE 66 (Nov. 2019); *see also* Corning Optical Commc'ns RF, LLC v. PPC Broadband, Inc., IPR2014-00441, Paper 19 (Oct. 30, 2014) (Representative).

2. Petitioner Reply

Petitioners can reply to arguments raised in the patent owner response.[39] Following the Supreme Court's decision in *SAS v. Iancu*, the Board also permits petitioners to address issues discussed in the institution decision.[40] The petitioner may submit rebuttal evidence to support its reply, including a new expert declaration.[41] At the same time, a petitioner may not submit new evidence or arguments that it could have presented earlier, such as to make a prima facie case of unpatentability.[42] The Board has warned that a reply that raises a new issue or belatedly presents evidence may not be considered.[43] For instance, the Board has indicated that a new rationale to combine prior art references is an improper new issue to raise in a reply.[44] Similarly, the Board has indicated that it is improper to provide new cited prior art references in a reply intended to "gap-fill" by teaching a claim element that was not present in the original prior art submitted with the petition.[45] But not all arguments that "could have been raised" in a petition are necessarily inappropriate for a reply. As the Board has explained, a petitioner cannot reasonably be expected to predict everything that a patent owner may present in its response and arguments.[46]

A reply is limited to 5,600 words[47] and is generally due three months after service of the patent owner response or a particular date set by the

39. 37 C.F.R. § 42.23(b); PATENT TRIAL AND APPEAL BOARD CONSOLIDATED TRIAL PRACTICE GUIDE 73 (Nov. 2019).

40. PATENT TRIAL AND APPEAL BOARD CONSOLIDATED TRIAL PRACTICE GUIDE 73 (Nov. 2019); SAS Inst. Inc. v. Iancu, 138 S. Ct. 1348 (2018).

41. PATENT TRIAL AND APPEAL BOARD CONSOLIDATED TRIAL PRACTICE GUIDE 73 (Nov. 2019); Belden Inc. v. Berk-Tek LLC, 805 F.3d 1064, 1077–78 (Fed. Cir. 2015).

42. PATENT TRIAL AND APPEAL BOARD CONSOLIDATED TRIAL PRACTICE GUIDE 73–74 (Nov. 2019).

43. *Id.* at 74.

44. *Id.*; Intelligent Bio-Sys., Inc. v. Illumina Cambridge Ltd., 821 F.3d 1359, 1369–70 (Fed. Cir. 2016).

45. PATENT TRIAL AND APPEAL BOARD CONSOLIDATED TRIAL PRACTICE GUIDE 74 (Nov. 2019); Genzyme Therapeutic Prods. Ltd. v. Biomarin Pharm. Inc., 825 F.3d 1360, 1365–69 (Fed. Cir. 2016).

46. *See Genzyme Therapeutic Prods. Ltd.*, 825 F.3d at 1367; Liberty Mut. Ins. Co. v. Progressive Cas. Ins. Co., CBM2012-00004, Paper 34 (Sept. 3, 2013).

47. 37 C.F.R. § 42.24(c)(1).

scheduling order.[48] In addition, a reply must include a listing of facts admitted, denied, or that otherwise cannot be admitted or denied if the patent owner response includes a listing of material facts.[49]

3. Patent Owner Sur-Reply

The scheduling order entered at institution normally authorizes a patent owner to file a sur-reply.[50] A sur-reply is limited to 5,600 words[51] and is generally due one month after service of the petitioner reply or by a particular date set by the scheduling order.[52] Usually, a sur-reply may only respond to arguments raised in the reply.[53] The Board has explained that responding to arguments does not mean proceeding in a new direction with a new approach, and they have warned that a sur-reply that raises a new issue or belatedly presents evidence may not be considered.[54] A sur-reply may not be accompanied by new evidence other than deposition transcripts of the cross-examination of any reply witness.[55] If the reply includes a listing of material facts, the sur-reply must include a listing of facts admitted, denied, or that otherwise cannot be admitted or denied.[56]

C. Discovery

Parties in an IPR or PGR are permitted to seek discovery of relevant evidence, including the deposition of witnesses that submit affidavits or declarations, evidence that is "otherwise necessary in the interest of justice" in IPRs, and evidence that is "directly related to factual assertions advanced

48. PATENT TRIAL AND APPEAL BOARD CONSOLIDATED TRIAL PRACTICE GUIDE 6–7 (Nov. 2019).
49. 37 C.F.R. § 42.23(a).
50. PATENT TRIAL AND APPEAL BOARD CONSOLIDATED TRIAL PRACTICE GUIDE 73–74 (Nov. 2019).
51. 37 C.F.R. § 42.24(c)(4).
52. PATENT TRIAL AND APPEAL BOARD CONSOLIDATED TRIAL PRACTICE GUIDE 6–7 (Nov. 2019).
53. *Id.* at 73–74.
54. *Id.*
55. 37 C.F.R. § 42.23(b).
56. *Id.* § 42.23(a).

by either party" in PGRs.[57] The statutory provisions for IPRs and PGRs caution against abusive or harassing discovery.[58] The party moving for additional discovery has the burden of proof in establishing entitlement to the requested relief.[59] Discovery is provided for in PTAB trials to develop the record and aid the Board in assessing the credibility of witnesses.[60] A party is not entitled to discovery except as provided for by the rules or as otherwise agreed to by the parties.[61] Parties are required to provide routine discovery and may agree to mandatory initial disclosures and additional discovery.[62] All other discovery must be made by motion.[63] The scheduling order and the rules establish a sequenced discovery process that will provide each party with a discovery period.[64]

1. Mandatory Initial Disclosures

Parties may agree to mandatory discovery in the form of initial disclosures.[65] Where the parties agree, there are two options available for initial disclosures.[66]

a. Option 1

Option 1 is modeled after Rule 26(a) of the Federal Rules of Civil Procedure.[67] This option requires disclosure of the name, address, and telephone number (if known) of "each individual likely to have discoverable information" and the subject of the information that may be used to support the disclosing

57. 35 U.S.C. §§ 316(a)(5), 326(a)(5); 37 C.F.R. §§ 42.51, 42.53.

58. *See* 35 U.S.C. §§ 316(a)(6), 326(a)(6); *see also* Bloomberg Inc. v. Markets-Alert Pty. Ltd., CBM2013-00005, Paper 32 (May 29, 2013) (Precedential); Garmin Int'l, Inc. v. Cuozzo Speed Techs. LLC, IPR2012-00001, Paper 26 (Mar. 5, 2013) (Precedential).

59. 37 C.F.R. § 42.20(c).

60. PATENT TRIAL AND APPEAL BOARD CONSOLIDATED TRIAL PRACTICE GUIDE 22 (NOV. 2019).

61. 37 C.F.R. § 42.51(b).

62. *Id.* § 42.51(a)(1), (b)(1), (b)(2).

63. *Id.* § 42.51(b)(2)(i).

64. PATENT TRIAL AND APPEAL BOARD CONSOLIDATED TRIAL PRACTICE GUIDE 22 (NOV. 2019).

65. 37 C.F.R. § 42.51(a)(1).

66. PATENT TRIAL AND APPEAL BOARD CONSOLIDATED TRIAL PRACTICE GUIDE 29–30 (Nov. 2019).

67. *Id.*

party's claims or defenses.[68] The subject of the information does not have to be disclosed if it will be used solely for impeachment.[69] Disclosure of a copy or description of the category and location of all documents that may be used to support the disclosing party's claims and defenses is also required unless the use would be solely for impeachment.[70] Documents include all electronically stored information and tangible things that a party has in its possession, custody, or control.[71]

b. Option 2

Option 2 is more extensive and generally requires the petitioner to identify persons and information relating to the basis of obviousness allegations, secondary considerations, and any allegations of prior nonpublished public disclosures.[72]

2. Routine Discovery

Routine discovery includes three general types: (1) exhibits cited in a paper or in testimony (unless it has already been served or the parties agree otherwise); (2) cross-examination of the other party's declarants; and (3) relevant information that is inconsistent with a position advanced by the party (concurrent with the filing of the documents that include the inconsistency).[73] Routine discovery is intended to place the parties on a level playing field and streamline the proceeding.[74] Board authorization is not required to conduct routine discovery.[75] The timelines for conducting routine discovery are generally set forth in the scheduling order.[76]

---

68. *Id.*
69. *Id.*
70. *Id.*
71. *Id.*
72. *Id.* at 30.
73. 37 C.F.R. § 42.51(b)(1); Patent Trial and Appeal Board Consolidated Trial Practice Guide 23 (Nov. 2019).
74. Patent Trial and Appeal Board Consolidated Trial Practice Guide 23 (Nov. 2019).
75. *Id.*
76. *Id.*

a. *Exhibits Cited*

Routine discovery requires that any exhibit cited in a paper or in testimony (e.g., expert declaration) must be served with the citing document unless it has already been served.[77] The rules allow for the parties to come to a separate agreement regarding serving exhibits.[78]

b. *Cross-Examination*

Cross-examination of testimony submitted via affidavit is authorized within a time period that will be set by the Board.[79] The cost for producing a witness for cross-examination will normally fall on the party presenting the direct testimony of the witness.[80] Additional information regarding depositions is provided in this chapter, section D.1.

c. *Inconsistent Information*

The rules require service of any relevant information that is "inconsistent with a position advanced by the party during the proceeding."[81] This discovery requirement does not include privileged material. Examples of inconsistent statements include any nonprivileged work done by or on behalf of a party that is inconsistent with statements in the party's expert affidavit or any nonprivileged evidence that is inconsistent with a patent owner's contention of unexpected results.[82] The requirement extends to "inventors, corporate officers, and persons involved in the preparation or filing of the documents or things."[83]

---

77. 37 C.F.R. § 42.51(b)(1)(i).
78. *Id.*
79. *Id.* §§ 42.51(b)(1)(ii), 42.53(d).
80. *Id.* § 42.53(g); PATENT TRIAL AND APPEAL BOARD CONSOLIDATED TRIAL PRACTICE GUIDE 23–24 (Nov. 2019); Invue Sec. Prod., Inc. v. Merch. Tech. Inc., IPR2013-00122, Paper 47, at 2–3 (Mar. 17, 2014).
81. 37 C.F.R. § 42.51(b)(1)(iii).
82. PATENT TRIAL AND APPEAL BOARD CONSOLIDATED TRIAL PRACTICE GUIDE 23 (Nov. 2019).
83. 37 C.F.R. § 42.51(b)(1)(iii).

3. Additional Discovery

Additional discovery goes beyond routine discovery.[84] For example, the production of documents referred to during cross-examination or documents produced during district court litigation but not in an IPR may be additional discovery.[85] Parties may agree to additional discovery, and when they do not agree, a party may move for additional discovery.[86] Opposed requests for additional discovery require a joint conference call with the Board to discuss the request and require approval from the Board before a party may file a motion for additional discovery.[87]

A party seeking additional discovery must show that the additional discovery is in the interests of justice for IPRs and for good cause for PGRs.[88] These two standards are closely related, but, on balance, the interests-of-justice standard is slightly higher than the good-cause standard.[89] In addition, additional discovery in PGR proceedings is limited to evidence directly related to factual assertions advanced by either party.[90]

To determine whether the requested additional discovery is in the interests of justice in an IPR, the Board considers five general factors:[91]

1. More than a possibility and mere allegation—The mere possibility of finding something useful, and the mere allegation that something useful will be found, is insufficient to show that additional

84. 77 Fed. Reg. 48,612, 48,636, Response to Comment 97 (Aug. 14, 2012); PATENT TRIAL AND APPEAL BOARD CONSOLIDATED TRIAL PRACTICE GUIDE 24–28 (Nov. 2019).

85. 77 Fed. Reg. 48,612, 48,641, Response to Comment 97 (Aug. 14, 2012).

86. 37 C.F.R. § 42.51(b)(2)(i); *see also* VirnetX, Inc. v. Mangrove Partners Master Fund, Ltd., 778 F. App'x 897, 903–04 (Fed. Cir. 2019) (finding the Board abused its discretion in not allowing patent owner the opportunity to file a motion for additional discovery).

87. 77 Fed. Reg. 48,612, 48,636, Response to Comment 97 (Aug. 14, 2012).

88. 37 C.F.R. § 42.51(b)(2); PATENT TRIAL AND APPEAL BOARD CONSOLIDATED TRIAL PRACTICE GUIDE 23 (Nov. 2019).

89. PATENT TRIAL AND APPEAL BOARD CONSOLIDATED TRIAL PRACTICE GUIDE 23 (Nov. 2019); Bloomberg Inc. v. Markets-Alert Pty. Ltd., CBM2013-00005, Paper 32 (May 29, 2013) (Precedential).

90. 37 C.F.R. §§ 42.51(b)(2)(i), 42.224(b).

91. Garmin Int'l, Inc. v. Cuozzo Speed Techs. LLC, IPR2012-00001, Paper 26 (Mar. 5, 2013) (Precedential); PATENT TRIAL AND APPEAL BOARD CONSOLIDATED TRIAL PRACTICE GUIDE 28 (Nov. 2019); *see also* Caterpillar Inc. v. Wirtgen Am., Inc., IPR2017-02188, Paper 40 (Oct. 29, 2018); Brunswick Corp. v. Volva Penta of the Ams., IPR2020-01512, Paper 25 (May 12, 2021).

discovery is in the interests of justice. The party requesting discovery should already be in possession of evidence tending to show beyond speculation that something useful will be uncovered.[92]

2. Litigation positions and underlying basis—Asking for the other party's litigation positions and the underlying basis for those positions is not necessary in the interests of justice. The Board has established rules for the presentation of arguments and evidence. There is a proper time and place for each party to make its presentation. A party may not attempt to alter the Board's trial procedures under the pretext of discovery.[93]
3. Ability to generate equivalent information by other means—Information a party can reasonably figure out or assemble without discovery would not be in the interests of justice to have produced by the other party. The Board will want to know the ability of the requesting party to generate the requested information without discovery.[94]
4. Easily understandable instructions—The questions should be easily understandable. For example, ten pages of complex instructions for answering questions are prima facie unclear. Such instructions are counterproductive and tend to undermine the responder's ability to answer efficiently, accurately, and confidently.[95]
5. Requests not overly burdensome to answer—The requests must not be overly burdensome to answer, given the expedited nature of IPRs and PGRs. The burden includes financial burden, burden on human resources, and burden on meeting the time schedule of the

---

92. *Garmin Int'l, Inc.*, IPR2012-00001, Paper 26; *see also* Kashiv Pharma, LLC v. Purdue Pharma L.P., IPR2018-00625, Paper 20 (July 31, 2018); Mylan Pharms. Inc. v. Allergan Inc., IPR2016-01127, Paper 28 (May 31, 2017); Corning Inc. v. DSM IP Assets B.V., IPR2013-00043, Paper 27 (June 21, 2013).

93. *Garmin Int'l, Inc.*, IPR2012-00001, Paper 26; *see also* St. Jude Med. LLC v. Snyders Heart Valve LLC, IPR2018-00105, Paper 37 (Oct. 18, 2018); *Caterpillar Inc.*, IPR2017-02188, Paper 40.

94. *Garmin Int'l, Inc.*, IPR2012-00001, Paper 26; *see also* Dynamic Air Inc. v. M-I Drilling Fluids UK Ltd., IPR2016-00260, Paper 39 (Nov. 30, 2016); *Caterpillar Inc.*, IPR2017-02188, Paper 40.

95. *Garmin Int'l, Inc.*, IPR2012-00001, Paper 26.

proceeding. Requests should be sensible and responsibly tailored according to a genuine need.[96]

The Board considers substantially similar factors for PGRs.[97] Factors 2–5 from *Garmin* for IPR proceedings and factors 2–5 from *Bloomberg* for PGR proceedings are substantially the same.[98] Factor 1 for both IPR and PGR proceedings requires a party to show more than a mere allegation that something useful may be found by the requested discovery.[99] For IPR proceedings, the requesting party should already have evidence that would tend to show "beyond speculation" that something useful will be discovered.[100] The Board emphasized that for something to be "useful," it must be "favorable in substantive value to a contention of the moving party" and not merely relevant.[101] For PGR proceedings, a "good cause" showing requires "the moving party to provide a specific factual reason" to expect that the requested discovery will be "useful."[102]

The Board has also allowed focused discovery into real parties in interest and evidence of secondary considerations of nonobviousness.[103] The Board has stated that such requests should be focused and narrow and be shown to have an impact on the merits of the final decision.[104]

96. *Id.*; PATENT TRIAL AND APPEAL BOARD CONSOLIDATED TRIAL PRACTICE GUIDE 24–28 (Nov. 2019).

97. PATENT TRIAL AND APPEAL BOARD CONSOLIDATED TRIAL PRACTICE GUIDE 23 (Nov. 2019); Bloomberg Inc. v. Markets-Alert Pty. Ltd., CBM2013-00005, Paper 32 (May 29, 2013) (Precedential); *Garmin Int'l, Inc.*, IPR2012-00001, Paper 26.

98. *Compare Garmin Int'l, Inc.*, IPR2012-00001, Paper 26, at 6–7, *with Bloomberg Inc.*, CBM2013-00005, Paper 32.

99. *Compare Garmin Int'l, Inc.*, IPR2012-00001, Paper 26, *with Bloomberg Inc.*, CBM2013-00005, Paper 32; PATENT TRIAL AND APPEAL BOARD CONSOLIDATED TRIAL PRACTICE GUIDE 23 (Nov. 2019).

100. *Garmin Int'l, Inc.*, IPR2012-00001, Paper 26.

101. *Id.*; *Bloomberg Inc.*, CBM2013-00005, Paper 32.

102. *Bloomberg Inc.*, CBM2013-00005, Paper 32.

103. PATENT TRIAL AND APPEAL BOARD CONSOLIDATED TRIAL PRACTICE GUIDE 28 (Nov. 2019).

104. Ventex Co. v. Columbia Sportswear N. Am., Inc., IPR2017-00651, Paper 40 (Dec. 19, 2017); Palo Alto Networks, Inc. v. Juniper Networks, Inc., IPR2013-00369, Paper 36 (Feb. 5, 2014); Medtronic, Inc. v. Robert Bosch Healthcare Sys., Inc., IPR2014-00488, Paper 25 (Nov. 5, 2014); Unified Patents v. Vilox Techs., IPR2018-00044, Paper 64 (Feb. 6, 2019).

4. Third-Party Discovery

It is expected that discovery, including production of documents and testimony needed for an IPR or PGR proceeding, will be within the control of the real parties in interest. The rules, however, allow for third-party discovery, which may be voluntary or compelled.[105] If voluntary, third-party discovery generally follows the procedures under section 42.51 (discovery) and section 42.53 (testimony).[106] For example, voluntary third-party testimony must be in the form of an affidavit or declaration.[107] If compelled, third-party discovery follows different procedures.[108]

A party seeking to compel testimony or production of documents must first seek Board authorization to file a motion for additional discovery to compel third-party discovery.[109] If granted, the party may then file a motion seeking a Board order authorizing the party to apply for a subpoena from a district court.[110] The motion must identify the witness by name or title for testimony or must identify the general nature of the document or thing for other discovery.[111] Motions for third-party discovery will be considered under the Board's articulated criteria for determining motions for additional in-party discovery.[112]

After the motion is granted, the party must then compel discovery by a subpoena under 35 U.S.C. § 24, because the Office does not have direct authority to issue a subpoena for compelling discovery.[113] Section 24 authorizes the clerk of any U.S. court in the district where the testimony is to be taken to issue a subpoena for any witness residing or in its territory for

105. 37 C.F.R. §§ 42.51–42.53; *see* Therriault v. Garbe, 53 U.S.P.Q.2d 1179, 1181 (B.P.A.I. 1999) (third-party discovery in interference).

106. 37 C.F.R. §§ 41.51, 42.53(a), (b).

107. *Id.* § 42.53(a).

108. *Id.* § 42.52.

109. *Id.* § 42.52(a).

110. Chi. Mercantile Exch., Inc. v. 5th Mkt., Inc., CBM2015-00061, Paper 25, at 6 (Nov. 18, 2015); Int'l Bus. Machs. Corp. v. Intell. Ventures I LLC, IPR2014-01385, Paper 26, at 10–11 (May 27, 2015).

111. 37 C.F.R. § 42.52(a).

112. PATENT TRIAL AND APPEAL BOARD CONSOLIDATED TRIAL PRACTICE GUIDE 24–28 (Nov. 2019).

113. 35 U.S.C. § 24; *Chi. Mercantile Exch., Inc.*, CBM2015-00061, Paper 25, at 4, 6; Therriault v. Garbe, 53 U.S.P.Q.2d 1179, 1182 (B.P.A.I. 1999).

testimony that is to be used in a contested case in the Office.[114] The testimony may be either ex parte, subject to subsequent cross-examination, or inter partes.[115] Motions to compel may be denied where a party does not first seek voluntary discovery.[116] When considering a motion to compel, the Board may consider whether a witness is under the opposing party's control;[117] where the witness resides;[118] whether a party relies directly or indirectly on particular evidence;[119] and whether a motion is sufficiently specific, not overly burdensome, and timely.[120] Motions to compel may be granted for cross-examination by deposition where a party submits declaratory evidence.[121]

Direct compelled testimony is taken in the form of a deposition transcript[122] with the opportunity for cross-examination and redirect examination, both also taken in the form of a deposition transcript.[123] Direct deposition testimony must be noticed at least ten days before the deposition and must serve a list and copy of all documents under a party's control that the party intends to rely on and a list and a proffer of reasonable access to documents not in the party's control.[124]

---

114. 35 U.S.C. § 24.

115. PATENT TRIAL AND APPEAL BOARD CONSOLIDATED TRIAL PRACTICE GUIDE 29 (Nov. 2019); *Therriault*, 53 U.S.P.Q.2d at 1186.

116. *See, e.g.*, Toshiba Corp. v. Optical Devices LLC, IPR2014-01445, Paper 14 (May 8, 2015).

117. *See* Mexichem Amanco Holdings S.A. de C.V. v. Honeywell Int'l, Inc., IPR2013-00576, Paper 36 (Sept. 5, 2014).

118. *Id.*

119. *Compare* Amneal Pharm., LLC v. Endo Pharm. Inc., IPR2014-00360, Paper 39 (Nov. 14, 2014) (denying motion to compel declarant from ex parte examination), *with* Ikaria, Inc. v. GeNO LLC, IPR2013-00253, Paper 20 (Apr. 1, 2014) (granting additional discovery).

120. *See* Int'l Bus. Machs. Corp. v. Intell. Ventures I LLC, IPR2014-01385, Paper 26 (May 27, 2015); *see also* SAP Am., Inc. v. Pi-NET Int'l, Inc., CBM2013-00013, Paper 25 (Oct. 17, 2013).

121. *See Int'l Bus. Machs. Corp.*, IPR2014-01385, Paper 26.

122. 37 C.F.R. § 42.53(a).

123. *Id.* § 42.53(c)(1).

124. *Id.* § 42.53(d)(3).

5. E-Discovery (Model Order in PTAB Guide Appendix)

The Office adopted a default Model Order Regarding E-Discovery to promote economic and procedural efficiency.[125] Except for routine discovery, the parties should enter this Model Order whenever seeking discovery of electronically stored information (ESI).[126] The Model Order supplements all other discovery rules and orders and can be modified only for good cause.[127] If desired, the parties should jointly submit proposed modifications within one month of the proceeding's start date or at the initial conference call, if earlier.[128]

Unless otherwise authorized by the Board or agreed to by the parties, ESI production does not include metadata.[129] Fields showing the date and time a document was sent and received, however, fall outside of this exception.[130] Except for routine discovery, ESI production does not include email or other forms of electronic correspondence.[131] To obtain production of email, parties must delineate specific email production requests and seek and obtain Board authorization.[132]

If ESI production is authorized or agreed to, any email production request must identify specific issues, such as the custodian, search terms, and time frame.[133] Each requesting party is limited to five custodians.[134] The parties may agree to modify this limit, but, without agreement, the Board will only consider requests for up to five additional custodians per party upon a showing of need based on size, complexity, and issues of the proceeding.[135] Similarly, production requests are limited to five search terms.[136] Again, the parties may agree to modify this limit, but the Board will consider con-

125. PATENT TRIAL AND APPEAL BOARD CONSOLIDATED TRIAL PRACTICE GUIDE 33–34 (Nov. 2019).
126. *Id.* at 33.
127. *Id.* at App'x C.
128. *Id.*
129. *Id.*
130. *Id.*
131. *Id.*
132. *Id.*
133. *Id.*
134. *Id.*
135. *Id.*
136. *Id.*

tested requests for up to five additional search terms based upon a showing of need.[137] The Model Order sets out several limitations regarding search terms and phrases: terms should be narrowly tailored to particular issues; indiscriminate terms, such as company name or product name, are inappropriate without narrowing search criteria; conjunctive combinations narrowing the search constitute one search term; and disjunctive combinations, which broaden the search, constitute separate search terms.[138] The Board will consider cost-shifting for disproportionate ESI production requests.[139]

6. Protective Orders

The record of a proceeding, including documents filed with the Board, will be made available to the public unless a party files, and has been granted, a motion to seal.[140] The Board will issue protective orders for good cause to protect a party from disclosing confidential information.[141] Protective orders may be issued forbidding disclosure or discovery; specifying terms of the disclosure or discovery; prescribing a method of discovery; forbidding or limiting discovery into certain matters; designating persons who may be present during discovery or who may have access to discovery; and requiring that certain discovery, such as depositions, trade secrets, research, or other commercial information, not be revealed or be revealed in a specified manner.[142]

A party seeking to seal a document may file a motion to seal, including a proposed protective order, at the same time as filing the document.[143] The document will be provisionally sealed and will remain sealed until the Board decides the motion.[144] The moving party shall include a copy of the

137. *Id.*
138. *Id.*
139. *Id.*
140. *Id.* at 19.
141. 37 C.F.R. § 42.54(a).
142. *Id.*
143. *Id.* § 42.14; PATENT TRIAL AND APPEAL BOARD CONSOLIDATED TRIAL PRACTICE GUIDE 19 (Nov. 2019).
144. PATENT TRIAL AND APPEAL BOARD CONSOLIDATED TRIAL PRACTICE GUIDE 19 (Nov. 2019).

proposed protective order. [145] Before a party to the proceeding may receive the confidential information, that party must certify that the party accepts and agrees to the terms of the proposed protective order.[146] The proposed protective order will remain in effect until superseded by an order issued by the Board.[147]

The Office has provided a default protective order.[148] The parties are encouraged to agree and stipulate to a protective order, which must be approved by the Board.[149] If the parties do not agree, the default protective order will be automatically entered.[150] Under the default order, a disclosing party must designate any document deemed to be confidential under the order, and such material will be limited to the parties, party representatives, and in-house counsel, as well as experts and other party employees if those individuals sign an acknowledgment stating they will comply with the protective order.[151] Employees of the Office who need access to the information, for example, members of the Board, the Director, and support personnel, shall have access to confidential information without signing an acknowledgment.[152] Non-Office support personnel, such as court reporters and other persons acting on behalf of the Office, shall also have access to confidential information without signing an acknowledgment.[153]

A petitioner may file a motion to seal and a proposed protective order concurrent with the filing of a petition.[154] The petitioner must file, but need not serve, the confidential information.[155] The institution of a trial will constitute a grant of the motion unless the Board orders otherwise.[156] Where a petitioner requests entry of the default protective order, the patent owner may access the confidential information before the trial is instituted only if

145. *Id.* at App'x B.
146. *Id.*
147. *Id.*
148. *Id.*
149. *Id.*
150. *Id.*
151. *Id.*
152. *Id.*
153. *Id.*
154. 37 C.F.R. § 42.55.
155. *Id.* § 42.55(a).
156. *Id.* § 42.55.

the patent owner agrees to the terms of the default order or obtains relief from the Board.[157] If the petitioner requests entry of another proposed protective order, the patent owner may access the confidential information before the trial is instituted only if the patent owner agrees to the terms of the proposed order, agrees to the terms of a jointly filed order, or obtains entry of another order, for example, the default protective order.[158]

After denial of a petition or after a final decision, a party may file a motion to expunge confidential information from the record.[159] A party to a settlement agreement may request that the settlement be treated as business confidential and kept separate from the patent files.[160]

7. Sanctions

All parties and individuals involved in IPRs and PGRs have a duty of candor and good faith to the Office during the proceeding.[161] By signing a paper or presenting or advocating to the Board, an attorney, registered practitioner, or unrepresented party attests to compliance with the Office's signature and certification requirements that all representations made to the Board are, to the best of the person's knowledge, information, and belief, formed after inquiry reasonable under the circumstances:

- not presented for any improper purpose, such as to harass, cause unnecessary delay, or needlessly increase the cost of a proceeding;
- include contentions warranted by existing law or by a nonfrivolous argument for extending, modifying, or reversing existing law;
- based on factual contentions that have evidentiary support; and
- based on denials of factual contentions warranted on the evidence.[162]

157. *Id.* § 42.55(a).
158. *Id.* § 42.55(b).
159. *Id.* § 42.56.
160. *Id.* § 42.74(c).
161. *Id.* § 42.11(a).
162. *Id.* §§ 42.11(c), 11.18(b).

By statute, the Board may impose sanctions.[163] By rule, the Board may impose sanctions for violating the required certification.[164] The Board may also impose sanctions for misconduct, including (1) failing to comply with a rule or order; (2) advancing a misleading or frivolous argument or request for relief; (3) misrepresenting a fact; (4) engaging in dilatory tactics; (5) abusing discovery; (6) abusing process; or (7) engaging in other improper use of the proceeding, including actions that harass or cause unnecessary delay or an unnecessary increase in the cost of the proceeding.[165] The Board can sanction a party for willfully misleading the Office that it is a proper petitioner when the party knew it was privy of a previously unsuccessful petitioner seeking review of the same patent claims.[166] The Board may also sanction a party for making repeated, unauthorized filings;[167] failing to timely respond to requests from opposing counsel or the Board;[168] failing to attend scheduled conference calls with the Board;[169] and failing to adhere to the rules governing depositions.[170] And the Board may impose sanctions for impeding the fair examination of a witness.[171]

The Board may issue sanctions sua sponte,[172] or an opposing party may seek authorization to file a motion for sanctions.[173] Sanctions may be sought at any time, including after the final written decision.[174] In addition, the matter may be submitted to the Office of Enrollment and Discipline.[175]

163. 35 U.S.C. §§ 316(6), 326(6).
164. 37 C.F.R. § 42.11(d)(1).
165. *Id.* § 42.12(a).
166. 77 Fed. Reg. 48,680, 48,695, Response to Comment 11 (Aug. 14, 2012).
167. SAP Am., Inc. v. Lakshmi Arunachalam, IPR2014-00413, Paper 23 (Dec. 5, 2014).
168. Facebook, Inc. v. TLI Commc'ns LLC, IPR2014-00566, Paper 11 (June 23, 2014).
169. Euro-Pro Operating LLC v. Acorne Enters., LLC, IPR2014-00351, Paper 20 (Aug. 5, 2014).
170. *See* Apple Inc. v. Smartflash LLC, IPR2014-00102, Paper 20 (Dec. 12, 2014); *see also* Medtronic, Inc. v. Troy R. Norred, M.D., IPR2014-00110, Paper 23 (Oct. 8, 2014); PATENT TRIAL AND APPEAL BOARD CONSOLIDATED TRIAL PRACTICE GUIDE 92, 100, 130 (Nov. 2019).
171. PATENT TRIAL AND APPEAL BOARD CONSOLIDATED TRIAL PRACTICE GUIDE 92, 100, 130 (Nov. 2019).
172. *SAP Am., Inc.*, IPR2014-00413, Paper 23.
173. 37 C.F.R. § 42.11(d)(2); *see also* Shire Dev. LLC v. LCS Grp., LLC, IPR2014-00739, Paper 14 (Dec. 23, 2014).
174. 77 Fed. Reg. 48,612, 48,630, Response to Comment 44 (Aug. 14, 2012).
175. *Id.*

Sanctions may include an order entering one or more of the following: (1) holding facts to have been established; (2) expunging or precluding a party from filing a paper; (3) precluding a party from arguing a particular issue; (4) precluding a party from requesting, obtaining, or opposing discovery; (5) excluding evidence; (6) providing for compensatory expenses, including attorneys' fees; (7) requiring terminal disclaimer of patent term; or (8) judgment in the trial or dismissal of the petition.[176]

D. Testimony

In trials before the Board, uncompelled direct testimony must be in the form of an affidavit or declaration.[177] All other testimony, including cross-examination, redirect examination, and compelled direct testimony, occurs by oral examination and is presented in the form of a deposition transcript.[178] Examination and cross-examination of a witness proceed as they would in a trial under the Federal Rules of Evidence.[179] In limited circumstances and on a case-by-case basis, the Board will permit live testimony at the hearing where the Board considers the demeanor of a witness critical to assessing credibility.[180]

1. Cross-Examination

Cross-examination of affidavit or declaration testimony (i.e., uncompelled direct testimony) prepared for the proceeding is routine discovery and specifically authorized under the rules.[181] Cross-examination of affidavit or declaration evidence that is not new testimony prepared for the proceeding, for example, preexisting declarations from prior Office proceedings (ex parte

176. 37 C.F.R. § 42.12(b).

177. 37 C.F.R. § 42.53(a); PATENT TRIAL AND APPEAL BOARD CONSOLIDATED TRIAL PRACTICE GUIDE App'x D (Nov. 2019).

178. 37 C.F.R. § 42.53(a); PATENT TRIAL AND APPEAL BOARD CONSOLIDATED TRIAL PRACTICE GUIDE App'x D (Nov. 2019).

179. PATENT TRIAL AND APPEAL BOARD CONSOLIDATED TRIAL PRACTICE GUIDE App'x D (Nov. 2019).

180. PATENT TRIAL AND APPEAL BOARD CONSOLIDATED TRIAL PRACTICE GUIDE 31–32 (Nov. 2019); K-40 Elecs., LLC v. Escort, Inc., IPR2013-00203, Paper 34 (May 21, 2014).

181. 37 C.F.R. § 42.51(b)(1)(ii).

examination, reexamination), as well as expert reports and deposition transcripts from litigations, is not provided under routine discovery.[182] A party seeking to cross-examine such a witness, however, may seek Board authorization to file a motion for additional discovery.[183] Any such motion must satisfy the Board's requirements for additional discovery.[184] The scope of cross-examination testimony is limited to the scope of the direct testimony.[185]

a. Timing and Logistics

Examination and cross-examination of a witness proceed as they would in a trial under the Federal Rules of Evidence.[186] For uncompelled direct testimony (affidavit or declaration testimony), the default deposition times are seven hours for cross-examination, four hours for redirect examination, and two hours for recross-examination.[187] The default time limits for compelled testimony are seven hours for direct examination, four hours for cross-examination, and two hours for redirect examination.[188] All parties must agree to a time and location before the taking of testimony.[189] The rules do not require a specific location for taking testimony.[190] And the parties may agree to take uncompelled deposition testimony outside the United States.[191] If the parties cannot agree, however, the parties must conference with the Board to determine a time and location.[192]

Cross-examination testimony should be in question-and-answer format and recorded by an officer authorized to take testimony under 35 U.S.C.

182. *Id.*; *see, e.g.*, CBS Interactive Inc. v. Helferich Patent Licensing, LLC, IPR2013-00033, Paper 85 (Sept. 3, 2013).

183. Mexichem Amanco Holdings S.A. de C.V. v. Honeywell Int'l, Inc., IPR2013-00576, Paper 31 (Aug. 26, 2014) (authorization granted).

184. *Id.*, Paper 36 (motion denied).

185. 37 C.F.R. § 42.53(d)(5)(ii).

186. PATENT TRIAL AND APPEAL BOARD CONSOLIDATED TRIAL PRACTICE GUIDE App'x D (Nov. 2019).

187. 37 C.F.R. § 42.53(c)(2).

188. *Id.* § 42.53(c)(1).

189. *Id.* § 42.53(d)(1).

190. *Id.* § 42.53(b)(2); PATENT TRIAL AND APPEAL BOARD CONSOLIDATED TRIAL PRACTICE GUIDE 33 (Nov. 2019).

191. 37 C.F.R. § 42.53(b)(3).

192. *Id.* § 42.53(d)(1); PATENT TRIAL AND APPEAL BOARD CONSOLIDATED TRIAL PRACTICE GUIDE 33 (Nov. 2019).

§ 23.[193] The witness shall read and sign a transcript of the testimony by affidavit unless the parties otherwise agree in writing or waive reading and signing on the record at the deposition or the witness refuses.[194] The officer shall prepare a certified transcript with a witness affidavit.[195] The transcript must also state, unless otherwise waived by the parties, (1) that the witness was duly sworn in, (2) that the transcript is a true and accurate record of the testimony given, (3) the name of the person recording the testimony, (4) the presence of any opponent, (5) the place where the deposition was taken and the day and hour when the deposition began and ended, (6) that the officer has no disqualifying personal or financial interest in a party, and (7) whether the witness refused to read or sign the transcript and the circumstance of such refusal.[196]

For direct deposition testimony (i.e., compelled testimony), the notice of deposition limits the scope of the testimony and must indicate (1) the time and place of the deposition, (2) the name and address of the witness, (3) a list of the relevant exhibits to be used during the deposition, and (4) a description of the scope and nature of the testimony to be elicited.[197] In addition, at least three business days before a conference regarding the time and place for a deposition for direct testimony, or if there is no conference, at least ten business days before the deposition, the party seeking the testimony must serve a list and copy of each document under the party's control and on which the party intends to rely and a list of, and proffer of reasonable access to, anything other than a document under that party's control on which the party intends to rely.[198] Additional details on compelled testimony, including compelled third-party testimony, are in this chapter, section C.4.

Cross-examination should ordinarily take place after any supplemental evidence relating to the direct testimony has been filed and more than a week before the filing date for any paper in which the cross-examination

193. 37 C.F.R. § 42.53(f)(1)–(2); PATENT TRIAL AND APPEAL BOARD CONSOLIDATED TRIAL PRACTICE GUIDE App'x D (Nov. 2019).
194. 37 C.F.R. § 42.53(f)(5).
195. *Id.* § 42.53(f)(6).
196. *Id.*
197. *Id.* § 42.53(d)(5)(i).
198. *Id.* § 42.53(d)(3).

testimony is expected to be used.[199] The party seeking a deposition must file a notice of deposition at least ten business days before taking the deposition.[200] The notice must list the time and place of the deposition and the manner in which the testimony will be recorded.[201] If a party objects to defects in a notice of deposition, the objections will be waived unless the objecting party promptly seeks authorization from the Board to file a motion to quash.[202]

b. Objections, Attorney Conduct, Witness Communication

The scope of cross-examination is limited to the scope of direct examination, that is, the scope of the affidavit or declaration.[203] The scope of redirect examination is limited to the scope of cross-examination, and the scope of recross-examination is limited to the scope of redirect examination.[204] The defending attorney may not interpret questions or help the witness respond.[205] Counsel may instruct a witness not to answer only when necessary to preserve privilege, enforce a Board-ordered limitation, or present a motion to limit or end the testimony.[206] Objections must be made on the record, and the examination will proceed subject to any objections.[207] If an objection is not made on the record during testimony or, if made, is not later preserved by filing a motion to exclude (according to the trial schedule), it is waived.[208]

Cross-examination may be ordered to take place in the presence of an administrative patent judge, which may occur at the deposition or oral argu-

---

199. *Id.* § 42.53(d)(2).
200. *Id.* § 42.53(d)(4).
201. *Id.* § 42.53(d)(5)(iii), (f).
202. *Id.* § 42.53(d)(6).
203. *Id.* § 42.53(d)(5)(ii).
204. FED. R. EVID. 611(b).
205. PATENT TRIAL AND APPEAL BOARD CONSOLIDATED TRIAL PRACTICE GUIDE App'x D (Nov. 2019).
206. *Id.*
207. *Id.*
208. 37 C.F.R. § 42.53(f)(8).

ment.[209] The Board may require live testimony when witness demeanor is of particular relevance, such as where misconduct is alleged.[210]

Objections must be stated concisely, in a nonargumentative form, without leading the witness.[211] Objections cannot suggest an answer to a witness.[212] Once the testimony is transcribed, the witness shall read and sign the transcript.[213] The transcript must be filed as an exhibit.[214] The Board has authority to impose sanctions on any person who impedes, delays, or frustrates the fair examination of a witness.[215]

Once cross-examination begins, and until cross-examination ends, counsel offering the witness on direct testimony cannot consult or confer with the witness regarding the substance of the testimony (whether already given or predicted) except to protect privilege, or suggest how a question should be answered.[216] Counsel shall not initiate a private conference or call for a break while a question is pending, except to determine whether privilege should be asserted.[217]

E. Forms of Evidence, Objections, Motions to Exclude, and Motions to Strike

The Federal Rules of Evidence generally apply to PTAB trials, except where modified to comport with practice before the Office.[218] For example, portions of the Federal Rules that apply to criminal proceedings do not apply, and a limited number of terms have been redefined to specifically apply to proceedings before the Office rather than before a U.S. court.[219]

---

209. PATENT TRIAL AND APPEAL BOARD CONSOLIDATED TRIAL PRACTICE GUIDE 31–32 (Nov. 2019).

210. *Id.*

211. *Id.* at App'x D.

212. *Id.*

213. 37 C.F.R. § 42.53(f)(5).

214. *Id.* § 42.53(f)(7).

215. PATENT TRIAL AND APPEAL BOARD CONSOLIDATED TRIAL PRACTICE GUIDE App'x D (Nov. 2019).

216. *Id.*

217. *Id.*

218. 37 C.F.R. § 42.62.

219. *Id.* § 42.62(b)–(c).

1. Forms of Evidence

Evidence in PTAB trials consists of affidavits, transcripts of depositions, documents, and things.[220] All evidence must be filed in the form of an exhibit.[221] Exhibits must be numbered sequentially, and each party must maintain a current exhibit list identifying each exhibit by number with a brief description of the exhibit.[222] If a party relies on a document or produces a document in a foreign language, then an English translation and an affidavit testifying to the accuracy of that translation must be provided.[223] English translations of all foreign-language documents are not necessarily required; however, documents produced under Rule 42.51 (uncompelled discovery) and any documents a party uses or relies on during the proceedings must be translated into English.[224] Other non-English-language documents produced under Rule 42.52 (compelled discovery) need not necessarily be translated into English.[225]

Evidence can be admitted only if it is taken, sought, or filed per the rules.[226] Certification is not necessary as a condition to admissibility for Office records that all parties have access to.[227] Generally, there is no concern with hearsay issues regarding admissibility of specifications or drawings from U.S. patent applications or issued patents.[228] Issues with hearsay arise when the materials are presented to prove the *truth* of the matter asserted.[229] A specification and drawing of a U.S. patent or patent application is admissible as evidence only to prove what the specification and drawing describe.[230] If there is data in the specification or drawing and the

220. *Id.* § 42.63(a).
221. *Id.*
222. *Id.* § 42.63(c), (e).
223. *Id.* § 42.63(b).
224. 77 Fed. Reg. 48,612, 48,645, Response to Comment 181 (Aug. 14, 2012).
225. *Id.*
226. 37 C.F.R. § 42.61(a).
227. *Id.* § 42.61(b).
228. *Id.* § 42.61(c); 77 Fed. Reg. 48,612, 48,645, Response to Comment 174 (Aug. 14, 2012).
229. 77 Fed. Reg. 48,612, 48,645, Response to Comment 174 (Aug. 14, 2012).
230. 37 C.F.R. § 42.61(c).

party intends to rely on that data, an affidavit by someone having firsthand knowledge of how the data was generated is needed.[231]

2. Objections

A party wishing to challenge the admissibility of evidence must object timely to the evidence.[232] Objections to evidence submitted with any paper prior to institution must be filed within ten business days of the institution of the trial.[233] After institution, any objection must be filed within five business days.[234] The objections must identify the grounds for objection with particularity to allow the possibility of correction in the form of supplemental evidence.[235] The party relying on evidence that has been objected to may respond to the objection by serving supplemental evidence within ten business days of service of the objection.[236]

3. Motions to Exclude

Objections to admissibility must be preserved by filing a motion to exclude the evidence.[237] Timing for filing the motion to exclude is set forth in the scheduling order,[238] and the motion can generally be filed without prior authorization from the Board.[239] A motion to exclude must address objections to exhibits in numerical order, identify where in the record the objection was originally made and where in the record the evidence was relied upon by an opponent, and explain each objection.[240] A motion to exclude

231. *Id.*

232. PATENT TRIAL AND APPEAL BOARD CONSOLIDATED TRIAL PRACTICE GUIDE 78–79 (Nov. 2019); 37 C.F.R. § 42.64.

233. 37 C.F.R. § 42.64(b); PATENT TRIAL AND APPEAL BOARD CONSOLIDATED TRIAL PRACTICE GUIDE 78–79 (Nov. 2019).

234. 37 C.F.R. § 42.64(b); PATENT TRIAL AND APPEAL BOARD CONSOLIDATED TRIAL PRACTICE GUIDE 78–79 (Nov. 2019).

235. 37 C.F.R. § 42.64(b).

236. *Id.*

237. *Id.* § 42.64(c); PATENT TRIAL AND APPEAL BOARD CONSOLIDATED TRIAL PRACTICE GUIDE 79 (Nov. 2019).

238. PATENT TRIAL AND APPEAL BOARD CONSOLIDATED TRIAL PRACTICE GUIDE 79 (Nov. 2019).

239. 37 C.F.R. § 42.64(c).

240. PATENT TRIAL AND APPEAL BOARD CONSOLIDATED TRIAL PRACTICE GUIDE 79 (Nov. 2019).

is for challenging the admissibility of evidence (e.g., hearsay or authentication) and is not the place to challenge the sufficiency of the evidence to prove a particular point.[241] The Board will generally wait until after the oral hearing and it has reviewed the entire record to decide a motion to exclude because the issue often becomes moot.[242] At the same time, in certain circumstances, where the evidence sought to be excluded is so central to the parties' dispute that the motion is unlikely to be mooted, the Board may decide it earlier, such as during a prehearing conference.[243]

4. Motions to Strike

When a party believes that the Board should disregard arguments, including improper arguments made on reply or late-filed evidence, the party may file a motion to strike.[244] When a party wishes to address the proper weight that the Board should give such arguments or late-filed evidence, then it may be appropriate to seek further briefing.[245]

The Board has indicated that because it is capable of identifying new issues and late-filed evidence, and disregarding them when weighing the evidence at the close of trial, striking the entirety or a portion of a party's brief is an exceptional remedy that it expects to grant only rarely.[246] But where there can be no dispute that an issue is new or evidence is presented late or where waiting until the close of the evidence to determine whether new issues or evidence has been presented would cause great injury to a party, the Board will consider the merits of a motion to strike.[247] A reply brief clearly presenting a new theory not included in prior briefing is a situation where a motion to strike is appropriate.[248] A new theory raised at oral argument is another situation where a motion to strike is appropriate.[249]

241. *Id.*
242. *Id.* at 79–80.
243. *Id.*
244. *Id.* at 80–81.
245. *Id.*
246. *Id.*
247. *Id.*
248. *Id.*
249. *Id.*

Chapter 6

Postinstitution: Motions to Amend

This chapter explores motions to amend following an institution decision. Briefing and discovery are explored in Chapter 5. Oral argument and requests for rehearing are discussed in Chapter 7.

A. Introduction

Motions to amend can be an important tool in post-grant proceedings. The process for seeking amendment has varied over time. The Office has issued several notices and rules and has implemented pilot programs that provide different avenues to seek amendment of a patent under review.

1. Overview and Brief History

The ability to seek amendment is part of the statutory scheme for both IPR and PGR proceedings.[1] But the procedures and applicable burdens of proof have shifted over time. Originally, the Board required patent owners to show that any substitute claims proposed in a motion to amend met the statutory requirements and separately show that they were patentable.[2] This was based, in part, on the procedural requirement that patent owners

1. *See* 35 U.S.C. §§ 316(d), 326(d).
2. 85 Fed. Reg. 82,923, 82,925 (Dec. 21, 2020).

file a motion proposing substitute claims and the general practice that a moving party bears the burden to show it is entitled to the relief it seeks.[3]

This early guidance was later challenged in *Aqua Products, Inc. v. Matal*.[4] There, the Federal Circuit ruled that in the absence of "considered statutory interpretation" by the Patent Office,[5] and in view of the statutory assignment of the burden of proof to petitioners,[6] the Patent Office could not require patent owners to show substitute claims were patentable.[7] The burdens and motion to amend practice have been the subject of several subsequent Board decisions and separate notices.[8] In December 2020, the Board issued its most comprehensive guidance and regulations regarding motions to amend since the America Invents Act (AIA) itself. These rules generally assign the ultimate burden to show any proposed substitute claims are unpatentable to a petitioner, although they do assign other burdens to the patent owner.[9]

Despite many changes over the years, several strategic and procedural considerations applicable to motions to amend have remained relatively constant.

2. Strategic Considerations

In considering whether to seek amendment (or whether to oppose a motion to amend or, indeed, whether to file a petition), the parties should consider the consequences of potential claim amendments. For example, motions to amend change the briefing schedule of a proceeding. In addition, motions to amend may create intervening rights and may create some procedural issues with parallel litigation, but they may also strengthen claims and focus infringement analyses. Patent owners should also consider (and petitioners

3. *Id.*
4. 872 F.3d 1290, 1318 (Fed. Cir. 2017) (en banc) (addressing Idle Free Sys., Inc. v. Bergstrom, Inc., IPR2012-00027, Paper 26 (June 11, 2013); MasterImage 3D, Inc. v. RealD Inc., IPR2015-00040, Paper 42 (July 15, 2015) (Precedential)).
5. *Id.* at 1324–25.
6. *Id.* at 1302 (citing 35 U.S.C. § 316(d), (e)).
7. *Id.* at 1327–28.
8. *E.g.*, Hunting Titan, Inc. v. DynaEnergetics Europe GmbH, IPR2018-00600, Paper 67 (July 6, 2020) (Precedential); Notice Regarding a New Pilot Program Concerning Motion to Amend Practice and Procedures in Trial Proceedings under the America Invents Act before the Patent Trial and Appeal Board, 84 Fed. Reg. 9,497 (Mar. 15, 2019).
9. 85 Fed. Reg. 82,923, 82,924 (Dec. 21, 2020).

should keep in mind) that other avenues for claim amendment like reexamination and reissue also exist.

a. Impact on Briefing Schedule

The parties should consider the logistics of filing and responding to motions to amend. Where a patent owner files a motion to amend, it may support its position with expert testimony.[10] The patent owner's initial paper is generally due with the patent owner response, but the motion to amend schedule may be offset from the regular briefing.[11] Like regular briefing, a petitioner may take deposition testimony of any patent owner expert and respond to the motion to amend with its own paper and its own expert declarations or additional art directed to the proposed substitute claims.[12] A petitioner's response or opposition is generally due along with the petitioner's reply, as it is finalizing its case, but again may be offset from the regular briefing schedule.[13] Similarly, the patent owner's opportunity to reply (and any expert or other rebuttal evidence) in support of its motion is generally due at the same time as its sur-reply to the petition.[14] And a petitioner's sur-reply to a motion to amend is due shortly thereafter.[15] In sum, parties in a proceeding with a motion to amend will generally face at least double the briefing and expert discovery (declarations and depositions) in an overlapping period with original briefing.

In addition, as discussed in greater detail later,[16] the Board's pilot program for motions to amend allows a patent owner to seek preliminary guidance from the Board on a first motion and respond to that guidance, including proposing a new set of substitute claims. This process can also be very condensed, and both parties should be prepared to handle the additional

---

10. *See* PATENT TRIAL AND APPEAL BOARD CONSOLIDATED TRIAL PRACTICE GUIDE 69 (Nov. 2019).

11. *See id.* at 95.

12. *Id.* at 72.

13. *See, e.g., id.* at 95.

14. *Id.*

15. *Id.*

16. *See infra* Chapter 6, section D.

briefing and, potentially, additional expert declarations and related depositions or even a second motion to amend.

b. Intervening Rights

The Doctrine of Intervening Rights protects a party who "finds its previously lawful activities rendered newly infringing under a modified patent."[17] There are two types of intervening rights. Absolute intervening rights protect a party from the amended claims when their now-infringing product was made or used before the amended claims issued, while equitable intervening rights protect a party that made substantial preparations to make or use a now-infringing product prior to issuance of the amended claims.[18] The application of either version of the doctrine prevents a patent owner from recovering damages for the otherwise infringing activity.[19]

Intervening rights are not unique to PGRs and IPRs; intervening rights can occur through reexamination and reissue. And not all claim amendments create intervening rights. If the amendments are "without substantive change," no intervening rights arise.[20] Courts focus on overall claim scope instead of the literal words of a claim to determine if there has been a substantive change.[21] Moreover, many PGR and IPR proceedings have copending proceedings, and a granted motion to amend substituting new patent claims (with corresponding cancellation of original patent claims) will affect litigation and require the parties to balance the risks and impact accordingly. Patent owners should consider whether an amendment will negate infringement on already existing products.[22] But the risk of forgoing damages on existing products, that is, because original claims are at risk of being found invalid, may be countered by the potential to recover damages

17. Marine Polymer Techs., Inc. v. HemCon, Inc., 672 F.3d 1350, 1361 (Fed. Cir. 2012).

18. *See id.* at 1361–62; 35 U.S.C. §§ 252, 307(b), 318(c).

19. The application and scope of both absolute and equitable intervening rights are case specific and depend on, among other things, the type of claims at issue, the effect of the amendment, and the alleged infringing activity.

20. Laitram Corp. v. NEC Corp., 163 F.3d 1342, 1346 (Fed. Cir. 1998) (quoting Seattle Box Co. v. Indus. Crating & Packing, Inc., 731 F.2d 818, 827 (Fed. Cir. 1984)).

21. *See, e.g.*, *Seattle Box Co.*, 731 F.2d at 827–28.

22. *See, e.g.*, *Laitram*, 163 F.3d at 1349 (ruling intervening rights barred damages claim where reexamination substantively changed claim scope).

on future products. Petitioners should be aware of a parallel concern—while a successful amendment may bar a patent owner from seeking damages for the petitioner's existing products, in the absence of equitable intervening rights, future products are not protected. Courts consider various factors in deciding whether equitable rights apply, including (1) the preparations made by the infringer before the amended claims issue, (2) whether the infringer received advice of counsel, (3) whether the infringer had existing orders, (4) whether the infringer can manufacture a noninfringing product, (5) whether the infringer has been able to recoup its investment, and (6) whether the infringer may seek equitable relief or whether it has unclean hands, for example due to willful infringement.[23]

Patent owners and petitioners alike should be aware that while intervening rights is primarily the province of district courts and infringement, the Board has occasionally considered whether amended claims are substantively identical to original claims. As set forth in the Consolidated Trial Practice Guide,[24] a patent owner "may request that the Board determine that the amended claim and original patent claim are substantially identical" for purposes of intervening rights.[25] For example, in *Google Inc. v. Contentguard Holdings, Inc.*,[26] the Board considered whether the patent owner's successfully amended claims were identical in scope to the original claims.[27] The Board determined that the substitute claim simply amended the claim to replace a term construed by the district court with the district court's construction of the term,[28] and the Board concluded that the patent owner's substitute claim was substantially identical to the original.[29] Parties

23. *See, e.g.*, Visto Corp. v. Sproqit Techs., Inc., 413 F. Supp. 2d 1073, 1090 (N.D. Cal. 2006) (noting factors); Mfr.'s Fin. Co. v. McKey, 294 U.S. 442, 449 (1935) ("[One] who seeks equity must do equity. . . ."); Shockley v. Arcan, Inc., 248 F.3d 1349, 1361 (Fed. Cir. 2001) ("The record, with its finding of willful infringement, amply supports the district court's discretion to deny Arcan access to equity.").

24. PATENT TRIAL AND APPEAL BOARD CONSOLIDATED TRIAL PRACTICE GUIDE (Nov. 2019).

25. *Id.* at 70.

26. Google Inc. v. Contentguard Holdings, Inc., No. CBM2015-00040, 2019 WL 764128 (Feb. 19, 2019).

27. *Id.* at *30–31.

28. *Id.* at *31.

29. *Id.*

seeking early resolution of intervening rights issues may consider requesting such a ruling from the Board.

c. *Availability of Other Proceedings*

Both parties should also be aware that patent owners have other avenues to amend their claims (or obtain claims of new scope).

The simplest option is to obtain a new patent. Where a challenged patent still has pending continuations, patent owners can take the petitioner's invalidity arguments into account when drafting new claims. Though patent owners may be bound by regulatory estoppel,[30] a patent applicant has a great deal of freedom to craft claims during normal examination. And while the Board has authority to take jurisdiction over pending applications,[31] the Board rarely does.

Another option is ex parte reexamination. During reexamination, patent owners may not enlarge the scope of the claims or introduce new matter unsupported by the specification, but otherwise patent owners have latitude to amend their claims.[32] The Board has discretion to stay a reexamination proceeding in parallel with an IPR or PGR,[33] but the Board also encourages patent owners to seek reexamination in some situations in lieu of motions to amend in an IPR or PGR.[34] Accordingly, timing matters—patent owners interested in seeking reexamination on a ground they believe will be the focus of an IPR may wish to seek reexamination as early as possible, for example, after receiving invalidity contentions but before an IPR or PGR is filed. Notably, patent owners may seek reexamination on grounds not addressed in an IPR or PGR final written decision even *after* a final written decision finding challenged claims unpatentable, so long as the reexamination request is made before the deadline to appeal (or before the Federal

30. *See supra* Chapter 2, section E.
31. *See* 35 U.S.C. § 325(d).
32. *See generally* MANUAL OF PATENT EXAMINING PROCEDURE § 2234 (9th ed., rev. Oct. 2019, last rev. June 2020).
33. 35 U.S.C. § 325(d); *see also supra* Chapter 2, section D; CBS Interactive Inc. v. Helferich Patent Licensing, LLC, IPR2013-00033, Paper 15 (Nov. 6, 2012) (order to stay a concurrent reexamination).
34. 84 Fed. Reg. 16,654, 16,655 (Apr. 22, 2019).

Circuit resolves any appeal, as applicable).[35] One strategy consideration to keep in mind: because successful reexamination does not result in a new patent (unlike reissue, discussed later),[36] a petitioner who was time barred from filing an IPR or PGR before the reexamination remains time barred after the reexamination (although that petitioner remains free to challenge validity of the reexamined patent in district court or by requesting a separate ex parte reexamination).[37]

Finally, patent owners can seek reissue. Like reexamination, a patent owner may seek a narrowing reissue at any time, even after a final written decision in an IPR or PGR.[38] Similar to reexamination, the Board may stay the reissue proceeding.[39] Unlike reexamination, which is based on a substantial new question of patentability, reissue is based on identifying an error or defect in the original patent that makes it "wholly or partly inoperative."[40] The error need not be related to prior art or invalidity, and the patent owner may seek amendment for any defect.[41] In addition, the failure to present narrower claims, without acknowledging any defect in the original claims, that is, presenting new dependent claims without amending independent claims, is a defect that can be corrected in reissue.[42] Notably, a successful reissue application yields a new patent—and a new nine-month window for PGR challenges (if a post-AIA patent) and a new (or restarted) statutory time bar for IPRs.[43] Additionally, a reissue application may be abandoned at any time, preserving the original patent as is,[44] and may be a reasonable option depending on the strength of the PGR or IPR grounds.

35. *Id.*

36. Biodelivery Scis. Int'l, Inc. v. Monosol RX, LLC, IPR2013-00316, Paper 28, at 3 (Nov. 13, 2013).

37. *Id.*

38. 35 U.S.C. § 251 (subsection (d) limiting a broadening reissue to being filed within two years of grant of the original patent).

39. *Id.*; *see also, e.g.*, Stride Rite Children's Grp., LLC v. Shoes by Firebug LLC, IPR2017-01810, Paper 23 (July 12, 2018) (order to stay a concurrent reissue).

40. *See generally* MANUAL OF PATENT EXAMINING PROCEDURE § 1401 (2020); *see also* 35 U.S.C. § 251.

41. 84 Fed. Reg. 16,654, 16,655 (Apr. 22, 2019).

42. *In re* Tanaka, 640 F.3d 1246, 1251 (Fed. Cir. 2011).

43. Eizo Corp. v. Barco N.V., IPR2014-00358, Paper 11, at 9–10 (July 23, 2014).

44. 37 C.F.R. § 1.178 (2021).

Each of these proceedings has different advantages and disadvantages when compared to post-grant amendment before the Board, and a given strategy may include one or more depending on the particular case. In addition, each can proceed in parallel with or be stayed in view of a PGR or IPR proceeding, which likewise raises strategic implications. In deciding to stay a parallel proceeding, the Board has outlined several factors it considers.[45] These include

- overlap of claims and whether the claims in the PGR or IPR are the same as or depend from claims at issue in the parallel proceeding;
- overlap of issues and whether the same grounds or same prior art is raised in the parallel proceeding;
- duplication of efforts and whether the parallel proceeding could result in inconsistent outcomes;
- whether amendment in one proceeding would affect claim scope in another proceeding;
- overall timeline, stage, and statutory deadline of the proceedings; and
- whether one proceeding would likely simplify issues in another proceeding.[46]

B. Statute and Regulations

Motions to amend in IPRs and PGRs are provided for by statute. 35 U.S.C. § 316(d) provides:

> (d) Amendment of the Patent.—
>
> (1) In general.—During an inter partes review instituted under this chapter, the patent owner may file 1 motion to amend the patent in 1 or more of the following ways:
>
> (A) Cancel any challenged patent claim.
>
> (B) For each challenged claim, propose a reasonable number of substitute claims.

45. 84 Fed. Reg. 16,654, 16,557 (Apr. 22, 2019).
46. *Id.*

(2) Additional motions.—Additional motions to amend may be permitted upon the joint request of the petitioner and the patent owner to materially advance the settlement of a proceeding under section 317, or as permitted by regulations prescribed by the Director.

(3) Scope of claims.—An amendment under this subsection may not enlarge the scope of the claims of the patent or introduce new matter.[47]

A virtually identical statute applies to PGR proceedings.[48] In implementing these statutes, the Patent Office has set forth a number of regulations governing motions to amend in IPR and PGR proceedings.[49] Most notably, 37 C.F.R. § 42.121, titled Amendment of the Patent, sets forth the procedure and burdens for a motion to amend; it states:

(a) Motion to amend. A patent owner may file one motion to amend a patent, but only after conferring with the Board.

(1) Due date. Unless a due date is provided in a Board order, a motion to amend must be filed no later than the filing of a patent owner response.

(2) Scope. A motion to amend may be denied where:

(i) The amendment does not respond to a ground of unpatentability involved in the trial; or

(ii) The amendment seeks to enlarge the scope of the claims of the patent or introduce new subject matter.

(3) A reasonable number of substitute claims. A motion to amend may cancel a challenged claim or propose a reasonable number of substitute claims. The presumption is that only one substitute claim would be needed to replace each challenged claim, and it may be rebutted by a demonstration of need.

47. 35 U.S.C. § 316(d).
48. *Id.* § 326(d).
49. *See* 37 C.F.R. § 42.1 *et seq.* (2021).

(b) Content. A motion to amend claims must include a claim listing, which claim listing may be contained in an appendix to the motion, show the changes clearly, and set forth:

(1) The support in the original disclosure of the patent for each claim that is added or amended; and

(2) The support in an earlier-filed disclosure for each claim for which benefit of the filing date of the earlier filed disclosure is sought.

(c) Additional motion to amend. In addition to the requirements set forth in paragraphs (a) and (b) of this section, any additional motion to amend may not be filed without Board authorization. An additional motion to amend may be authorized when there is a good cause showing or a joint request of the petitioner and the patent owner to materially advance a settlement. In determining whether to authorize such an additional motion to amend, the Board will consider whether a petitioner has submitted supplemental information after the time period set for filing a motion to amend in paragraph (a)(1) of this section.

(d) Burden of Persuasion. On a motion to amend:

(1) A patent owner bears the burden of persuasion to show, by a preponderance of the evidence, that the motion to amend complies with the requirements of paragraphs (1) and (3) of 35 U.S.C. 316(d), as well as paragraphs (a)(2), (a)(3), (b)(1), and (b)(2) of this section;

(2) A petitioner bears the burden of persuasion to show, by a preponderance of the evidence, that any proposed substitute claims are unpatentable; and

(3) Irrespective of paragraphs (d)(1) and (2) of this section, the Board may, in the interests of justice, exercise its discretion to grant or deny a motion to amend only for reasons supported by readily identifiable and persuasive evidence of record. In doing so, the Board may make of record only readily identifiable and persuasive evidence in a related proceeding before the Office or evidence that a district court can judicially notice.

> Where the Board exercises its discretion under this paragraph, the parties will have an opportunity to respond.[50]

A parallel, virtually identical, regulation applies in PGR proceedings.[51] These statutes and regulations set forth both procedural and substantive requirements for motions to amend. Procedurally, a patent owner must

- confer with the Board prior to filing any motion to amend;[52]
- cancel one or more challenged claims or propose a "reasonable number" of substitute claims (generally presumed to be one replacement claim for each challenged claim);[53] and
- include a claim listing identifying the support in the original disclosure for each new or amended claim and the support in any earlier disclosure for the claimed priority date.[54]

And, of course, the motion to amend must be timely filed under the scheduling order for the proceeding[55] or the requirements of the particular pilot program[56] and must conform to the Board's style,[57] page or word-number requirements,[58] and general formatting and filing requirements.[59]

Substantively, the motion must

- respond to a ground of unpatentability involved in the trial[60] and
- not expand the claims' scope or introduce new subject matter.[61]

The patent owner bears the burden of showing compliance with these statutory and regulatory requirements,[62] but the petitioner bears the burden

50. 37 C.F.R. § 42.121(d)(3) (2021).
51. *Id.* § 42.221(d)(3).
52. *See id.* §§ 42.121(a), 42.221(a). This often occurs in a conference call.
53. *See id.* §§ 42.121(a)(3), 42.221(a)(3).
54. *See id.* §§ 42.121(b), 42.221(b).
55. *See id.* §§ 42.121(a)(1), 42.221(a)(1).
56. *See infra* Chapter 6, section D.
57. *See* 37 C.F.R. § 42.22 (2021) (requiring certain sections in any motion).
58. *See id.* § 42.24.
59. *See id.* § 42.6 (setting forth, among other things, typeface, margin, signature, filing, and service requirements).
60. *See id.* §§ 42.121(a)(2)(i), 42.221(a)(2)(i).
61. *See id.* §§ 42.121(a)(2)(ii), 42.221(a)(2)(ii); 35 U.S.C. §§ 316(d)(3), 326(d)(3).
62. *See* 37 C.F.R. §§ 42.121(d)(1), 42.221(d)(1) (2021).

of showing that any proposed substitute claims are not patentable.[63] Though the focus of the amendment process is on responding to a ground of unpatentability raised in the underlying proceeding,[64] amendments can encompass more, and the Board can review the patentability of proposed substitute claims more generally. For example, a patent owner may also amend claims to bolster patent eligibility even if not raised (in a PGR) or applicable to original claims (in an IPR),[65] and the Board may review the substitute claims, including original or added elements with respect to all patentability requirements, including indefiniteness and patent eligibility, even though those criteria may not be at issue in a particular proceeding, that is, in an IPR.[66] As of March 31, 2020, 53 percent of motions to amend denied on statutory grounds were denied for reasons other than anticipation or obviousness.[67]

C. Burdens of Persuasion

Throughout an IPR or PGR proceeding, the ultimate burden of proving unpatentability by a preponderance of evidence rests with the petitioner.[68] This is true for the original patent claims and substitute claims as well, although historically patent owners bore the burden to show substitute claims were patentable. Nonetheless, an unopposed motion to amend is not automatically granted,[69] and the Board itself may independently assess the patentability of substitute claims when there is no opposition or a clearly

63. *See id.* §§ 41.121(d)(2), 42.221(d)(2).

64. *See id.* §§ 42.121(a)(2)(i), 42.221(a)(2)(i).

65. Lectrosonics, Inc. v. Zaxcom, Inc., IPR2018-01129, Paper 15, at 5–6 (Feb. 25, 2019).

66. Uniloc 2017 LLC v. Hulu, LLC, 966 F.3d 1295, 1304 (Fed. Cir. 2020) (noting Board must consider the patentability of substitute claims generally); *see also* Nike, Inc. v. Adidas AG, 955 F.3d 45, 51 (Fed. Cir. 2020) (ruling the Board is not "constrained to arguments and theories raised by the petitioner" in deciding motions to amend).

67. *Patent Trial and Appeal Board Motion to Amend Study, Installment 6: Update through March 31, 2020*, at 9, USPTO, https://www.uspto.gov/sites/default/files/documents/20200709-PTAB-PTAB%20MTA%20Study%20Installment%206%20%20%2820200629%29-IQ_813950-Final.pdf.

68. 35 U.S.C. §§ 316(e), 326(e).

69. 85 Fed. Reg. 82,923, 82,924 (Dec. 21, 2020).

inadequate opposition. Moreover, patent owners bear an initial burden to show a motion to amend meets statutory and regulatory requirements.[70]

1. Overview of Patent Office Rules

Following several challenges, various decisions, and stakeholder comments, the Patent Office announced new regulations for seeking amendment in IPR and PGR proceedings in late 2020.[71] Effective January 20, 2021, these new rules revised the burdens for motions to amend "to expressly assign to the petitioner the burden of showing the unpatentability of substitute claims proposed in a motion to amend . . . [and] to expressly assign to the patent owner the burden of showing that a motion to amend complies with certain statutory and regulatory requirements for such a motion."[72] And, according to the rules, the Board may, "in the interest of justice," exercise discretion in granting or denying a motion to amend.[73] Thus, the patent owner, the petitioner, and the Board each play a part.

2. Patent Owner and Petitioner Burdens of Proof and Persuasion

Under the rules, the patent owner must show that the proposed substitute claims comply with statutory and regulatory requirements,[74] including the following:

- the motion cancels a challenged patent claim and proposes a reasonable number of substitute claims;[75]
- the proposed substitute claims do not enlarge the scope of the claims or introduce new matter;[76]
- the motion to amend (and the proposed substitute claims) responds to a ground of unpatentability involved in the trial;[77]

---

70. *Id.*
71. *Id.*
72. *Id.* at 82,923.
73. *Id.*
74. *Id.*; *see also* 37 C.F.R. §§ 42.121(d)(1), 42.221(d)(1) (2021).
75. 35 U.S.C. §§ 316(d)(1), 326(d)(1); *see also* 37 C.F.R. §§ 42.121(a)(3), 42.221(a)(3) (2021).
76. 35 U.S.C. §§ 316(d)(3), 326(d)(3); *see also* 37 C.F.R. §§ 42.121(a)(2)(ii), 42.221(a)(2)(ii) (2021).
77. 37 C.F.R. §§ 42.121(a)(2)(i), 42.221(a)(2)(i) (2021).

- the motion sets forth the support in the original specification for the amendments;[78] and
- the motion includes a claim listing identifying support in any earlier-filed disclosures, to the extent the patent owner asserts an earlier filing date, that is, claims priority.[79]

The patent owner must show compliance with each of these requirements by a preponderance of evidence.[80] The petitioner, in turn, must show that any proposed substitute claims are unpatentable.[81] Like the patent owner, the petitioner must make this showing by a preponderance of the evidence.[82]

As a practical matter, the Board first determines whether the patent owner meets the statutory and regulatory requirements before considering the patentability of the proposed substitute claims.[83] In the Board's view, the patent owner, as drafter of the substitute claims and written description, can best explain why the number of substitute claims is reasonable, why the substitute claims do not enlarge the scope of the claims, and how the written description supports the substitute claims.[84] The Board then considers whether the petitioner has met its burden to show unpatentability.[85]

3. The Board's Discretion

Beyond the parties' burdens, the rules allow the Board to exercise discretion to grant or deny motions to amend "in the interests of justice" for either party.[86] The notice emphasizes, however, that the Board may only do so "for reasons supported by readily identifiable and persuasive evidence of record in the proceeding."[87] In rare instances, the Board may add to the record but, again, only using "readily identifiable and persuasive evidence in a related proceeding before the Office or evidence that a district court can judicially

78. *Id.* §§ 42.121(b)(1), 42.221(b)(1).
79. *Id.* §§ 42.121(b)(2), 42.221(b)(2).
80. 85 Fed. Reg. 82,923, 82,924 (Dec. 21, 2020).
81. *Id.*; *see also* 37 C.F.R. §§ 42.121(d)(2), 42.221(d)(2) (2021).
82. 85 Fed. Reg. 82,923, 82,924 (Dec. 21, 2020).
83. *Id.* at 82,928.
84. *Id.* at 82,928–29 (Office response to comment 1).
85. *Id.*
86. *Id.* at 82,928; *see also* 37 C.F.R. §§ 42.121(d)(3), 42.221(d)(3) (2021).
87. 85 Fed. Reg. 82,923, 82,924 (Dec. 21, 2020).

notice."[88] For example, the Board may consider the patent's prosecution history or the record in another proceeding challenging the patent.[89] The Board expects to exercise its discretion only rarely—for example, where the petitioner does not oppose the motion to amend or where the patent owner fails to address a statutory or regulatory requirement with which the amendment obviously complies.[90] And should the Board exercise discretion, the parties are guaranteed an opportunity to respond.[91]

4. Major Decisions (Federal Circuit and Board)

When introducing the December 2020 rules, the Board emphasized that they comply with *Aqua Products, Inc. v. Matal*,[92] *Lectrosonics, Inc. v. Zaxcom, Inc.*,[93] and *Hunting Titan, Inc. v. DynaEnergetics Europe GmbH*.[94] The rules pull heavily from the holdings of these cases, and the rationale behind the decisions may shed additional light on the Board's practices.

The rule that the petitioner bears the burden to show substitute claims unpatentable comes from *Aqua Products*. In *Aqua Products*, the full Federal Circuit determined that, in the absence of formal rulemaking to the contrary, the Patent Office could not require patent owners to prove patentability of proposed substitute claims.[95] In *Aqua Products*, the Board had found that the motion to amend complied with the procedural requirements.[96] But applying the then-applicable rules, the Board denied the motion to amend because it concluded the patent owner failed to prove that the substitute claims were patentable.[97] The court considered whether the Board improperly denied the motion, in part by placing the burden on the patent owner.[98]

88. *Id.*
89. *Id.* at 82,927.
90. *Id.* at 82,924.
91. *Id.*
92. Aqua Prods., Inc. v. Matal, 872 F.3d 1290 (Fed. Cir. 2017) (en banc).
93. Lectrosonics, Inc. v. Zaxcom, Inc., IPR2018-01129, Paper 15 (Feb. 25, 2019) (Precedential).
94. Hunting Titan, Inc. v. DynaEnergetics Europe GmbH, IPR2018-00600, Paper 67 (July 6, 2020) (Precedential).
95. *Aqua Prods.*, 872 F.3d at 1327.
96. *Id.*
97. *Id.*
98. *Id.* at 1297.

On appeal, a divided en banc court reversed the Board.[99] A plurality of the court agreed that the AIA unambiguously placed the burden of proving unpatentability on petitioners for all issues, that is, for original and substitute claims.[100] A majority of the court, however, determined that even if the statute was ambiguous (with respect to the burden for substitute claims), the Office had not adopted an interpretation that was entitled to deference.[101] The majority acknowledged that the Office may promulgate rules implementing the AIA,[102] but because the Office had not issued any rule specifically assigning the burden of proof for a motion to amend to the patent owner, the court held that the Office could not place the burden of proof on the patent owner.[103]

Lectrosonics built on *Aqua Products* and the issue of burdens in a motion to amend. *Lectrosonics*, a precedential decision, divided the burdens between patent owner and petitioner, allocating those burdens in the same way the December 2020 rules do. The Board followed the court's holding and rationale in *Aqua Products* and placed the burden to show substitute claims are unpatentable on the petitioner but distinguished that burden from the burden to show substitute claims comply with statutory and regulatory requirements, which it placed on the patent owner.[104] The Board also provided general guidance on motions to amend.[105] It explained that as a threshold matter before considering patentability, "the Board first must determine whether the motion to amend meets the statutory and regulatory requirements."[106] But, noting the *Aqua Products* analysis, the Board also stated that "a patent owner does not bear the burden of persuasion to demonstrate the patentability of substitute claims presented in a motion to amend."[107] And it explained that "the Board determines whether substitute

99. *Id.* at 1327.
100. *Id.* at 1315.
101. *Id.*
102. *See, e.g.*, *id.* at 1315–16.
103. *Id.* at 1327.
104. Lectrosonics, Inc. v. Zaxcom, Inc., IPR2018-01129, Paper 15, at 4 (Feb. 25, 2019) (Precedential).
105. *Id.* at 2.
106. *Id.* at 4.
107. *Id.*

claims are unpatentable by a preponderance of the evidence based on the entirety of the record, including any opposition made by the petitioner."[108]

The Board then discussed the threshold requirements for a motion.[109] It noted that "to the extent a patent owner seeks to propose more than one substitute claim for each cancelled claim, the patent owner should explain in the motion to amend the need for the additional claims and why the number of proposed substitute claims is reasonable" and should "specifically identify" each challenged claim a substitute claim is intended to replace," in order to meet the reasonable claims requirement.[110] The Board also explained that "every word added to or removed from a claim" need not be added or removed solely to overcome an instituted ground.[111] Rather, the Board noted, additional modifications to address, for example, eligibility or written description issues, "serve[] the public interest by helping to ensure the patentability of amended claims."[112] The Board noted that a patent owner can avoid improperly enlarging claims if it does not "remove a feature of the claim in a manner that broadens the scope of the claims" and "add[s] a novel and nonobvious feature or combination to avoid the prior art in an instituted ground of unpatentability."[113] The Board did caution patent owners, however, that in setting forth written description and priority support for substitute claims, "citation should be made to the original disclosure of the application, as filed, rather than to the patent as issued," the "written description support must be set forth in the motion to amend itself, not the claim listing," and support must be shown "for each proposed substitute claim as a whole, and not just the features added by the amendment," including for dependent claims.[114] The Board "strongly suggest[ed]" the use of brackets and underlining in the required claim listing to show changes in the substitute claim as compared to the original claim.[115]

108. *Id.*
109. *Id.* at 4–10.
110. *Id.* at 5.
111. *Id.*
112. *Id.* at 6.
113. *Id.* at 6–7.
114. *Id.* at 8.
115. *Id.* at 8–9.

Finally, the rules implement the exercise of discretion discussed by the Board in *Hunting Titan*. In *Hunting Titan*, also precedential, the Board addressed its ability to raise issues sua sponte when addressing motions to amend.[116] The patent owner filed a motion to amend with proposed substitute claims.[117] The petitioner opposed the motion, but its opposition "presented only obviousness arguments, without alleging that the proposed substitute claims were anticipated by the prior art of record."[118] In its final written decision, the Board denied the motion to amend, finding that the proposed substitute claims were anticipated by the same reference that it also found anticipated the original claims.[119]

The patent owner objected, requesting rehearing and Precedential Opinion Panel (POP) review to address whether the Board may raise a ground of unpatentability against proposed substitute claims not developed by the petitioner and whether the parties are entitled to an opportunity to respond to such Board-raised grounds.[120] In its decision, the POP confirmed that the Board may, "in rare circumstances, raise a ground of unpatentability that a petitioner did not advance, or insufficiently developed."[121] The POP reasoned that the Federal Circuit confirmed the Board's ability to raise such grounds in addressing motions to amend.[122] But it ruled that the Board is not obligated to independently examine every proposed substitute claim.[123] And, it reasoned, the Board should do so only rarely. The POP identified several possible situations where it would be appropriate for the Board to raise grounds of unpatentability sua sponte, such as where the petitioner has ceased to participate in the proceeding, the petitioner chooses not to oppose the motion to amend, or the record evidence so clearly provides

116. Hunting Titan, Inc. v. DynaEnergetics Europe GmbH, IPR2018-00600, Paper 67, at 4–5, 13, 25 (July 6, 2020) (Precedential); *see also Patent Trial and Appeal Board Boardside Chat: Recent Developments for AIA Trials* 18, 21, USPTO (Jan. 28, 2021), https://www.uspto.gov/sites/default/files/documents/20200128_ptab_boardside_chat.pdf.

117. *Hunting Titan, Inc.*, IPR2018-00600, Paper 67, at 2.

118. *Id.*

119. *Id.* at 2–3.

120. *Id.* at 3.

121. *Id.* at 4.

122. *Id.* at 7–8 (citing Nike, Inc. v. Adidas AG, 955 F.3d 45, 51 (Fed. Cir. 2020)).

123. *Id.* at 10–12.

evidence of unpatentability that the Board should "take it up in the interest of supporting the integrity of the patent system."[124] The POP found that such circumstances were not present in *Hunting Titan*. It noted that the petitioner "vigorously prosecuted" its case but "affirmatively chose not to raise [the] particular anticipation ground" relied on by the Board as a matter of strategy.[125] And it stated that the record did not provide the type of readily identifiable and persuasive evidence of anticipation necessary to justify the Board's intervention—certain claim limitations were not clearly disclosed in the reference.[126]

The POP further explained that even if the Board should have raised anticipation on its own, the parties lacked fair notice, as mandated by due process considerations.[127] The POP separately ruled that the Board cannot raise a ground of unpatentability for the first time in a final written decision.[128] Nor can the Board adopt a ground of unpatentability against a substitute claim that was asserted against an original claim without providing separate notice to the parties.[129] Whenever the Board raises an issue, the parties are entitled to an opportunity to be heard,[130] and the POP noted several possible ways the Board can provide the required notice and accompanying opportunity to be heard. For example, the Board may request "supplemental briefing from the parties regarding [the Board's] proposed ground for unpatentability" or may request the parties discuss the Board's ground of unpatentability asserted against the substitute claim at an oral hearing.[131]

D. Pilot Program

Overlapping with these cases and development of the regulations, the Board implemented a pilot program for motions to amend in March 2019 that

124. *Id.* at 12–13.
125. *Id.* at 19–20.
126. *Id.* at 20–21.
127. *Id.* at 22.
128. *Id.*
129. *Id.* at 14–15.
130. *Id.* at 14.
131. *Id.* at 15–16.

applies to all AIA proceedings instituted on or after March 15, 2019.[132] In addition to a standard motion to amend, the Motion to Amend Pilot Program provides patent owners the option to receive preliminary guidance from the Board on a proposed set of substitute claims. The preliminary guidance will consider any opposition to the motion filed by the petitioner.[133] And, after receiving the preliminary guidance, the patent owner can file a revised motion to amend.[134]

1. Procedure and Timeline

The procedure and timeline for filing of a motion to amend under the Motion to Amend Pilot Program progress in substantially the same way as under prior procedures but can include additional briefing depending on how the patent owner decides to proceed.[135] And a patent owner must still confer with the Board before filing any motion to amend, even though filing one such motion is a matter of right.

At institution, the Board will issue a scheduling order setting forth the dates for motion to amend briefing.[136] The patent owner's motion to amend will be due on the same day as its response to the petition, which is typically 12 weeks after the institution decision, and the petitioner's opposition to the motion to amend will be due on the same day as its reply to the petition, which is typically 12 weeks later.[137] If the patent owner requests preliminary guidance, the Board will issue its guidance within four weeks after the petitioner's opposition to the motion to amend.[138] The preliminary guidance will "focus on the limitations added . . . and will not address the patentability of the originally challenged claims."[139] It will provide "an initial discussion about whether there is a reasonable likelihood that the [motion]

132. Notice Regarding a New Pilot Program Concerning Motion to Amend Practice and Procedures in Trial Proceedings under the America Invents Act before the Patent Trial and Appeal Board, 84 Fed. Reg. 9,497 (Mar. 15, 2019).

133. *Id.*

134. *Id.*

135. *Id.* at 9,500.

136. *Id.*

137. *Id.*

138. *Id.*

139. *Id.*

meets statutory and regulatory requirements . . . and provide an initial discussion about whether [an opposition] establishes a reasonable likelihood that the substitute claims are unpatentable."[140] Similar to an institution decision, the preliminary guidance will not be binding.[141]

If the patent owner chooses to file a reply to the petitioner's opposition to the motion to amend and the Board's preliminary guidance (if requested), instead of filing a revised motion to amend, the due date for the reply will be the same date as the patent owner's sur-reply to its response, which is typically six weeks after the petitioner's opposition.[142] This timeline is depicted in Figure 6.1.[143]

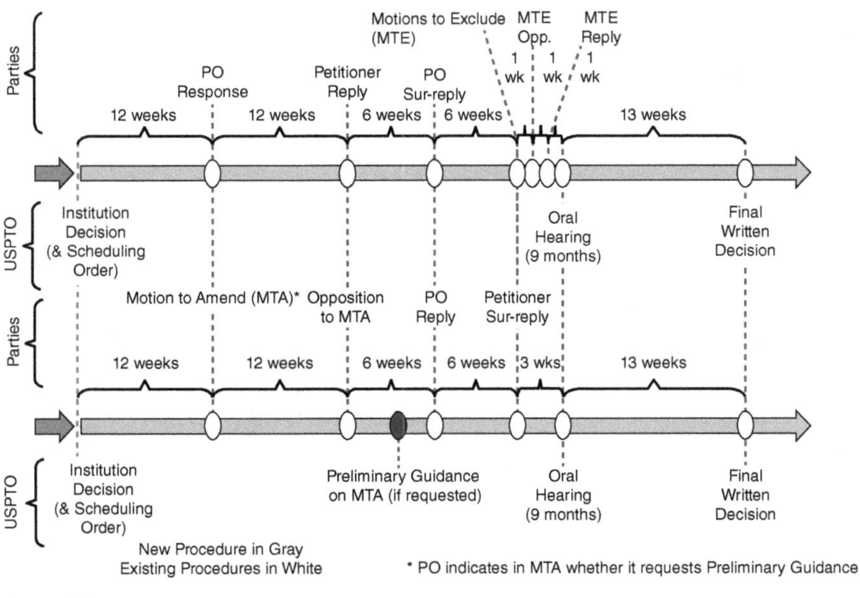

Figure 6.1

140. *Id.*
141. *Id.*
142. *Id.* at 9,500–01.
143. *Id.* at 9,506.

If the patent owner chooses to file a revised motion to amend in view of the petitioner's opposition and the Board's preliminary guidance, the revised motion to amend will be due at the same time as the patent owner's sur-reply, which is typically six weeks after the petitioner's opposition.[144] The revised motion to amend must include "one or more new proposed substitute claims in place of previously presented substitute claims."[145] After the patent owner files a revised motion to amend, the Board will issue a revised scheduling order typically in line with the timeline depicted in Figure 6.2.[146] The revised scheduling order will set the dates for addressing the revised motion to amend, including the petitioner's opposition, the patent owner's reply, the petitioner's sur-reply, and the oral hearing. A patent owner can also withdraw an initial motion to amend, in which case no further briefing will be authorized and the Board will not address the motion in the final written decision.[147]

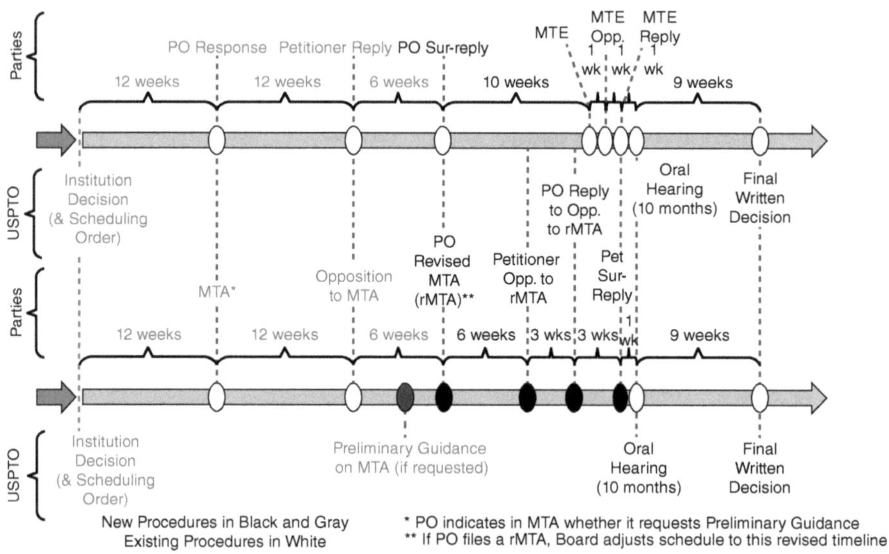

Figure 6.2

144. *Id.* at 9,501.
145. *Id.*
146. *Id.* at 9,507.
147. *Id.* at 9,502.

While the parties have general flexibility to stipulate to new due dates for the briefing concerning the original claims, that is, the patent owner's response, the petitioner's reply, and the patent owner's sur-reply, there are limits to adjusting the briefing schedule for motions because of the overall schedule (including oral hearing) as well as receiving preliminary guidance on a first motion to amend. Thus, the briefing schedule, including discovery periods, for original claims may be offset from the schedule for substitute claims.

2. Evidentiary Considerations

Generally, new evidence, including new prior art and new witness declarations, may be submitted with every paper in the motion to amend process, except for the sur-reply.[148] A sur-reply may only include cross-examination deposition transcripts, that is, deposition testimony from witness declarations submitted with a reply.[149] This allows for serial attempts for the parties to draw out and test positions. It also creates the possibility for numerous expert depositions. In view of the short, three-week deadlines later in the schedule, parties should meet and confer as soon as practicable to confirm deposition scheduling and to make any declarants available for deposition. The Board has explained that "any unavailability [of deponents] will not be a reason to adjust the schedule for briefing on a or revised [motion to amend] absent extraordinary circumstances."[150]

E. Other Issues

1. Written Description, Enablement, Indefiniteness, and Patent Eligibility

Unlike PGR petitions, which may raise any ground of unpatentability, IPR petitions are limited to raising grounds of unpatentability based on prior art patents and printed publications.[151] The grounds of unpatentability

148. *Id.* at 9,500.
149. *Id.*
150. *Id.*
151. *Compare* 35 U.S.C. § 321(b), *with* 35 U.S.C. § 311(b).

that may be raised against proposed amended claims, however, are not limited to grounds of unpatentability based on prior art patents and printed publications.[152] Petitioners may also raise challenges under, inter alia, 35 U.S.C. §§ 101 and 112. Consistent with the allocation of burdens between a patent owner and petitioner,[153] the petitioner bears the burden to show unpatentability for questions of indefiniteness, enablement, and patent eligibility, just as it does for prior art questions of unpatentability.[154] It is important to keep in mind, however, that patent owners bear the burden of showing substitute claims do not enlarge the scope of the original claims and do not introduce new matter,[155] effectively placing the burden on patent owners to show written description.

The Board has addressed whether proposed amended claims comply with 35 U.S.C. § 112 in a number of proceedings.[156] Regarding indefiniteness, the Board has historically applied the indefiniteness standard set forth in *In re Packard* in IPRs involving unexpired patents, which is different from the *Nautilus* standard applied in district court.[157] The Board applied the *Packard* standard because, for several years, the Board also applied the broadest rea-

152. Amazon.com, Inc. v. Uniloc Lux. S.A., IPR2017-00948, Paper 34, at 5 (Jan. 18, 2019) (Precedential) ("By its terms, § 311(b) limits a petitioner to requesting cancellation of *existing* claims of a patent only under § 102 and § 103 . . . . It does not, however, limit the grounds of unpatentability that can be raised in response to proposed substitute amended claims presented in a motion to amend.").

153. Aqua Prods., Inc. v. Matal, 872 F.3d 1290 (Fed. Cir. 2017) (en banc).

154. Bosch Auto. Serv. Sols., LLC v. Matal, 878 F.3d 1027, 1039–40 (Fed. Cir. 2017), *as amended on reh'g in part* (Mar. 15, 2018).

155. 85 Fed. Reg. 82,923, 82,927 (Dec. 21, 2020) (citing 35 U.S.C. §§ 316(d), 326(d); 37 C.F.R. § 42.121(a)(2), (a)(3), (b)(1), (b)(2) (2021), or § 42.221(a)(2), (a)(3), (b)(1), (b)(2) (2021)).

156. *See, e.g.*, Apple Inc. v. Valencell, Inc., IPR2017-00315, Paper 13, at 44 (May 31, 2018) ("[W]e agree with Petitioner that the proposed substitute claims do not pass muster under 35 U.S.C. § 112 because they are indefinite."); Cook Grp., Inc. v. Bos. Sci. Scimed, Inc., IPR2017-00440, Paper 92 (Dec. 28, 2018) ("[W]e determine, based on the final record before us, that Petitioner has not shown, by a preponderance of the evidence, that proposed substitute claims 21, 30, and 38 are unpatentable for failing to comply with the requirements of 35 U.S.C. § 112, ¶¶ 1, 2."); Intel Corp. v. Alacritech, Inc., IPR2017-01409, Paper 79, at 24 (Nov. 14, 2018) ("[W]e are not persuaded by Petitioner that substitute claims 61–78 are indefinite under 35 U.S.C. § 112, second paragraph.").

157. *In re* Packard, 751 F.3d 1307, 1322 (Fed. Cir. 2014) (Plager, J., concurring) ("[A] claim is indefinite when it contains words or phrases whose meaning is unclear."); Nautilus, Inc. v. Biosig Instruments, Inc., 134 S. Ct. 2120, 2129 (2014).

sonable interpretation standard when construing claims. Under the *Packard* standard, "a claim is indefinite when it contains words or phrases whose meaning is unclear."[158] This contrasts with the indefiniteness standard district courts apply. In later cases, however, the Board has applied both the *Packard* and the *Nautilus* indefiniteness standards in addressing indefiniteness.[159] And in January 2021, the Office stated, by memorandum, that the Board will "follow *Nautilus* in AIA post-grant proceedings."[160] Until the Office sets forth formal regulations addressing indefiniteness in PGRs and IPRs, parties should consider addressing indefiniteness under both *Packard* and *Nautilus*.

The Board has also addressed whether proposed amended claims comply with 35 U.S.C. § 101.[161] In *Amazon.com*, for example, the Board concluded that the petitioner failed to show that the proposed amended claims were obvious under 35 U.S.C. § 103 but found the proposed amended claims recited patent-ineligible subject matter under 35 U.S.C. § 101.[162] The Board agreed with an earlier district court finding, affirmed by the Federal Circuit, that the original patent claims were directed to patent-ineligible subject matter under 35 U.S.C. § 101 and found that the proposed amended claims were no different for purposes of 35 U.S.C. § 101.[163]

Moreover, while the primary focus of a motion to amend is to present amendments that are responsive to the instituted ground of unpatentability

---

158. *In re Packard*, 751 F.3d at 1322.

159. *Apple Inc.*, IPR2017-00315, Paper 13, at 44 (applying both *Packard* and *Nautilus*); Shure Inc. v. Clearone, Inc., IPR2017-01785, Paper 91, at 18 (Jan. 24, 2019) ("Although the phrase is broad, it does not fail to 'inform those skilled in the art about the scope of the invention with reasonable clarity,' nor is it unclear.") (citing Nautilus, Inc. v. Biosig Instruments, Inc., 572 U.S. 898, 910 (2014); *In re Packard*, 751 F.3d at 1314); Flir Sys., Inc. v. Garmin Switz. GmbH, IPR2017-00946, Paper 38, at 52 (July 10, 2018) ("We determine, based on the record of this proceeding, that Petitioner has not shown, by a preponderance of the evidence, that proposed claims 73 and 74 are unpatentable as indefinite under 35 U.S.C. § 112, ¶ 2, under either *Packard* or *Nautilus*.").

160. USPTO Memorandum, Approach to Indefiniteness under 35 U.S.C. § 112 in AIA Post-Grant Proceedings 5 (Jan. 6, 2021).

161. Amazon.com, Inc. v. Uniloc Lux. S.A., IPR2017-00948, Paper 31, at 60 (Aug. 1, 2018) (Precedential).

162. *Id.*

163. *Id.* ("Patent Owner's proposed amendments do not change the character of the claims such that they are not abstract.").

and petitioners can raise non-prior-art grounds against substitute claims in IPR proceedings, patent owners should also consider amendments to address potential issues under 35 U.S.C. §§ 101 and 112.[164]

2. Antedating References

As part of a motion to amend, patent owners may attempt to avoid prior art by establishing a date of invention that is earlier than the critical date of the reference. One way to remove a reference as prior art is to "swear behind" the reference by demonstrating an earlier conception and reduction to practice or an earlier conception coupled with diligence to reduction to practice from a time prior to the conception by another.[165] Another way to remove a reference is to claim the benefit of priority of an earlier-filed application that describes the claimed invention in sufficient detail to demonstrate possession of the claimed invention.

For original claims challenged in a petition, the Federal Circuit has held that (under 35 U.S.C. § 316(e)) the petitioner bears the ultimate burden of persuasion to prove unpatentability by a preponderance of the evidence.[166] But the burden of production may shift between the parties. In particular, the petitioner bears the initial burden of production to demonstrate that a reference constitutes prior art with respect to the claimed invention, and if the petitioner meets its burden of production, the burden of production shifts to the patent owner to demonstrate a date of invention that is earlier than the critical date of the reference.[167]

For substitute claims proposed in a motion to amend, however, the patent owner bears the burden to show that the proposed amended claims comply with statutory and regulatory requirements.[168] These requirements

---

164. W. Digit. Corp. v. Spex Techs., Inc., IPR2018-00082, Paper 13, at 6 (Apr. 25, 2018) (Informative) ("[O]nce a proposed claim includes amendments to address a prior art ground in the trial, a patent owner also may include additional limitations to address potential § 101 or § 112 issues, if necessary.").

165. Pre-AIA 35 U.S.C. § 102(g).

166. Dynamic Drinkware, LLC v. Nat'l Graphics, Inc., 800 F.3d 1375, 1378, 1380 (Fed. Cir. 2015).

167. *Id.*

168. Lectrosonics, Inc. v. Zaxcom, Inc., IPR2018-01129, Paper 15, at 4 (Feb. 25, 2019) (Precedential).

include showing, inter alia, that the original specification (and any priority application relied on) provides sufficient written description to support each substitute claim. In particular, the motion to amend "must set forth written description support for each proposed substitute claim as a whole, and not just the features added by the amendment," and this requirement "applies equally to independent claims and dependent claims, even if the only amendment to a dependent claim is in the identification of the claim from which it depends."[169] Accordingly, if the patent owner files a motion to amend, the patent owner bears the burden of demonstrating that the proposed amended claims are entitled to the benefit of priority of an earlier-filed application, whereas the petitioner bears the burden of demonstrating that the original claims are *not* entitled to the benefit of priority of an earlier-filed application. Patent owners also bear the burden when seeking to antedate references on both original[170] and substitute[171] claims. Additionally, patent owners seeking to swear behind a reference should be cognizant that adding limitations in substitute claims may result in a later conception or reduction-to-practice date, which may be different compared to original claims.

169. *Id.* at 8.

170. *See, e.g.*, Motorola Mobility LLC v. Intell. Ventures II LLC, IPR2014-00504, Paper 84, at 14–15 (Mar. 13, 2020).

171. *See, e.g.*, Apple Inc. v. Valencell, Inc., IPR2017-00315, Paper 45, at 44 (May 31, 2018).

Chapter 7

Postinstitution: Oral Argument, Rehearing, Precedential Opinion Panel

This chapter explores oral argument, requests for rehearing, and the Precedential Opinion Panel. Briefing and discovery are discussed in Chapter 5, and motions to amend are explored in Chapter 6.

A. Oral Argument

1. Argument Procedures

The statute provides "either party with the right to an oral hearing as part of the proceeding."[1] Thus, any party can request a hearing before a panel of judges.[2] The request must be filed as a separate paper and must specify the issues to be argued.[3] The requesting party can recommend a time and date for the hearing, but the Board will then set them.[4] In certain circumstances (e.g., during the COVID-19 pandemic), the Board has authorized virtual

---

1. 35 U.S.C. §§ 316(a)(10), 326(a)(10).
2. 37 C.F.R. § 42.70(a); Patent Trial and Appeal Board Consolidated Trial Practice Guide 81–86 (Nov. 2019).
3. *Id.*
4. *See, e.g.*, 77 Fed. Reg. 48,612, 48,646, Response to Comment 193 (Aug. 14, 2012).

hearings in which the judges and the parties participate by WebEx®.[5] Subject to the parties' objection, the hearing is generally open to the public and can be broadcasted by teleconference and/or WebEx®.[6] The Board expects that lead counsel for both parties will be present at the hearing unless good cause is shown for their absence.[7] Lead counsel is not required to argue, as arguments may be presented by any attorney of record.[8] If more than one attorney plans to argue, the Board requests that the parties keep distractions to a minimum when changing presenters.[9]

During the hearing, the petitioner, having the burden to prove unpatentability, usually presents its arguments first, followed by the patent owner.[10] The Board generally allows both parties to reserve time for rebuttal arguments regardless of whether there is a motion to amend.[11] As with most oral arguments before the Board, the judges of the panel may ask questions that direct the discussion. Any rebuttal evidence must be submitted prior to the hearing, as the hearing should reflect oral arguments made and supported in the existing record.[12] When the Board grants a hearing, it will set the amount of time each party will have to present its case.[13]

A party may use demonstratives during the hearing. The rules require that a party must serve its demonstratives at least seven business days before the

---

5. *See, e.g.*, ByteDance Ltd. v. Triller Inc., IPR2021-00099, Paper 24 (Dec. 10, 2021). *See also* Agilent Techs., Inc. v. Bio-Rad Labs., Inc., IPR 2019-00271, Paper 20 (Mar. 13, 2020); Red Diamond, Inc. v. S. Visions LLP, PGR2019-00045, Paper 35 (July 27, 2020).

6. SAP Am., Inc. v. Versata Dev. Grp., Inc., CBM2012-00001, Paper 61 (Apr. 8, 2013).

7. Cyanotech Corp. v. Bd. of Trs. of the Univ. of Ill., IPR2013-00401, Paper 50 (June 18, 2014).

8. *Id.*

9. *Id.*

10. *SAP Am., Inc.*, CBM2012-00001, Paper 66.

11. *See, e.g.*, ByteDance Ltd. v. Triller Inc., IPR2021-00099, Paper 24 (Dec. 10, 2021); *see also* Qualcomm Inc. v. Monterey Rsch., LLC, IPR2021-00130, Paper 25 (Feb. 16, 2022); Apple, Inc. v. LBT IP I LLC, IPR2020-01190, Paper 38 (Nov. 24, 2021).

12. PATENT TRIAL AND APPEAL BOARD CONSOLIDATED TRIAL PRACTICE GUIDE 81–86 (Nov. 2019); *see also* Level 3 Commc'ns, LLC v. AIP Acquisition LLC, IPR2013-00296, Paper 42, at 9–10 (Oct. 8, 2014) (sustaining petitioner's objections to new case law and arguments raised by patent owner for the first time at the oral hearing), *aff'd*, 622 F. App'x 905 (Fed. Cir. 2015).

13. Petroleum Geo-Servs. Inc. v. Westerngeco LLC, IPR2014-00687, Paper 97, at 2 (July 16, 2015) (granting 90 minutes total time for each side in a hearing covering three related, but not joined, cases); K40 Elecs., LLC v. Escort, Inc., IPR2013-00240, Paper 26, at 2 (May 15, 2014) (granting 60 minutes to each side in a hearing for two joined cases); *SAP Am., Inc.*, CBM2012-00001, Paper 62.

hearing and file them no later than the time of the hearing.[14] Generally, the Board specifies the procedure for filing and serving demonstratives in the order authorizing the oral hearing.[15] The Board often requires the parties to file demonstratives on the same day that the parties serve them or a few days later[16] and may allow the parties to stipulate to a different date for serving demonstratives.[17] If a party intends to use electronic demonstratives (e.g., a PowerPoint presentation), they should arrange for such accommodations (e.g., projector and screen, etc.) with the Board prior to the hearing.

A party must request the equipment for demonstratives in writing at least three days in advance of the scheduled hearing, so it can be set up prior to the hearing.[18] At the Alexandria hearing rooms, the Board has an easel, an Elmo projector, a laptop projector, and a screen, which may be requested for oral arguments.[19] For Microsoft PowerPoint and other computer-based presentations, the party must provide its own laptop. Animation and video demonstratives cannot be presented at a hearing without specific prior authorization.[20] Internet access may not be available in the hearing rooms—all information must be stored on the party's laptop (e.g., a hard drive, flash drive, or CD).[21] If a party plans to appear from a hearing room in a satellite USPTO location, the party may contact the Hearings Clerk for any questions about available equipment.[22]

---

14. 37 C.F.R. § 42.70(b).

15. *See, e.g.*, CBS Interactive Inc. v. Helferich Patent Licensing LLC, IPR2013-00033, Paper 118 (Oct. 23, 2013).

16. Organik Kimya AS v. Rohm & Haas Co., IPR2014-00185, Paper 49, at 2 (Jan. 9, 2015) (requiring exhibits to be filed five days in advance of hearing); Chi. Mercantile Exch., Inc. v. 5th Mkt., Inc., CBM2014-00114, Paper 28 (Apr. 15, 2015) (requiring demonstratives to be filed three days before hearing).

17. *SAP Am., Inc.*, CBM2012-00001, Paper 62.

18. *Use of Demonstratives and Exhibits*, USPTO, https://www.uspto.gov/page/use-demonstratives-and-exhibits (last visited Apr. 21, 2022).

19. *Id.*

20. *Id.*

21. *Id.*

22. *Id.*

Parties cannot include live testimony except under circumstances approved by the Board.[23] Either party may request live testimony.[24] In appropriate cases, the Board may authorize or even require live testimony.[25] For example, the Board may require live testimony where the Board considers the demeanor of a witness critical to assessing credibility.[26] In considering requests for live testimony, the Board will make a case-by-case determination and will consider factors such as the importance of the testimony and whether the witness is a fact or expert witness.[27]

The Board has granted live testimony at an oral argument where the patent owner requested permission to present the testimony of its principal fact witness, the sole inventor of the challenged patent, who had previously submitted declarations on antedating of the references.[28] In that case, the Board concluded that the witness's testimony was "key, and may well be case-dispositive."[29] In contrast, the Board has denied a request for live testimony of an expert witness where the credibility or demeanor of the expert went only to the weight of evidence and had no bearing on the scientific reliability of the facts.[30] Where the Board allows such testimony, it does not appear willing to hear additional direct testimony, as that is fixed on the record.[31] Indeed, the Board has issued a precedential decision denying

---

23. PATENT TRIAL AND APPEAL BOARD CONSOLIDATED TRIAL PRACTICE GUIDE 31–32, 85–86 (Nov. 2019).

24. *Id.*; *see also* 80 Fed. Reg. 50,720, 50,736 (Aug. 20, 2015).

25. *See* 37 C.F.R. § 42.53(a).

26. *See* PATENT TRIAL AND APPEAL BOARD CONSOLIDATED TRIAL PRACTICE GUIDE 31–32, 85–86 (Nov. 2019); *but see* Petroleum Geo-Servs. Inc. v. Westerngeco LLC, IPR2014-00687, Paper 97, at 2–3 (July 16, 2015) (denying patent owner's request to present live testimony regarding secondary considerations because petitioner's arguments did attack witness credibility).

27. PATENT TRIAL AND APPEAL BOARD CONSOLIDATED TRIAL PRACTICE GUIDE 31–32, 85–86 (Nov. 2019).

28. K40 Elecs., LLC v. Escort, Inc., IPR2013-00203, Paper 34 (May 21, 2014) (Precedential).

29. *Id.*

30. Edmund Optics, Inc. v. Semrock, Inc., IPR2014-00599, Paper 55, at 4–5 (May 13, 2015).

31. *K40 Elecs., LLC*, IPR2013-00203, Paper 34, at 4 (allowing 30 minutes for cross-examination and 30 minutes for redirect).

a request for the inventor to participate in a hearing without being counsel of record or having previously submitted a declaration.[32]

2. Demonstratives

Demonstratives are not evidence, cannot include new evidence, and cannot refer to evidence that—although in the record—was not discussed in a previously filed paper.[33] Demonstratives may not include any new arguments, and they must fairly characterize the record.[34] A party should include a proper citation to the evidence in the record for each demonstrative slide to show that the demonstrative slide does not present new argument or new evidence.[35] "A party should be able to point specifically to a sentence or two, or even a paragraph, in an appropriate paper to support a demonstrative slide."[36] Different characterizations of the evidence and different inferences drawn from the evidence are new arguments.[37] A party's reliance on declaration testimony in a manner not already presented is a new argument.[38] Demonstratives cannot be used as an opportunity for additional briefing. "There is no proper basis for presenting such additional 'briefings' as demonstrative exhibits, especially if such demonstrative exhibits are to be kept in the official record."[39] Demonstratives cannot present argument based on evidence that was not specifically discussed in any paper before the Board, even if that evidence is already in the record.[40]

---

32. DePuy Synthes Prods., Inc. v. Medidea, L.L.C., IPR2018-00315, Paper 29 (Jan. 23, 2019).

33. St. Jude Med., Cardiology Div., Inc. v. Bd. of Regents of the Univ. of Mich., IPR2013-00041, Paper 65 (Jan. 27, 2014); Organik Kimya AS v. Rohm & Haas Co., IPR2014-00185, Paper 49 (Jan. 9, 2015); EMC Corp. v. Pers. Web Techs., LLC, IPR2013-00085, Paper 70 (Dec. 13, 2013); PATENT TRIAL AND APPEAL BOARD CONSOLIDATED TRIAL PRACTICE GUIDE 84 (Nov. 2019).

34. *St. Jude Med., Cardiology Div., Inc.*, IPR2013-00041, Paper 65; PATENT TRIAL AND APPEAL BOARD CONSOLIDATED TRIAL PRACTICE GUIDE 84 (Nov. 2019).

35. CBS Interactive Inc. v. Helferich Patent Licensing, LLC, IPR2013-00033, Paper 118, at 4 (Oct. 23, 2013).

36. *Id.*

37. *Id.*

38. Medtronic, Inc. v. Barry, IPR2015-00783, Paper 48, at 3 (May 13, 2016).

39. *CBS Interactive Inc.*, IPR2013-00033, Paper 118.

40. St. Jude Med., Cardiology Div., Inc. v. Bd. of Regents of the Univ. of Mich., IPR2013-00041, Paper 65, at 2–3 (Jan. 27, 2014).

Because demonstratives are filed as a single paper, the Board has discretion whether to allow presentation of all or none of the slides, if it would be burdensome to sift through a party's objections.[41] The Board allows the parties to file objections to demonstratives, and the oral argument order typically sets forth a particular panel's method for handling those objections.[42] For example, the Board may require the parties to initiate a conference call prior to the hearing to resolve any outstanding objections.[43] The Board also may permit the parties to file objections prior to the hearing and, if necessary, will conduct a conference call to resolve those objections prior to the hearing.[44] Alternatively, the Board may reserve its resolution of any objections until after the oral hearing.[45]

Parties should bear in mind that some judges may appear remotely from other locations.[46] It is incumbent on the parties to ensure that any demonstratives used during an oral hearing are visible and available to all judges on the panel.[47] For example, demonstrative exhibits displayed on an easel or via a projector may not be able to be seen by judges participating remotely.[48] Those remote judges will refer to the electronic copy of the demonstrative exhibit provided by the party in advance or to a copy of the relevant document as it appears in the record.[49] As such, parties should also clearly identify during the oral hearing any demonstrative exhibit to which they are referring to enable all judges participating in the hearing to follow along with the argument being presented.[50] It is important for the parties to number the demonstrative slides.

41. *CBS Interactive Inc.*, IPR2013-00033, Paper 118.

42. *See, e.g.*, *id.*

43. *See, e.g.*, Chi. Mercantile Exch., Inc. v. 5th Mkt., Inc., CBM2014-00114, Paper 28 (Apr. 15, 2015).

44. *See, e.g.*, Organik Kimya AS v. Rohm & Haas Co., IPR2014-00185, Paper 49 (Jan. 9, 2015).

45. *Id.*

46. *Use of Demonstratives and Exhibits*, USPTO, https://www.uspto.gov/page/use-demonstratives-and-exhibits (last visited Apr. 21, 2022).

47. *Id.*

48. *Id.*

49. *Id.*

50. *Id.*

3. Legal Experience Advancement Program

The Legal Experience Advancement Program (LEAP) is a program developed and implemented by the Office to provide training and oral advocacy opportunities for less experienced advocates to gain practical experience in proceedings before the Board.[51] LEAP went into effect on May 15, 2020. It is open to any patent agent or attorney with three or fewer substantive oral arguments in any federal tribunal, including the Board.[52] To participate in LEAP, a practitioner must submit a Request and a Verification form to the Board at least five business days before the hearing.[53] Practitioners must not submit a Request or Verification form until the Board has assigned an oral hearing date for the proceeding in which LEAP participation is requested.[54] If a hearing date has not been assigned, the request will be denied as premature.[55]

A LEAP practitioner may conduct the entire oral argument or may share time with other counsel, provided that the LEAP practitioner is offered a meaningful and substantive opportunity to argue.[56] It remains within the party's discretion as to the type and quantity of oral argument that will be conducted by the LEAP practitioner.[57] For example, a LEAP practitioner might present the party's entire argument or might argue a more limited issue, for example, claim construction arguments, motions to exclude evidence, or patentability arguments.[58] Regardless of whether a LEAP practitioner conducts the entire argument, the Board will permit more experienced counsel to assist a LEAP practitioner, if necessary, during oral argument and to clarify any statements on the record before the conclusion of the oral argument.[59] Parties who participate in the program may be granted

51. *Legal Experience and Advancement Program (LEAP)*, USPTO, https://www.uspto.gov/patents/ptab/leap (last visited Apr. 21, 2022).

52. *Id.*

53. *Id.*

54. *Id.*

55. *Id.*

56. *Id.*

57. *Id.*

58. *Id.*

59. *Id.*

up to 15 minutes additional argument time depending on the length of the proceeding and the Board's hearing schedule.[60]

B. Rehearing Procedures

A party dissatisfied with a decision may file a single request for rehearing without prior authorization from the Board.[61] Any request must be filed within 14 days of the entry of a nonfinal decision or a decision to institute a trial as to at least one ground of unpatentability asserted in the petition or within 30 days of the entry of a final decision or a decision not to institute a trial.[62] The party seeking rehearing bears the burden to show where the decision should be modified.[63] The request "must specifically identify all matters the party believes the Board misapprehended or overlooked, and the place where each matter was previously addressed in a motion, an opposition, or a reply."[64] The Board reviews the decision for an abuse of discretion.[65]

The Board has explained that a request for rehearing of a decision is "not an opportunity to express disagreement with a decision" or "to re-argue a case."[66] The Board will not consider new arguments presented for the first time in a request for rehearing.[67] The Board also will not allow a party to use a request for rehearing to pursue an argument that it previously waived.[68] The Board has granted rehearing when the Board overlooked or misappre-

60. *Id.*
61. 37 C.F.R. § 42.71(d).
62. *Id.* § 42.71(d)(1)(2).
63. *Id.* § 42.71(d).
64. *Id.*
65. 37 C.F.R. § 42.71(c).
66. Corning Inc. v. DSM IP Assets B.V., IPR2013-00043, IPR2013-00044, Paper 101, at 2 (Aug. 12, 2014), *aff'd*, 616 F. App'x 421 (Fed. Cir. 2015); SAP Am., Inc. v. Versata Dev. Grp., Inc., CBM2012-00001, Paper 81, at 5 (Sept. 13, 2013).
67. Elec. Frontier Found. v. Pers. Audio, LLC, IPR2014-00070, Paper 45, at 4 (July 17, 2015); Autoquip Inc. v. Graco Minn., Inc., IPR2013-00452, Paper 20, at 3–4 (Apr. 16, 2015); *Corning Inc.*, IPR2013-00043, IPR2013-00044, Paper 101, at 6–7 (reasoning that party cannot use a rehearing to incorporate new arguments from a related IPR); *SAP Am., Inc.*, CBM2012-00001, Paper 81, at 7.
68. *SAP Am., Inc.*, CBM2012-00001, Paper 81, at 3–4.

hended a distinction between the challenged claims.[69] Alternatively, rather than seeking rehearing by the Board, a party dissatisfied with a final written decision may request review by the Director, under the interim Director review procedure, as discussed next. Also, a party dissatisfied with a final written decision of the Board may directly appeal that decision to the U.S. Court of Appeals for the Federal Circuit or may appeal following a decision on a request for rehearing or decision on Director review, as discussed in Chapter 8.[70]

The Office has implemented an interim procedure for Director review, following the Supreme Court's decision in *United States v. Arthrex*.[71] In *Arthrex*, the Supreme Court held "that 35 U.S.C. § 6(c) is unenforceable as applied to the Director insofar as it prevents the Director from reviewing the decisions of the PTAB on his own. The Director may engage in such review and reach his own decision."[72] Thus, *Arthrex* provides the Director authority to unilaterally review a PTAB final decision by rehearing. Following that decision, the Office implemented an interim Director review procedure.[73] Under this procedure, the Director may review a final written decision on the Director's own accord or in response to a party's request for Director review.[74] Parties may request Director review of a final written decision in an inter partes review or a post-grant review within 30 days of entry of a final written decision by concurrently entering a Request for Rehearing by the Director into the PTAB's filing system—PTAB E2E—and submitting a notification of the Request for Rehearing by the Director to the Office by email.[75] A party cannot make new arguments or submit new evidence with

69. Valeo N. Am., Inc. v. Magna Elecs., Inc., IPR2014-00220, Paper 61 (July 14, 2015) (concluding that Board misapprehended that claim 9 was narrower than claim 7 and as a result could not be held unpatentable for the "same reasons" as claim 7).

70. 35 U.S.C. §§ 319, 329 (referencing 35 U.S.C. §§ 141–144); 35 U.S.C. § 141(c); Versata Dev. Grp. v. SAP Am., Inc., 793 F.3d 1306 (Fed. Cir. 2015).

71. *Interim Process for Director Review*, USPTO, https://www.uspto.gov/patents/patent-trial-and-appeal-board/interim-process-director-review (last visited May 23, 2022); United States v. Arthrex, Inc., 141 S. Ct. 1041 (2021).

72. *Arthrex, Inc.*, 141 S. Ct. 1041.

73. *Interim Process for Director Review*, *supra* note 71.

74. *Id.*

75. *Id.*; *Arthrex Q&As*, USPTO, https://www.uspto.gov/patents/patent-trial-and-appeal-board/procedures/arthrex-qas (last updated Dec. 4, 2021).

a Request for Rehearing by the Director.[76] Once the request is submitted, the Director may deny or partially or entirely grant the request.

Through March 7, 2022, Director rehearing was granted three times:

- Proppant Express Invs., LLC v. Oren Techs., LLC, IPR2018-00733, Paper 95 (Nov. 18, 2021) (Director vacated and remanded the Board's unpatentability finding because it failed to give the necessary weight to objective evidence of nonobviousness).
- Ascend Performance Materials Ops. LLC v. Samsung SDI Co., Ltd., IPR2020-00349, Paper 57 (Nov. 1, 2021) (Director vacated and remanded the Board's unpatentability finding because it failed to address the claims in view of their corresponding priority date).
- Apple Inc. v. Personalized Media Comm'cns, LLC, IPR2016-00754, Paper 50 (Mar. 3, 2022) (Director vacated and remanded the Board's unpatentability finding so it could address its claim construction in light of a Federal Circuit decision in another case between the parties).

C. Precedential Opinion Panel

The Precedential Opinion Panel (POP) is a special type of panel created by the Office on September 20, 2018.[77] The POP members are selected by the Director and by default shall consist of the Director, the Commissioner for Patents, and the Chief Judge of the PTAB. The three members of the POP may each decide to delegate their authority in certain circumstances.[78] The Director (or the Director's delegate) may determine that a panel of more than three members is appropriate in certain circumstances.[79] The POP may be convened to rehear matters in pending trials and appeals on issues of exceptional importance and may assist the Director in determining

76. *Arthrex Q&As*, *supra* note 75.

77. *Revisions to Standard Operating Procedures: Paneling and Precedential Decisions*, USPTO, https://www.uspto.gov/patents/ptab/procedures/revisions-standard-operating (last visited Apr. 25, 2022).

78. STANDARD OPERATING PROCEDURE 2 (rev. 10): PRECEDENTIAL OPINION PANEL TO DECIDE ISSUES OF EXCEPTIONAL IMPORTANCE INVOLVING POLICY OR PROCEDURE 4 (Sept. 20, 2018) [hereinafter SOP 2].

79. *Id.*

whether a decision previously issued by the Board should be designated as precedential or informative.[80]

The POP is intended to establish binding agency authority concerning major policy or procedural issues or other issues of exceptional importance in the limited situations where it is appropriate to create such binding agency authority through adjudication before the Board.[81] For example, and among other things, the POP may be used to address constitutional questions; important issues regarding statutes, rules, and regulations; important issues regarding binding or precedential case law; or issues of broad applicability to the Board. The POP also may be used to resolve conflicts between Board decisions, to promote certainty and consistency, or to rehear any case it determines warrants the Panel's attention.[82]

A party to a proceeding may recommend POP review of a particular Board decision in that proceeding.[83] The recommendation must be submitted by email.[84] The recommendation must identify with particularity the reasons for recommending POP review and must be accompanied by a request for rehearing filed with the Board, which must satisfy the requirements of 37 C.F.R. § 41.52(a) or § 42.71(d), as applicable, including the due dates set forth therein. Counsel for all other parties must be included as recipients of the email.[85] In addition, the email must contain a statement of counsel stating the counsel's belief that the Board's decision is contrary to a specific decision; is contrary to a specific provision, statute, or regulation; or requires an answer to one or more precedent-setting questions of exceptional importance.[86]

A screening committee will review the recommendation and forward its recommendation to the Director.[87] The Director will convene a POP to

80. *Revisions to Standard Operating Procedures*, *supra* note 77.
81. SOP 2, *supra* note 78, at 3.
82. *Id.* at 3–4.
83. *Id.* at 5.
84. *Id.*
85. *Id.*
86. *Id.* at 5–6.
87. *Id.* at 6.

decide whether to grant rehearing and, if rehearing is granted, to render a decision on rehearing in the case.[88]

If POP review is ordered, the POP will identify the issues the POP intends to resolve and the composition of the panel, may request additional briefing on identified issues, may authorize the filing of amicus briefs, and may order an oral hearing.[89] Once the case has been assigned to the POP, the POP will render a decision in the case resolving the identified issues.[90] The decisions resulting from POP review will be designated as precedential, informative, or routine.[91] A precedential decision, as the name indicates, is binding agency authority for similar future matters.[92] A decision is designated as informative when it meets certain criteria, for example, (1) providing Board norms on recurring issues; (2) providing guidance on issues of first impression to the Board; (3) providing guidance on Board rules and practices; or (4) providing guidance on issues that may develop through analysis of recurring issues in many cases (e.g., factors to consider on institution decisions).[93] Every Board decision, other than a POP decision, is a routine decision until it is designated as precedential or informative.[94] If the Director determines that a particular Board decision should no longer be designated as precedential or informative, the subject Board decision will be de-designated.[95] The Chief Judge will notify the Board that the decision has been de-designated, the decision will be removed from the Board's Precedential and Informative Decisions web page, and the public will be notified that the decision has been de-designated.[96]

Through early 2022, POP was ordered in five cases:[97]

88. *Id.* at 7.
89. *Id.*
90. *Id.*
91. *Id.* at 8–9.
92. *Id.*
93. *Id.*
94. *Id.* at 8.
95. *Id.* at 8, 12.
96. *Id.*
97. *Precedential Opinion Panel*, USPTO, https://www.uspto.gov/patents/ptab/decisions/precedential-opinion-panel (last visited Apr. 25, 2022).

- Toshiba Am. Elec. Components, Inc. v. Monument Peak Ventures, LLC, IPR2021-00330, Paper 20 (Jan. 14, 2022) (AIA § 312(a)(1), Fedwire confirmation as evidence supporting payment of petition filing fee) (Precedential).
- Hunting Titan, Inc. v. DynaEnergetics Europe GmbH, IPR2018-00600, Paper 67 (July 6, 2020) (AIA § 316(d), Board may raise a ground of unpatentability that a petitioner did not advance against substitute claims under certain rare circumstances) (Precedential).
- GoPro, Inc. v. 360Heros, Inc., IPR2018-01754, Paper 38 (Aug. 23, 2019) (AIA § 315(b), one-year time bar triggered after the service of a complaint, regardless of whether the serving party lacked standing to sue or the pleading was otherwise deficient) (Precedential).
- Hulu, LLC, v. Sound View Innovations, LLC, IPR2018-01039, Paper 29 (Dec. 20, 2019) (AIA § 311(b), for purposes of institution, a petitioner must show a reasonable likelihood that an asserted reference qualifies as a printed publication) (Precedential).
- Proppant Express Invs., LLC v. Oren Techs. LLC, IPR2018-00914, Paper 38 (Mar. 13, 2019) (AIA § 315(c), same party and issue joinder) (Precedential).

Chapter 8

Appeals[1]

The Leahy-Smith America Invents Act (AIA) provides for direct appeal from the Board to the Federal Circuit from a final written decision.[2] During fiscal years 2012–2013, less than 150 matters per year from the Office were appealed to the Federal Circuit.[3] By 2021, the number of appeals increased to over 500 appeals per year.[4]

The Federal Circuit and Supreme Court have decided several important issues that affect these proceedings, including the Federal Circuit's jurisdiction to hear certain issues on appeal, the relevant standards of review on appeal, and the appropriate stay analysis for district court cases that have parallel PTAB proceedings.

A. Standing and Jurisdiction to Appeal

1. Standing to Appeal

Because the Constitution limits judicial power to cases or controversies,[5] a party must have Article III standing before a federal court will consider the

---

1. The authors thank J. Derek McCorquindale, Jason Romrell, Michelle Rice, Yicong Du, and Melissa Santos for their significant contributions in developing this chapter.

2. 35 U.S.C. §§ 319, 329.

3. *See Appeals Filed in Major Origins*, U.S. Ct. App. for the Fed. Cir., https://cafc.uscourts.gov/wp-content/uploads/reports-stats/Historical_Caseload_by_Origin_FY21.pdf (last visited May 23, 2022).

4. *Id.*

5. U.S. Const. art. III, § 2.

merits of a case. To establish standing, a party seeking judicial review must have (1) suffered an injury in fact (2) that is fairly traceable to the opposing party's challenged conduct and (3) that would likely be redressed by a favorable judicial decision.[6] Standing requirements, however, do not apply to parties appearing before administrative agencies, such as the USPTO.[7] Thus, no standing is necessary to appear before the Board. When seeking judicial review of an adverse Board decision, however, an appellant must supply proof of standing for the Federal Circuit to consider the appeal.[8]

Since 2019, the Supreme Court has denied several certiorari petitions[9] seeking review of the Federal Circuit's dismissal of appeals from the Board based on lack of standing, most recently in *Argentum*.[10] The Federal Circuit's case law therefore remains controlling on standing.

a. *General Legal Standards*

An appellant bears the burden to show standing. To do so, it must create a sufficient evidentiary record in the Federal Circuit if standing is not self-evident from the record before the Board. Standing is self-evident and unlikely to be challenged when, for example, a patent owner has lost an IPR challenge or when a petitioner has lost an IPR challenge to a patent that it has been accused of infringing. When the record before the Board is inadequate, however, the appellant must supplement the record with additional evidence to substantiate its entitlement to judicial review.[11] This additional evidence may take the form of declarations and documents establishing injury in fact. In *E.I. du Pont*,[12] for example, DuPont and ADM submitted declaration testimony regarding their construction of a pilot plant that potentially implicated the patent at issue. The court found that DuPont and

6. Spokeo, Inc. v. Robins, 136 S. Ct. 1540, 1547 (2016).
7. Consumer Watchdog v. Wis. Alumni Rsch. Found., 753 F.3d 1258, 1261 (Fed. Cir. 2014).
8. *Id.*; *see also* Phigenix, Inc. v. ImmunoGen, Inc., 845 F.3d 1168, 1171–72 (Fed. Cir. 2017).
9. *See, e.g.*, Gen. Elec. Co. v. Raytheon Techs. Corp., 140 S. Ct. 2820 (2020); JTEKT Corp. v. GKN Auto. Ltd., 139 S. Ct. 2713 (2019); RPX Corp. v. ChanBond LLC, 139 S. Ct. 2713 (2019).
10. Argentum Pharms. LLC v. Novartis Pharms. Corp., 141 S. Ct. 1685 (2021).
11. AVX Corp. v. Presidio Components, Inc., 923 F.3d 1357, 1362 (Fed. Cir. 2019).
12. E.I. du Pont de Nemours & Co. v. Synvina C.V., 904 F.3d 996 (Fed. Cir. 2018).

ADM had established standing to appeal and reversed the Board's decision, holding all challenged claims unpatentable for obviousness.

With respect to timing, because standing is a threshold question over the court's power to hear a case, generally an appellant must identify or submit evidence in support of standing at the first appropriate time, whether in response to a motion to dismiss or in the appellant's opening brief.[13] Standing must also be maintained throughout an appeal to avoid mootness. For example, in *Momenta*,[14] Momenta appealed after an unsuccessful IPR challenge to Bristol-Meyer Squibb's patent on abatacept. During the appeal, Momenta withdrew development of its abatacept biosimilar. Bristol-Meyer Squibb challenged Momenta's standing based on a Momenta press release and statement filed with the Securities and Exchange Commission regarding termination of relevant commercial activities. The Federal Circuit dismissed Momenta's appeal, holding that the cessation of potentially infringing activities meant that Momenta no longer had the potential for injury, depriving it of standing to appeal.[15]

b. Proving or Challenging Injury in Fact

The injury requirement remains a focal point of the standing analysis. To show an injury, an appellant must demonstrate "an invasion of a legally protected interest" that is "concrete and particularized" and "actual or imminent, not conjectural or hypothetical."[16] The injury requirement, and standing in general, has primarily been a concern for petitioners before the Board.

Patent owners generally will have standing to appeal Board decisions that hold their patent claims unpatentable. The injury to a patent owner should be self-evident given the potential loss of its patent rights. Patent owners, however, should be mindful that they must also maintain standing throughout an appeal. For example, transfer of patent rights, such as

13. *See, e.g.*, *Phigenix, Inc.*, 845 F.3d at 1173; Apple Inc. v. Qualcomm Inc., 992 F.3d 1378, 1382 (Fed. Cir. 2021).

14. Momenta Pharm., Inc. v. Bristol-Myers Squibb Co., 915 F.3d 764 (Fed. Cir. 2019).

15. *Id.* at 770.

16. Lujan v. Defenders of Wildlife, 504 U.S. 555, 560–61 (1992) (internal quotation marks omitted).

assignment to a third party, could moot any injury and deprive the (now former) patent owner of standing.

A patent challenger seeking to appeal an unfavorable Board decision must submit sufficient evidence demonstrating injury to obtain review at the Federal Circuit. If the appellant has been accused of infringing the challenged patent, it can show injury based on this potential infringement liability. Absent existing infringement allegations, patent-challenger appellants have sought to establish injury based on the risk of current or future infringement, economic harm, competitive or reputational injury, and the estoppel effect under 35 U.S.C. § 315. However, of these various arguments, evidence of potential infringement liability has been most persuasive in establishing standing to appeal.

i. Potential Infringement Liability

Whether an appellant is currently engaged in potentially infringing activities is a primary injury-in-fact consideration. For example, in *Google*,[17] LGE and Google appealed after unsuccessfully challenging a patent directed to location information services. Recognizing that both appellants currently marketed and sold products implicating the patent, the Federal Circuit found their risk of infringement to be concrete and substantial.

A lack of current infringing activity does not preclude standing. However, if an appellant relies on potential future infringement liability as a basis for injury in fact, it must show concrete plans for future activity that would likely lead to an infringement claim. For example, in *GE v. UTC*,[18] the Federal Circuit rejected GE's injury argument based on future harm, because GE did not demonstrate definite plans to use the claimed features of the challenged patent, and the patent owner had not sued or threatened to sue GE based on that patent. In contrast, the court later found standing in *GE v. Raytheon*,[19] because GE supplied sufficient evidence showing its concrete plans, raising a future infringement risk, and addressed the evidentiary

17. Google LLC v. Conversant Wireless Licensing S.A.R.L., 753 F. App'x 890 (Fed. Cir. 2018).
18. General Elec. Co. v. United Techs. Corp., 928 F.3d 1349 (Fed. Cir. 2019).
19. General Elec. Co. v. Raytheon Techs. Corp., 983 F.3d 1334 (Fed. Cir. 2020).

deficiencies in the previous appeal. GE provided evidence showing it had conceived a design that would arguably fall within the scope of the claims, alleged ongoing expenditures to refine that design, and identified a program where it submitted that design for bidding.[20]

To prove an injury through potential infringement liability, an appellant must also show an infringement risk borne by and personal to the appellant itself. That is, the appellant must be the entity that has performed or will perform the allegedly infringing activity and that would bear the potential liability for any infringement. For instance, in *Argentum v. Novartis*,[21] Argentum appealed a Board decision upholding the patentability of a Novartis patent related to Novartis's Gilenya® drug. Argentum argued that because it was pursuing a potentially infringing generic version of Gilenya®, it faced an imminent litigation threat. Argentum's CEO, however, testified that the Abbreviated New Drug Application (ANDA) for the generic drug would be filed by Argentum's partner KVK and, when that occurred, Novartis would sue KVK, not Argentum. The court therefore rejected Argentum's infringement-risk argument based on the lack of any evidence that Argentum itself bore any infringement liability or risk.

An appellant's standing evidence must sufficiently describe the potentially infringing product features or other activities to enable the court to assess the infringement risk. In *Pfizer v. Chugai*,[22] for instance, Pfizer appealed the Board's decisions upholding the patentability of two Chugai patents. To show injury, Pfizer argued that Chugai might accuse Pfizer's rituximab biosimilar product of infringing those patents. Pfizer submitted evidence that the FDA had approved its biosimilar and that it planned to sell the biosimilar in the United States. The court held, however, that Pfizer failed to show any infringement risk because its evidence did not allow the court to evaluate whether it practiced or intended to practice the patented methods in making the biosimilar product. *Apple v. Qualcomm*[23] provides another example stressing the importance of a sufficient evidentiary showing

20. *Id.* at 1344.
21. Argentum Pharm. LLC v. Novartis Pharm. Corp., 956 F.3d 1374 (Fed. Cir. 2020).
22. Pfizer Inc. v. Chugai Pharm. Co., 812 F. App'x 979 (Fed. Cir. 2020).
23. Apple Inc. v. Qualcomm Inc., 992 F.3d 1378 (Fed. Cir. 2021).

when relying on potential infringement risk. There, Apple appealed from the Board's decisions upholding validity of certain Qualcomm patents. To show standing, Apple argued that Qualcomm might sue Apple after a license involving those patents expires. The court found that the alleged possibility of suit was too speculative to confer standing. It held that Apple "provide[d] no evidence that it intends to engage in any activity that may give rise to an infringement suit . . . when the license expires." Additionally, the "declarations Apple submitted as evidence of standing [did not] even mention the patents at issue" and were "devoid of any of the specificity necessary to establish an injury in fact."[24] To cure the deficiencies of its evidence, Apple asked the court to take judicial notice that Apple would continue to sell its smartphones. The court rejected that request, stating that "[w]hat products and product features Apple may be selling at the expiration of the license agreement years from now are not the kind of undisputed facts we may take judicial notice of because they may be reasonably questioned."[25]

In evaluating injury contentions based on infringement risk, the court has also considered the parties' past conduct, such as previous activities and suits involving the challenged patent. Past potentially infringing activities, even if discontinued, may still create a controversy of "sufficient immediacy and reality" between the parties to confer standing.[26] For example, if the statute of limitations has not run, a patent owner may still assert infringement. "[T]he mere fact that [past] actions have not continued to the present does not necessarily dissipate a controversy over those actions."[27]

A patent owner's past infringement allegations against an appellant or a third party carrying similar products and its refusal to grant a covenant not to sue can help prove that the appellant's infringement risk is not spec-

24. *Id.* at 1384.
25. *Id.* at 1384–85.
26. Grit Energy Sols., LLC v. Oren Techs., LLC, 957 F.3d 1309, 1320 (Fed. Cir. 2020).
27. *Id.*

ulative or conjectural.[28] On the other hand, if the patent owner grants the appellant a covenant not to sue, the appeal may be mooted.[29]

In *Adidas v. Nike*,[30] for example, the court held that Adidas had standing to appeal the Board's decisions upholding the patentability of two Nike patents, although Nike had not sued or threatened to sue Adidas for infringement. The court pointed out that in 2012, Nike had asserted that Adidas's Primeknit footwear infringed one of its German patents and that Nike had expressed its intent to "protect [its] rights globally in the future against further infringing acts" by Adidas.[31] Nike had also asserted one of the challenged U.S. patents against a third-party product similar to Adidas's footwear. In addition, Nike had refused to grant Adidas a covenant not to sue, which confirmed that Adidas's risk of infringement was "concrete and substantial."[32]

ii. Economic Harm

Appellants have so far had little success in relying on economic harm to establish standing to appeal to the Federal Circuit. To prove an injury through economic harm, an appellant must show investments or losses that directly implicate, or are caused by, the challenged patent. Conclusory statements of economic harm will not pass muster under the court's scrutiny.

An appellant must detail any investments or losses that can be tied to its development of potentially infringing products or design-arounds, separate from costs attributed to unrelated products. This evidence can include, for example, documentation of changes to product features, facilities, or activities to avoid the patent; business plans discussing such changes; and directly associated expenses. On the other hand, when an appellee seeks to

28. *See, e.g.*, Choirock Contents Factory Co. v. Saucier, 801 F. App'x 754, 762 (Fed. Cir. 2020) (holding that the patent owner's past allegations against another entity carrying similar toy products as the appellant, and its refusal to grant appellant a covenant not to sue, showed the appellant's risk of liability was "not conjectural or hypothetical").

29. *See, e.g.*, PPG Indus. v. Valspar Sourcing, Inc., 679 F. App'x 1002 (Fed. Cir. 2017) (concluding that, although PPG did initially have standing to bring the appeal, the controversy as to the patented subject matter had been mooted by Valspar's unilateral covenant not to sue).

30. Adidas AG v. Nike, Inc., 963 F.3d 1355 (Fed. Cir. 2020).

31. *Id.* at 1357.

32. *Id.*

refute an appellant's economic injury arguments, the appellee should attack any general claims of economic harm as insufficiently tied to the challenged patent. In *GE v. UTC*,[33] for example, the court rejected GE's broad claim of economic loss as lacking support and thus insufficient to confer standing. The court found that GE had provided no "details" such as an "accounting for the additional research and development costs" caused by the challenged patent or any evidence that it actually designed a product covered by the challenged patent.[34]

The court reiterated the stringent evidentiary demands for economic injury in *Argentum v. Novartis*.[35] There, Argentum asserted that it would incur significant economic losses given its investments in developing a generic drug and preparing an ANDA. To support its position, Argentum submitted declarations from its CEO and the CEO of KVK, Argentum's manufacturing and marketing partner. The court found that evidence insufficient. Referring to admissions in the declarations, the court pointed out that Argentum's purported investments included KVK's renovation of manufacturing facilities intended for other drugs, not only the generic drug at issue. The court found that Argentum had provided only "generalities" about its invested resources, costs, and joint development efforts with KVK and that such general statements failed to show that Argentum had invested in the generic drug at issue.[36] Citing its CEO's testimony, Argentum also asserted that it would suffer lost profits of $10 to $50 million per year once the FDA approved the ANDA. The court, however, rejected that assertion as "both conclusory and speculative."[37]

iii. Estoppel Injury

Section 315 of the Patent Act limits the ability of a petitioner in a PTAB proceeding to subsequently assert any patentability challenges that the petitioner raised or could have raised in the proceeding. Appellants have often

33. Gen. Elec. Co. v. United Techs. Corp., 928 F.3d 1349 (Fed. Cir. 2019).
34. *Id.* at 1354.
35. Argentum Pharm. LLC v. Novartis Pharm. Corp., 956 F.3d 1374 (Fed. Cir. 2020).
36. *Id.* at 1378.
37. *Id.*

raised this potential estoppel effect in their injury arguments. The Federal Circuit, however, has consistently held that, if an appellant is not engaged in any activities that could give rise to infringement liability, the potential estoppel effect under section 315 does not constitute an injury sufficient to support standing.

The court has reiterated this principle in several cases.[38] In *Pfizer v. Chugai*,[39] for instance, Pfizer contended that the estoppel effect of section 315 enhanced its stake in the outcome of the case and helped show injury. The court rejected that contention, holding that "the estoppel provision does not constitute an injury in fact" when there was "no evidence that [Pfizer] was or is engaged in any activity that would give rise to a possible infringement suit."[40] In *Google v. Conversant*,[41] estoppel injury was also alleged, and there the court held that standing was established. Importantly, however, the court had already found that LGE and Google had engaged in potentially infringing activities such that their risk of infringement was concrete and substantial.

iv. Other Types of Injury

In the pharmaceutical area, the listing of an innovator drug company's patent in the FDA's Orange Book may help create a cognizable injury. In *Amerigen v. UCB*,[42] UCB owned a patent related to Toviaz®, which was listed in the Orange Book, and Amerigen had submitted a Paragraph III certification for the patent, which meant that the FDA would approve Amerigen's ANDA for a competing drug only after the patent expired. After unsuccessfully challenging the patent in an IPR, Amerigen appealed. The Federal Circuit held that Amerigen had a concrete, economic interest in future sales of its tentatively approved drug and therefore had demonstrated a sufficiently immediate controversy for standing. The court explained that if Amerigen

38. *See, e.g.*, AVX Corp. v. Presidio Components, Inc., 923 F.3d 1357, 1362–63 (Fed. Cir. 2019).

39. Pfizer Inc. v. Chugai Pharm. Co., 812 F. App'x 979 (Fed. Cir. 2020).

40. *Id.* at 982.

41. Google LLC v. Conversant Wireless Licensing S.A.R.L., 753 F. App'x 890 (Fed. Cir. 2018).

42. Amerigen Pharm. Ltd. v. UCB Pharma GmbH, 913 F.3d 1076 (Fed. Cir. 2019).

successfully challenged the patent and had it delisted from the Orange Book, it could potentially launch its proposed generic drug product at a substantially earlier date.

Some appellants have argued injury in fact based on the potential effect of Board decisions on the appellant's (usually the patent challenger's) ability to compete in the market. However, if the appellant is not engaged in conduct implicating the patent (or does not have nonspeculative plans to do so), the alleged competitive harm may be insufficient to constitute the concrete interest required for standing. For example, in *AVX v. Presidio*,[43] IPR petitioner AVX appealed from the Board's decision upholding a capacitor patent owned by competitor Presidio. In support of standing, AVX submitted a declaration from its general counsel explaining AVX's investment in capacitors, previous litigations between the two competitors, and his belief that the threat of future litigation over the challenged patent was substantial. The Federal Circuit rejected AVX's argument that the Board's decision reduced AVX's ability to compete with Presidio, concluding that AVX had no present or nonspeculative interest in engaging in conduct even arguably covered by the patent claims.[44] The court explained that government action upholding patent claims covering precisely defined product features did not harm a party simply because it was a competitor. Rather, a patent claim could have a harmful competitive effect if the challenger was using the claimed features or planned to do so in competition.[45]

The Federal Circuit considered potential reputational injury in *RPX v. Chanbond*,[46] where RPX asserted that the Board's decision injured its reputation for successfully challenging patents in IPR proceedings. To support its position, RPX submitted a declaration from its Senior Vice President of Client Relations in arguing that the Board's unfavorable determination tarnished its reputation in successfully challenging patents. The court, however, rejected this reputational injury argument based on insufficient evidence to quantify the injury or show concrete and particularized harm. It remains

43. AVX Corp. v. Presidio Components, Inc., 923 F.3d 1357 (Fed. Cir. 2019).
44. *Id.* at 1363.
45. *Id.* at 1365.
46. RPX Corp. v. Chanbond LLC, 780 F. App'x 866 (Fed. Cir. 2018).

unclear whether reputational injury alone (without economic harm) could meet the injury-in-fact requirement when adequately proved through persuasive documentary and/or testimonial evidence. In most cases where standing has been disputed and found, however, injury in fact has been based at least in part on economic injury related to potential infringement liability.

c. *Timing Considerations*

To maintain an appeal, an appellant must show that standing exists at all stages of an appeal. Cessation of potentially infringing activities during an appeal may moot the appellant's injury and deprive it of standing to maintain the appeal.[47] An appellant must also establish that standing existed when the appeal began, that is, when the notice of appeal was filed. Subsequent activities, even if concerning an injury, will likely not suffice absent proof of an injury at the outset of the appeal.

In *Pfizer v. Chugai*,[48] for instance, the court held that Pfizer failed to establish an injury at the beginning of the appeal. Pfizer had filed its notice of appeal in January 2019. To show standing, Pfizer argued that the FDA had approved its potentially infringing rituximab biosimilar product in July 2019 and that it planned to sell the product in 2020. However, because Pfizer did not establish its activities or plans before July 2019, it failed to show any injury when the appeal began in January 2019. Pfizer contended at oral argument that it was "self-evident to the parties" that there was "a product at issue" when the appeal began.[49] The court rejected that argument, holding that it was not self-evident "to the court" and that it was Pfizer's responsibility to "submit evidence to make its standing evident" to the court.[50]

To maintain an appeal, an appellant must present sufficient evidence, supplementing the PTAB record as necessary, to demonstrate standing at all stages of the appeal. Where possible, a prospective petitioner should also consider strategically planning the timing for initiating PTAB proceedings

47. Momenta Pharm., Inc. v. Bristol-Myers Squibb Co., 915 F.3d 764, 770 (Fed. Cir. 2019).
48. Pfizer Inc. v. Chugai Pharm. Co., 812 F. App'x 979 (Fed. Cir. 2020).
49. *Id.* at 981.
50. *Id.*

and related commercial activities, such that in case of an unfavorable Board decision (typically about 18 months from the PTAB petition filing), sufficient evidence can be presented to show injury when a future appeal begins. An appellee, on the other hand, should investigate the appellant's activities before and during the appeal to identify any potential deficiencies in demonstrating standing at all stages of the appeal.

2. Decisions to Institute

A determination on whether to institute a trial is final and nonappealable.[51] The Federal Circuit has confirmed that a party cannot take a direct appeal from a decision on whether to institute.[52] Although a petitioner can request that a panel rehear the decision not to institute, the panel's determination is nonappealable.[53] The Federal Circuit and the Supreme Court have also made it clear that parties cannot challenge institution decisions even as part of appeals after the Board issues final written decisions.[54] The Supreme Court held that "where a patent holder merely challenges the Patent Office's 'determin[ation] that the information presented in the petition . . . shows that there is a reasonable likelihood' of success 'with respect to at least 1 of the claims challenged,' § 314(a), or where a patent holder grounds its claim in a statute closely related to that decision to institute *inter partes* review, § 314(d) bars judicial review."[55] In a recent Supreme Court decision, the Court denied judicial review of the Board's decision to institute IPR upon finding that the time bar of 35 U.S.C. § 315(b) did not apply because the § 315(b) time bar for IPR is a statute closely related to IPR institution.[56] In light of this Supreme Court decision, the Federal Circuit ruled in a later case that judicial review is barred for the Board's threshold determination, as part of the decision to institute covered business method (CBM) review,

51. 35 U.S.C. §§ 314(d), 324(e).
52. St. Jude Med., Cardiology Div., Inc. v. Volcano Corp., 749 F.3d 1373 (Fed. Cir. 2014).
53. 35 U.S.C. §§ 314(d), 324(e); *see also* 37 C.F.R. § 42.4(a) (2021) ("The Board institutes the trial on behalf of the Director.").
54. *In re* Cuozzo Speed Techs., LLC, 793 F.3d 1268, 1273 (Fed. Cir. 2015), *aff'd*, 136 S. Ct. 2131 (2016).
55. Cuozzo Speed Techs., LLC v. Lee, 136 S. Ct. 2131, 2142 (2016).
56. Thryv, Inc. v. Click-to-Call Techs., LP, 140 S. Ct. 1367 (2020).

that the challenged patent qualifies as a CBM patent.[57] The Supreme Court left open the possibility of appeals that implicate constitutional questions or other statutes less closely related to the one barring review of institution decisions.[58]

The Federal Circuit has thus far rejected all attempts to obtain review of institution and noninstitution decisions through writs of mandamus.[59] But the court held that judicial review could be available through mandamus when necessary to protect the court's prospective jurisdiction.[60] The prospective jurisdiction is triggered when a party takes a preliminary step that might lead to appellate jurisdiction in the Federal Circuit, such as filing a petition for IPR.[61] The court has also suggested that mandamus may be available to challenge the PTO's decision to grant a petition to institute inter partes review after the Board's final decision in situations where the PTO has clearly and indisputably exceeded its authority.[62] Mandamus is an extraordinary remedy permitted only when (1) the petitioner has shown a "clear and indisputable right to relief," (2) the petitioner lacks adequate alternative means to obtain the relief requested, and (3) the issuance of a writ is appropriate under the circumstances.[63]

The Board's decision to institute a PTAB trial has been collaterally attacked in actions filed at the U.S. District Court for the Eastern District of Virginia, but so far, those cases have been dismissed. In one action, the plaintiff argued that the Office had exceeded its authority under the AIA by instituting review of a patent.[64] The district court dismissed the action.[65] In another action, the plaintiff challenged the Board's interpretation of "covered

---

57. SIPCO, LLC v. Emerson Elec. Co., 980 F.3d 865, 868–70 (Fed. Cir. 2020).

58. *Cuozzo Speed Techs.*, 136 S. Ct. at 2141–42.

59. *In re* Dominion Dealer Sols., LLC, 749 F.3d 1379 (Fed. Cir. 2014); *In re* Procter & Gamble Co., 749 F.3d 1376 (Fed. Cir. 2014); *In re* MCM Portfolio, LLC, 554 F. App'x 944 (Fed. Cir. 2014); *In re* Power Integrations, Inc., 899 F.3d 1316 (Fed. Cir. 2018).

60. Mylan Labs. Ltd. v. Janssen Pharmaceutica, N.V., 989 F.3d 1375 (Fed. Cir. 2021).

61. *Id.*

62. *In re* Cuozzo Speed Techs., LLC, 793 F.3d 1268, 1274 (Fed. Cir. 2015).

63. Cheney v. U.S. Dist. Ct. for D.C., 542 U.S. 367, 381 (2004).

64. Mentor Graphics Corp. v. Rea, No. 1:13-cv-00328, Complaint at 1–2 (E.D. Va. Apr. 29, 2013).

65. *See* Mentor Graphics Corp. v. Rea, No. 1:13-cv-518, 2013 WL 3874522, at *3 (E.D. Va. July 25, 2013).

business method patents" and the grounds for a CBM-PGR.[66] The district court dismissed that action as well,[67] and the Federal Circuit affirmed.[68]

3. PTAB Motion Rulings

The Federal Circuit has reviewed several types of motion rulings encompassed in final written decisions. For example, it reviewed the Board's decision to deny a party's motion to submit supplemental information under 37 C.F.R. § 42.123(a).[69] The court has also reviewed motions to amend claims.[70]

Motion rulings not included in the final written decision are not final,[71] and the statutory framework does not provide an interlocutory mechanism for appealing these rulings.[72] A party seeking relief from a discovery ruling could seek mandamus relief. However, the Federal Circuit has not granted mandamus relief in any Board proceeding.[73] The rules do allow a party to seek rehearing of a decision on procedural rules by a panel of the Board.[74] The statutory framework does not exclude the procedural rules from appellate review, but it also does not expressly permit direct appeal.

As noted in Chapter 5, section C.4, in some instances, discovery disputes can occur in federal court. For example, if a panel of the Board grants authorization to conduct third-party discovery, a party may be able to use the procedures of 35 U.S.C. § 24 to obtain a subpoena through the federal courts. In those situations, the scope of the subpoena would be resolved by the federal court and would be appealable.

---

66. Versata Dev. Grp. Inc. v. Rea, 959 F. Supp. 2d 912 (E.D. Va. 2013).
67. *Id.* at 927.
68. *See* Versata Dev. Corp. v. Lee, 793 F.3d 1352, 1354 (Fed. Cir. 2015) ("[S]ince the attempt by Versata to obtain judicial review of the PTAB's decision to institute a CBM review in this case was addressed to the PTAB's determinations at the decision to institute stage, the district court was correct in barring judicial review pursuant to subsection 324(e).").
69. Redline Detection, LLC v. Star Envirotech, Inc., 811 F.3d 435 (Fed. Cir. 2015).
70. Aqua Prods., Inc. v. Matal, 872 F.3d 1290 (Fed. Cir. 2017).
71. 37 C.F.R. § 42.71(b).
72. 35 U.S.C. §§ 314(d), 324(e).
73. *In re* Dominion Dealer Sols., LLC, 749 F.3d 1379 (Fed. Cir. 2014); *In re* Procter & Gamble Co., 749 F.3d 1376 (Fed. Cir. 2014); *In re* MCM Portfolio, LLC, 554 F. App'x 944 (Fed. Cir. 2014); Mylan Labs. Ltd. v. Janssen Pharmaceutica, N.V., 989 F.3d 1375 (Fed. Cir. 2021).
74. 37 C.F.R. §§ 41.125, 42.71(d).

4. Final Determinations

Final determinations from the Board can be appealed to the Federal Circuit.[75] Any party to the underlying proceeding can be a party to the appeal.[76]

The rules also provide for rehearing after a final determination.[77]

5. Constitutional Challenges

The Federal Circuit held that it maintains exclusive jurisdiction over constitutional challenges to acts of Congress pertaining to patents.[78] In *MadStad*, the court determined that a constitutional challenge to the AIA's first-to-file provisions was properly before it: "[T]his appeal 'arise[s] under' an Act of Congress relating to patents within the meaning of both 28 U.S.C. §§ 1338 and 1295(a)(1) and that we, thus, may properly exercise jurisdiction over this appeal."[79] While the question of arising under jurisdiction in a similar context had been implicitly decided 30 years earlier,[80] the court applied the four-part jurisdictional analysis required by *Gunn v. Minton*, 133 S. Ct. 1059 (2013), in the context of the AIA.[81] Thus, a claim attacking the constitutionality of the AIA is one arising under that act of Congress within the meaning of 28 U.S.C. §§ 1295 and 1338 and is exclusively appealable to the Federal Circuit.

The Federal Circuit has addressed several constitutional challenges relating to Board proceedings. It rejected a patent owner's argument that inter partes review violates Article III and the Seventh Amendment.[82] The court also concluded that the AIA and due process rights are not violated by having the PTO Director delegate the institution decision to the Board or by having a PTAB panel that instituted an IPR also decide its merits in the

75. 35 U.S.C. §§ 319, 329; *In re* Cuozzo Speed Techs., LLC, 793 F.3d 1268, 1272 (Fed. Cir. 2015) ("We have jurisdiction to review the Board's final decision under 28 U.S.C. § 1295(a)(4)(A).").

76. 35 U.S.C. §§ 319, 329.

77. 37 C.F.R. § 42.71(d)(2).

78. MadStad Eng'g, Inc. v. Lee, 756 F.3d 1366 (Fed. Cir. 2014).

79. *Id.* at 1371.

80. *See* Patlex Corp. v. Mossinghoff, 758 F.2d 594, 596 (Fed. Cir. 1985) (considering whether "certain provisions of the patent reexamination statute and implementing regulations" were unconstitutional under the Fifth and Seventh Amendments of the U.S. Constitution).

81. *MadStad Eng'g, Inc.*, 756 F.3d at 1369–70.

82. MCM Portfolio LLC v. Hewlett-Packard Co., 812 F.3d 1284 (Fed. Cir. 2015).

final written decision.[83] Recently, the Supreme Court ruled that the appointments of administrative patent judges (APJs) were unconstitutional under the Appointment Clause of Article II of the U.S. Constitution.[84] As a remedy, the Court ruled that the final written decisions of APJs must be subject to review by the Director of the USPTO.[85] In response to this decision, the USPTO has implemented an interim procedure whereby review of a Board final decision may be initiated sua sponte by the Director or requested by a party to a Board proceeding.[86] At this time, a party may request Director review of a final written decision in an IPR or PGR by filing a request for rehearing by the Director and concurrently submitting a notification of that request to the Office.[87] The Supreme Court left open the question of the precise effect of § 314(d) on appeals that implicate constitutional questions.[88]

B. Considerations on Appeal

1. Selecting Issues and Requested Relief for Appeal

Deciding what issues to raise on appeal is one of the most important strategic decisions in any appeal. The court will generally decline to address matters that have not been addressed and decided by the Board.[89] When selecting issues, advocates should also consider the applicable standard of review, which affects the amount of deference the Federal Circuit must give to Board decisions.[90] For example, it would be advantageous to raise issues of law whenever possible on appeal, such as claim construction or statutory interpretation. Since the court reviews these issues de novo and

83. Ethicon Endo-Surgery, Inc. v. Covidien LP, 812 F.3d 1023 (Fed. Cir. 2016).
84. United States v. Arthrex, Inc., 141 S. Ct. 1970 (2021).
85. *Id.*
86. *USPTO Issues Information on Implementation of the Supreme Court's Decision in U.S. v. Arthrex, Inc.* (June 29, 2021), USPTO, https://www.uspto.gov/about-us/news-updates/uspto-issues-information-implementation-supreme-courts-decision-us-v-arthrex.
87. *Id.*
88. Cuozzo Speed Techs., LLC v. Lee, 136 S. Ct. 2131, 2141–42 (2016).
89. Sec. & Exch. Comm'n v. Chenery Corp., 318 U.S. 80, 87 (1943) ("The grounds upon which an administrative order must be judged are those upon which the record discloses that its action was based.").
90. *See infra* Chapter 8, section C.

gives no deference to the Board, the appellant has a better chance to have the Board's decision reversed.

It is also generally desirable to limit the number of issues appealed. Presenting only the strongest issues on appeal permits the appellant to fully address the facts and law surrounding the appealed issues and prevents the weak issues from discrediting or drowning out the strong ones.

Asking for appropriate relief can also play an important role in an appeal. In certain cases, the Federal Circuit may be reluctant to reverse a decision outright but may be willing to vacate the decision and remand the case to the Board to readdress select issues in view of the court's guidance.

2. Requirements for Filing a Notice of Appeal

A notice of appeal must be filed with the Director and the Board no later than 63 days after the final Board decision or after the Board acts on a timely filed request for rehearing.[91] An extension of time may be requested.[92] The appellant must also simultaneously send the clerk of the Federal Circuit a copy of the notice.[93]

Any notice of cross-appeal is controlled by Rule 4(a)(3) of the Federal Rules of Appellate Procedure.[94]

3. Appeal Schedule

Once a notice of appeal is filed, the appeal is docketed at the Federal Circuit.[95] The Director of the PTO has 40 days to send the certified list and copy of the decision or order appealed to the court.[96] Currently, data from the Federal Circuit suggest that an appeal takes about 14 months to complete from the date the case has been docketed until decision.[97] The

91. 37 C.F.R. §§ 90.2, 90.3.
92. *Id.* § 90.3.
93. FED. CIR. R. 15(a)(1).
94. 37 C.F.R. § 90.3.
95. FED. CIR. R. 15(b)(1).
96. FED. CIR. R. 17(b)(1).
97. *See Median Disposition Time for Cases Decided by Merits Panels (2012–2021)*, U.S. CT. APP. FOR THE FED. CIR., https://cafc.uscourts.gov/wp-content/uploads/reports-stats/disposition-time/06_Med_Disp_Time_MERITS_table.pdf (last visited May 16, 2022).

reversal rate was approximately 9 percent over a 12-month period ending September 2021.[98]

4. Motion Practice on Appeal

Motion practice is governed by Federal Rule of Appellate Procedure 27 and Federal Circuit Rule 27. An application for an order or other relief is made by motion unless these rules prescribe another form.[99] Any party may file a response to a motion.[100] The response must be filed within 10 days after service of the motion unless the court shortens or extends the time.[101] Any reply to a response must be filed within seven days after service of the response.[102]

Motions are not required for the case to progress through the court of appeals to a final disposition on the merits.[103] The clerk's office explains that "[a] motion, however, is required to be filed to request permission to or to take an action that is otherwise not allowed by the rules."[104] The clerk of court's delegated ability "to act on procedural or unopposed nonprocedural motions includes the authority to grant or deny the requested relief in whole or in part or to refer the motion to a judge or a panel."[105] Examples of procedural motions include motions for extensions of time, motions to reform the caption, motions to withdraw counsel, and motions for leave to proceed in forma pauperis.[106] Examples of nonprocedural motions include motions to dismiss, motions to remand, motions to transfer, motions to summarily affirm, motions for stays of injunctions, motions for injunctions, motions to strike, motions for leave to intervene, and motions for leave to file briefs as amici curiae.[107]

---

98. *Reports & Statistics*, U.S. Ct. App. for the Fed. Cir., https://cafc.uscourts.gov/wp-content/uploads/reports-stats/appeals/AppealsFY2021.pdf (last visited May 16, 2022).
99. Fed. R. App. P. 27(a)(1).
100. Fed. R. App. P. 27(a)(3).
101. *Id.*
102. *Id.*
103. *Life of an Appeal*, U.S. Ct. App. for the Fed. Cir., https://cafc.uscourts.gov/wp-content/uploads/RulesProceduresAndForms/FilingResources/Life_of_an_Appeal_Narrative_and_flowchart.pdf (last visited Apr. 26, 2022).
104. *Id.*
105. Fed. Cir. R. 27, Practice Notes.
106. *Id.*
107. *Id.*

C. Standards of Review

1. Standard of Review of Claim Construction

In IPRs and PGRs, the Board construes patent claims under the same standard used in district court—the *Phillips* standard.[108] Under the *Phillips* standard, claim construction should primarily be determined using intrinsic evidence, and then, if needed, the Board may consider extrinsic evidence to determine the meaning of claim language.[109] Examples of intrinsic evidence include the patent's claim language, specification, and prosecution history, while extrinsic evidence includes, for example, dictionaries and treatises.[110] The Board's claim construction determination, which is a question of law, is reviewed at the Federal Circuit de novo with underlying factual determinations reviewed for substantial evidence.[111] Previously, the Federal Circuit applied two different standards of review to claim-construction decisions by the Board.[112]

2. Standard of Review of Invalidity Determinations

The Federal Circuit treats obviousness, indefiniteness, and lack of enablement as questions of law and reviews them de novo.[113] Underlying factual inquiries, however, are reviewed for substantial evidence.[114] Anticipation and lack of written description are also reviewed for substantial evidence, as they are questions of fact.[115]

108. 37 C.F.R. §§ 42.100(b), 42.200(b); Phillips v. AWH Corp., 415 F.3d 1303, 1317 (Fed. Cir. 2005).

109. *Id.*

110. *Id.* at 1317–18.

111. *In re* Cuozzo Speed Techs., LLC, 793 F.3d 1268, 1279–80 (Fed. Cir. 2015) (citing Teva Pharm. USA, Inc. v. Sandoz, Inc., 135 S. Ct. 831, 841 (2015)).

112. Flo Healthcare Sols., LLC v. Kappos, 697 F.3d 1367, 1376–80 (Fed. Cir. 2012) (Plager, J., providing additional views), 1380–83 (Newman, J., providing additional views).

113. Celgene Corp. v. Peter, 931 F.3d 1342, 1349 (Fed. Cir. 2019) (obviousness); *In re* Gartside, 203 F.3d 1305, 1316 (Fed. Cir. 2000) (obviousness); Exxon Rsch. & Eng'g Co. v. United States, 265 F.3d 1371, 1376 (Fed. Cir. 2001) (indefiniteness); Enzo Biochem, Inc. v. Calgene, Inc., 188 F.3d 1362, 1369 (Fed. Cir. 1999) (lack of enablement).

114. *In re Gartside*, 203 F.3d at 1316.

115. *In re* Gleave, 560 F.3d 1331, 1334–35 (Fed. Cir. 2009) (anticipation); *In re* Curtis, 354 F.3d 1347, 1352 (Fed. Cir. 2004) (lack of written description).

Substantial evidence is such relevant evidence as a reasonable mind might accept as adequate to support a conclusion.[116] "[T]he possibility of drawing two inconsistent conclusions from the evidence does not prevent an administrative agency's finding from being supported by substantial evidence."[117]

3. Standard of Review of Office Rules

The Office's interpretations of its own rules are entitled to "substantial deference" and will be accepted unless they are plainly erroneous or inconsistent with the rules.[118]

4. Standard of Review for Constitutional Challenges

The Federal Circuit treats constitutional challenges as questions of law and reviews them de novo.[119]

D. Other Strategic Considerations

1. Making a Record for Appeal

Preparation for an appeal should begin during the Board trial phase. Apart from select matters subject to judicial notice,[120] an appeal is limited to the record established during the PTAB trial.[121] Therefore, practitioners should ensure that the record includes all facts (supported by admissible evidence) and legal positions (supported by statutes, regulations, and case law) necessary for an eventual appeal. Practitioners should ensure that they have raised all arguments that they may later wish to raise on appeal.

---

116. *In re* Chevalier, 500 F. App'x 932, 934 (Fed. Cir. 2013) (nonprecedential) (quoting Consol. Edison Co. v. NLRB, 305 U.S. 197, 229 (1938)).

117. *In re Chevalier*, 500 F. App'x at 934 (quoting Consolo v. Fed. Mar. Comm'n, 383 U.S. 607, 620 (1966)).

118. *In re* DBC, 545 F.3d 1373, 1378 (Fed. Cir. 2008) (citing Woodford v. Ngo, 548 U.S. 81, 90, 126 S. Ct. 2378 (2006)); Eli Lilly & Co. v. Bd. of Regents of Univ. of Wash., 334 F.3d 1264, 1266 (Fed. Cir. 2003); *see also* Microsoft Corp. v. Proxyconn, Inc., 789 F.3d 1292, 1307 (Fed. Cir. 2015), *overruled by* Aqua Prod., Inc. v. Matal, 872 F.3d 1290 (Fed. Cir. 2017).

119. Celgene Corp. v. Peter, 931 F.3d 1342, 1357 (Fed. Cir. 2019).

120. *See, e.g.*, Versata Software, Inc. v. Callidus Software, Inc., 771 F.3d 1368, 1372 (Fed. Cir. 2014), *vacated*, 780 F.3d 1134 (Fed. Cir. 2015) (taking judicial notice of status of copending proceeding).

121. *See* FED. R. APP. P. 16.

The Federal Circuit will generally decline to address matters that have not already been argued by the appellant before the Board and decided by the Board.[122] But an appellee may have additional flexibility on appeal as it can defend the Board's decision on "any ground that is supported by the record."[123] As the Federal Circuit has frequently noted, it "review[s] judgments, not opinions."[124]

Even if an issue is generally appealable, the Federal Circuit may not address it if the appealing party previously waived its arguments on the issue. For example, a party may waive arguments by not timely making them to the Board.[125] Further, a party may waive arguments by not citing the rule at issue to the Board, because the Board would not have been on notice of what is at issue.[126] Accordingly, parties should raise arguments and cite rules at issue to the Board as early as possible to avoid waiving arguments.

2. Third-Party/Government Participation

The Federal Circuit has determined that pre-AIA versions of 35 U.S.C. §§ 141 and 315 do not allow the third-party requester in an inter partes reexamination to appeal unfavorable patentability determinations by the Board absent a showing of constitutional "injury-in-fact."[127] Consumer Watchdog—a "not-for-profit public charity dedicated to providing a voice for taxpayers and consumers"[128]—was deemed to lack standing before the Article III court of appeal, notwithstanding that the reexamination statute permitted it to participate in proceedings before the USPTO. According to

122. Sec. & Exch. Comm'n v. Chenery Corp., 318 U.S. 80, 87 (1943) ("The grounds upon which an administrative order must be judged are those upon which the record discloses that its action was based."); *cf. In re* Skvorecz, 580 F.3d 1262, 1267 n.2 (Fed. Cir. 2009) ("Because this aspect is a matter of law, it does not raise an issue of the Chenery doctrine.").

123. Rexnord Indus., LLC v. Kappos, 705 F.3d 1347, 1356 (Fed. Cir. 2013).

124. Gen. Mills, Inc. v. Hunt-Wesson, Inc., 103 F.3d 978, 981 (Fed. Cir. 1997) (citing Chem. Eng'g Corp. v. Essef Indus., Inc., 795 F.2d 1565, 1572 (Fed. Cir. 1986)).

125. *In re* DBC, 545 F.3d 1373, 1378, 1380 (Fed. Cir. 2008) ("It is well-established that a party generally may not challenge an agency decision on a basis that was not presented to the agency."); Lingamfelter v. Kappos, 513 F. App'x 934, 938 (Fed. Cir. 2012).

126. Lingamfelter v. Kappos, 513 F. App'x 934, 938 (Fed. Cir. 2012).

127. Consumer Watchdog v. Wis. Alumni Rsch. Found., 753 F.3d 1258, 1260 (Fed. Cir. 2014).

128. *Id.* at 1259–60.

the Federal Circuit, a "statutory grant of a procedural right, e.g., right to appeal, does not eliminate the requirements of Article III."[129] Specifically addressing the injury-in-fact requirement, the court suggested that alleging some requester activities that could give rise to an infringement suit, some involvement in research, or some commercial activities involving the patents might suffice as a constitutional matter. But the court determined that Consumer Watchdog could not establish such facts in its case.[130]

Government participation in appeals of Board final written decisions is discretionary. The USPTO and the United States typically participate in matters they view as being of potential legal significance. The Federal Circuit, moreover, may request government briefing on certain issues.

3. The Preclusive Effect of Divergent District Court and Office Decisions

Because concurrent litigation and post-grant proceedings can proceed independently, absent a stay of the litigation, there is a risk of divergent outcomes in the district court and before the Board. For example, claims could be held valid and infringed by a federal court yet be held unpatentable by the Board. These decisions may be appealed at different times to the Federal Circuit. This raises the question: What is the preclusive effect of these divergent decisions?

A Federal Circuit opinion affirming a Board's final determination of unpatentability is preclusive in any later district court proceeding.[131] Similarly, the Office is bound by a Federal Circuit opinion affirming a determination of invalidity at the district court.[132] But a judgment of validity at the district court does not preclude a later finding of unpatentability at

129. *Id.* at 1262 (citing Lexmark Int'l, Inc. v. Static Control Components, Inc., 134 S. Ct. 1377, 1386 (2014)).

130. *Id.* ("Consumer Watchdog is not engaged in any activity that would give rise to a possible infringement suit.").

131. *See, e.g.*, Translogic Tech., Inc. v. Hitachi, Ltd., 250 F. App'x 988 (Fed. Cir. 2007) (vacating and remanding for dismissal a district court opinion finding patents valid and infringed in light of the Federal Circuit's prior decision affirming BPAI decision finding patents obvious).

132. *See, e.g.*, MANUAL OF PATENT EXAMINING PROCEDURE § 2286(IV) (2020) (discussing the effect of a Federal Circuit holding on claim validity).

the Office.[133] Indeed, the Federal Circuit recently held that a district court judgment of infringement may be set aside when the patent claims are subsequently held unpatentable by the Office if the judgment of infringement has not been made final.[134]

E. En Banc Review

An en banc hearing or panel hearing is not favored and typically will not be ordered unless it is necessary to maintain uniformity of the court's decisions and the proceeding involves a question of exceptional importance.[135] If a litigant wants to challenge a motions panel's decision on a dispositive motion, a rehearing en banc may be proper.[136] Parties may petition for a panel rehearing or rehearing en banc.[137] Questions of exceptional importance must be concisely stated.

A petition that an appeal be heard initially en banc must be filed by the date when the appellee's brief is due.[138] A petition for rehearing en banc must be filed within the time stated by Federal Rule of Appellate Procedure 35 for filing a petition.[139]

Once a petition for en banc hearing or panel hearing has been submitted, a response addressing whether rehearing should be granted or denied must be filed within 14 days. En banc consideration requires a majority of active circuit judges to agree to hear or rehear a case en banc.[140]

---

133. *See, e.g., In re Baxter Int'l, Inc.*, 678 F.3d 1357, 1365 (Fed. Cir. 2012) (affirming the Board decision of unpatentability after affirming a district court finding of validity); *In re* Swanson, 540 F.3d 1368, 1377 (Fed. Cir. 2008) (affirming a Board finding of invalidity after affirming a district court decision that the same claims were not invalid in light of the same art).

134. *See* Fresenius USA, Inc. v. Baxter Int'l, 721 F.3d 1330, 1340–45 (Fed. Cir. 2013) (holding that under the reexamination statute, the cancellation of claims by the Office is binding on a district court infringement litigation where a decision had been rendered but was not final).

135. *See* FED. R. APP. P. 35(a), 40; *see also* Mendel v. Morgan Keegan & Co. Inc., 700 F. App'x 994 (11th Cir. 2017) (court held that since appellant's brief did not comply with FED. R. APP. P. 35, appellant's request for an en banc hearing would not be considered).

136. Wallace v. FedEx Corp., 764 F.3d 571, 583 (6th Cir. 2014).

137. *See* FED. R. APP. P. 35(b).

138. *See* FED. R. APP. P. 35(c).

139. *See id.*

140. Cafeteria & Rest. Workers Union, Loc. 473, AFL-CIO v. McElroy, 284 F.2d 173, 189 (D.C. Cir. 1960).

Chapter 9

Other Motions Practice

A. Motions Practice

By statute, a patent owner may file one motion to amend.[1] Motions to amend are addressed in Chapter 6. A party requesting other types of relief during a proceeding can do so by filing a motion.[2] Various types of motions are possible, including motions to seal, motions for joinder, motions to file supplemental information, motions for judgment based on supplemental information, motions for sanctions, and motions for additional briefing, among other relief.[3] Parties must seek Board authorization before filing a motion[4] except where impractical (e.g., motions to seal and motions filed with a petition) or where authorization is automatically granted by the rules or in the scheduling order (e.g., motions to exclude).[5] Authorization for motions can also be provided during the proceeding after conferring with the Board.[6]

1. 35 U.S.C. §§ 316(d), 326(d).
2. 37 C.F.R. § 42.20(a); Patent Trial and Appeal Board Consolidated Trial Practice Guide 37 (Nov. 2019).
3. Patent Trial and Appeal Board Consolidated Trial Practice Guide 19, 22, 24, 29, 48, 76, 79, 80, 91 (Nov. 2019).
4. *Id.* at 37–38.
5. *Id.* at 37, 66.
6. *Id.* at 37–38.

Most of the business of a PTAB trial is conducted through telephone conferences with the Board. To request a conference for a particular case, a party must contact the Board by email at Trials@uspto.gov. The email should copy the other parties to the proceeding and indicate the relief being requested or the subject matter of the conference call. The Board expects that the parties will meet and confer regarding the topics in the email before contacting the Board. All substantive communications with the Board must include all parties.[7] Ex parte communications are generally not permitted.[8] Emails to the Board should not contain substantive arguments.

Parties can expect conference calls with the Board to cover most issues raised during the trial.[9] During these calls, parties should be prepared to address their specific issues concisely and have an understanding of relevant patent trial rules.[10] The Board expects that counsel attending a conference call has the authority to participate on behalf of the respective party.[11] Any counsel who does not have power of attorney, or who has not appeared pro hac vice, may not be able to attend or participate in discussions with the Board.[12] The Board may grant the requested relief during the conference call or even in response to the email requesting a conference call.

A party filing a motion must file it as a separate paper.[13] The motion must contain a statement of precise relief requested, a statement of the reasons for relief,[14] and any additional showing required by the Board.[15] The burden of proof rests with the moving party to establish that they are entitled to relief.[16] A statement of material facts is not required.[17] By default, the opposing party can file an opposition to the motion, and the party requesting relief can file a subsequent reply.[18] The Board has the authority to adjust

7. *Id.* at 9–10.
8. *Id.*
9. *Id.*
10. *Id.*
11. *Id.* at 9–11.
12. *See* 37 C.F.R. § 42.10(c).
13. *Id.* § 42.22(a).
14. *Id.* § 42.22(a)(1)–(2).
15. *Id.* § 42.22(d).
16. *Id.* § 42.20(c).
17. *Id.* § 42.22(c).
18. *Id.* § 42.23.

briefing as necessary.[19] Again, by default, motions, other than motions to amend, are limited to 15 pages.[20] Corresponding oppositions are limited to 15 pages.[21] Corresponding replies are limited to five pages.[22]

The Board may take up petitions or motions in any order and may grant, deny, or dismiss any petition or order.[23] A decision on a motion without a judgment is not final for the purposes of judicial review.[24] If a decision is not a panel decision, the adversely affected party may request rehearing before the panel.[25] The request for rehearing may be made without prior authorization and must be made within 14 days of the decision.[26] The request does not toll other times for taking actions.[27] The panel will review the decision for an abuse of discretion.[28]

B. Settlement and Termination

The parties can agree to settle a proceeding.[29] The settlement can be either preinstitution[30] or postinstitution.[31] If the settlement is reached postinstitution, the Board has discretion to terminate the proceeding or render a judgment regarding jurisdiction, patentability, or Office practice.[32] Generally, the Board expects that proceedings will terminate after the parties reach a settlement.[33] If the Board decides to proceed to a final written decision, the Board may terminate the involvement of the petitioner but still allow the

19. *Id.* § 42.20(d).
20. *Id.* § 42.24(a)(1)(v).
21. *Id.* § 42.24(b)(3).
22. *Id.* § 42.24(c)(2).
23. *Id.* § 42.71(a).
24. *Id.* § 42.71(b).
25. *Id.*
26. *Id.* § 42.71(d)(1).
27. *Id.* § 42.71(d).
28. *Id.* § 42.71(b).
29. 35 U.S.C. §§ 317(a), 327(a); 37 C.F.R. § 42.74(a)–(b).
30. Int'l Bus. Mach. Corp. v. Fin. Sys. Tech. (Intell. Prop.) Pty., IPR2013-00078, Paper 7 (Feb. 8, 2013) (Representative).
31. Macauto U.S.A. v. BOS GmbH & KG, IPR2012-00004, Paper 21 (Feb. 4, 2013) (Representative).
32. 37 C.F.R. § 42.74(a).
33. *Id.* § 42.20(a); PATENT TRIAL AND APPEAL BOARD CONSOLIDATED TRIAL PRACTICE GUIDE 86 (Nov. 2019).

patent owner to request an oral hearing.[34] Termination due to a settlement has no statutory estoppel effect.[35]

Any agreement between the parties to terminate the proceeding must be in writing, and a true copy of the agreement must be filed with the Board.[36] The Board will not accept redacted versions.[37] However, the parties can file a written request along with the agreement to treat the agreement as business confidential.[38] In addition to filing the written agreement, the parties must also file a joint motion to terminate that explains why termination is appropriate.[39] Until the Board terminates the proceeding, all due dates remain in effect.[40]

Like all motions, prior Board authorization is needed before the joint motion can be filed, even if the Board has not yet issued its institution decision.[41]

C. Supplemental Briefing

A party may file a motion to submit supplemental information after institution.[42] The party must seek authorization to file the motion within one month of the trial institution date,[43] and the supplemental information must

34. 35 U.S.C. §§ 317(a), 327(a); Interthinx, Inc. v. Corelogic Sols., LLC, CBM2012-00007, Paper 47 (Nov. 12, 2013).

35. 35 U.S.C. §§ 317(a), 327(a); 77 Fed. Reg. 48,612, 48,649, Response to Comment 218 (Aug. 14, 2012).

36. 35 U.S.C. §§ 317(b), 327(b); *see also* Hyundai Motor Am., Inc. v. Clear with Computs., LLC, IPR2013-0104, Paper 16, at 3 (July 3, 2013) (requiring the parties to "certify in writing that no other written or oral agreements or understandings, including any collateral agreements, between them" are made as part of the contemplated termination of the proceeding before the Board).

37. *See, e.g.*, Monsanto Co. v. Pioneer Hi-Bred Int'l, Inc., IPR2013-00022, Paper 39 (Apr. 3, 2013).

38. 37 C.F.R. § 42.74(c).

39. *See, e.g.*, Monsanto Co., IPR2013-00022, Paper 39.

40. *See, e.g.*, Kyocera Corp. v. ADC Tech. Inc., IPR2013-00107, Paper 23 (June 24, 2013) (Representative).

41. *See* 37 C.F.R. § 42.20; *see also* JST Performance, Inc. v. Koninklijke Philips N.V., IPR2015-00308, Paper 11 (Feb. 27, 2015).

42. 37 C.F.R. §§ 42.123(a), 42.223(a).

43. *Id.* §§ 42.123(a)(1), 42.223(a)(1).

be relevant to a claim for which the trial has been instituted.[44] The Board has indicated that supplemental information must relate to a ground of unpatentability that was instituted and cannot change those grounds or the evidence initially presented.[45] Even when all the requirements have been met, however, the Board has denied requests where the petitioner "sought to use the supplemental information at issue to bolster the challenges presented originally in the Petition, based on feedback gleaned from the institution decision."[46] The Board has also indicated that even if a request is made within the one-month period, the Board may not grant it to ensure timely conclusion of the proceeding.[47]

A party may submit supplemental information more than one month after institution, but the party must show why the supplemental information could not have reasonably been obtained earlier and that consideration of the supplemental information would be in the interests of justice.[48] The Board has held that information "could not have been obtained earlier" where it did not exist before; for example, where a document published after the filing of the relevant paper.[49] According to the Board, prior knowledge of a reference, however, does not entirely foreclose submission of supplemental information relating to it.[50] The Board has also construed Rule 42.123(b)

44. *Id.* §§ 42.123(a)(2), 42.223(a)(2).

45. Palo Alto Networks, Inc. v. Juniper Networks, Inc., IPR2013-00369, Paper 37, at 3 (Feb. 5, 2014) (allowing submission of information about the public availability of the alleged prior art); *see also* Mitsubishi Plastics, Inc. v. Celgard, LLC, IPR2014-00524, Paper 30, at 4 (Nov. 28, 2014).

46. *Mitsubishi Plastics, Inc.*, IPR2014-00524, Paper 30, at 5 (refusing to allow submission of expert declarations from related IPRs where one declaration was by an entirely different expert and the other, although from the same expert, was materially different than the one submitted in the present IPR); B/E Aerospace, Inc. v. MAG Aerospace Indus., IPR2014-01510, Paper 37, at 5 (May 26, 2015) ("The filing of a petition for *inter partes* review should not be turned into a two-stage process, first to elicit a claim interpretation by the Board, and second to complete the petition on the basis of that claim interpretation.").

47. *See* Palo Alto Networks, Inc., IPR2013-00369, Paper 37, at 4.

48. 37 C.F.R. §§ 42.123(b)–(c), 42.223(b)–(c).

49. Shire Dev. LLC v. Lucerne Bioscis., LLC, IPR2014-00739, Paper 23 (Mar. 12, 2015) (allowing submission of press release published after the filing of the patent owner response); *but see* Endo Pharms., Inc. v. Depomed, Inc., IPR2014-00652, Paper 47, at 3 (Apr. 21, 2015) (denying submission and reasoning that although hearing demonstratives and transcript from a related IPR could not have been obtained earlier, the underlying evidence could have been).

50. Edmund Optics, Inc. v. Semrock, Inc., IPR2014-00599, Paper 44, at 3 (May 5, 2015) (allowing submission of information relating to a recently discovered discrepancy in previously

to include information that could not have been obtained without a subpoena.[51] The Board has even waived that requirement where the petitioner repeatedly and in good faith tried to obtain the information sought to be submitted and the information was otherwise in the interest of justice.[52]

The Board has considered information to be "in the interest of justice" when it specifically responds to an opponent's challenge.[53] The Board has also indicated that submitted information is in the interest of justice where it assists in determining whether the scientific evidence that is submitted in an IPR is reliable.[54] The Board has also admitted supplemental information where it was contrary and not cumulative to positions taken on the record.[55] In doing so, the Board explained that information that is cumulative and not competent is not in the interest of justice.[56]

When considering motions for supplemental information, the Board also considers whether the opposing party would be prejudiced by the information. For example, the Board has concluded that there is no prejudice where the information was served on the opposing party and where there remains time to consider and respond to that information.[57] Conversely, the Board has concluded that voluminous information sought to be introduced late in the proceeding is prejudicial.[58]

known document); *but see* Ericsson Inc. v. Intell. Ventures LLC, IPR2014-00921, Paper 24, at 3 (Mar. 30, 2015) (concluding that a document "recently discovered" did not comply with the "could not have been obtained" requirement).

51. IBM Corp. v. Intell. Ventures LLC, IPR2014-01385, Paper 19, at 4–5 (May 4, 2015).

52. Biomarin Pharm. Inc. v. Genzyme Therapeutic Prods. Ltd., IPR2013-00534, Paper 80, at 5 (Jan. 7, 2015) (waiving "could not have been obtained" requirement).

53. *IBM Corp.*, IPR2014-01385, Paper 19, at 5 ("Because Petitioner's evidence responds to an objection by Patent Owner regarding the public availability of a prior art reference, we further determine that Petitioner has shown sufficiently that submitting this evidence is in the interests-of-justice.").

54. *Edmund Optics, Inc.*, IPR2014-00599, Paper 44, at 4.

55. Shire Dev. LLC v. Lucern Bioscis., LLC, IPR2014-00739, Paper 23 (Mar. 12, 2015).

56. *See id.*; Endo Pharms., Inc. v. Depomed, Inc., IPR2014-00652, Paper 48, at 3 (Apr. 21, 2015).

57. *See, e.g.*, Palo Alto Networks, Inc. v. Juniper Networks, Inc., IPR2013-00369, Paper 37, at 5 (Feb. 5, 2014); IBM Corp. v. Intell. Ventures LLC, IPR2014-01385, Paper 19, at 5 (May 4, 2015).

58. *Endo Pharms., Inc.*, IPR2014-00652, Paper 47, at 5.

Index

About the ABA Section of Intellectual Property Law

From its strength within the American Bar Association, the ABA Section of Intellectual Property Law (ABA-IPL) advances the development and improvement of intellectual property laws and their fair and just administration. The Section furthers the goals of its members by sharing knowledge and balanced insight on the full spectrum of intellectual property law and practice, including patents, trademarks, copyright, design, and trade secrets. Providing a forum for rich perspectives and reasoned commentary, ABA-IPL serves as the ABA voice of intellectual property law within the profession, before policy makers, and with the public.

ABA Section of Intellectual Property Law (ABA-IPL)
Order today! Call 800-285-2221
Monday-Friday, 8:00 a.m. – 5:00 p.m., CT
or visit www.ambar.org/iplbooks.

Qty	Title	Regular Price	ABA-IPL Member Price	Total
____	ADR Advocacy, Strategies, and Practices for Intellectual Property and Technology Cases, 2nd Ed. (5370231)	$149.95	$119.95	$______
____	ANDA Litigation, 3rd Ed. (5370243)	$379.00	$295.95	$______
____	Antitrust Issues in Intellectual Property Law (5370222)	$149.95	$119.95	$______
____	Arbitrating Patent Disputes (5370229)	$89.95	$74.95	$______
____	Careers in IP Law (5370204) (The ebook is complimentary with ABA-IPL Section membership)	$24.95	$16.95	$______
____	Commercialization of IP Rights in China (5370241)	$119.95	$95.95	$______
____	Computer Games and Immersive Entertainment, 2nd Ed. (5370239)	$89.95	$69.95	$______
____	Copyright Litigation Strategies (5370228)	$369.00	$285.00	$______
____	Copyright Remedies (5370208)	$89.95	$74.95	$______
____	Copyright Termination Law (5370226)	$139.95	$109.95	$______
____	Crash Course on U.S. Patent Law (5370221)	$39.95	$34.95	$______
____	The DMCA Handbook, 2nd Ed. (5370234)	$79.95	$64.95	$______
____	The Essential Case Law Guide to PTAB Trials (5370233)	$249.95	$199.95	$______
____	The Essentials of Japanese Patent Prosecution (5370245)	$149.95	$119.95	$______
____	Intellectural Property and Technology Due Diligence (5370236)	$219.95	$179.95	$______
____	The Intellectual Property Law Handbook, 2nd Ed. (5620154)	$139.95	$109.95	$______
____	IP Attorney's Handbook for Insurance Coverage in Intellectual Property Disputes, 2nd Ed. (5370210)	$139.95	$129.95	$______
____	IP Protection in China (5370217)	$139.95	$109.95	$______
____	IP Strategies for Medical Device Technologies (5370238)	$149.95	$119.95	$______
____	IP Valuation for the Future (5370237)	$89.95	$59.95	$______
____	The Law of Trade Secret Litigation Under the Uniform Trade Secrets Act, 2nd Ed. (5370242)	$369.95	$295.95	$______
____	A Lawyer's Guide to Section 337 Investigations before the U.S. International Trade Commission, 4th Ed. (5370240)	$139.95	$109.95	$______
____	Legal Guide to Video Game Development, 2nd Ed. (5370227)	$74.95	$59.95	$______
____	A Legal Strategist's Guide to Trademark Trial and Appeal Board Practice, 4th Ed. (5370247)	$179.95	$144.95	$______
____	New Practitioner's Guide to Intellectual Property (5370198)	$89.95	$69.95	$______
____	Patent Freedom to Operate Searches, Opinions, Techniques, and Studies (5370230)	$139.95	$109.95	$______
____	Patent Neutral (5370232)	$89.95	$69.95	$______
____	Patent Trial Advocacy Casebook, 3rd Ed. (5370124)	$149.95	$119.95	$______
____	Patently Persuasive (5370206)	$129.95	$99.95	$______
____	The Practitioner's Guide to the PCT (5370205)	$139.95	$109.95	$______
____	The Practitioner's Guide to Trials Before the Patent Trial and Appeal Board, 3rd Ed. (5370258)	$169.95	$139.95	$______